# Public Service Management and Asylum

Co-production occurs when citizens actively participate in the design and delivery of public services. The concept and its practice are of increasing interest among policymakers, public service managers and academics alike, with co-production often being described as a revolutionary solution to public service reform.

*Public Service Management and Asylum: Co-production, Inclusion and Citizenship* offers a comprehensive exploration of co-production from the public administration and service management perspectives. In doing so, it discusses the importance of both streams of literature in providing a holistic understanding of the concept, and, based on this integration, it offers a model which differentiates co-production on five levels. The first three refer to the role of the public service user in the design and delivery of services (co-construction, participative co-production and co-design) and the other two focus on inter-organisational relationships (co-management and co-governance). This model is applied to the case of asylum seekers in receipt of social welfare benefits in Scotland to explore the implications for social inclusion and citizenship. It argues that as public service users, asylum seekers will always play an active role in the process of service production and while co-production does not provide asylum seekers with legal citizenship status, if offers an opportunity for asylum seekers to act like citizens and supports their inclusion into society. It will be of interest to researchers, academics, policymakers, public services managers and students in the fields of public management, public administration and organisational studies.

**Kirsty Strokosch** is a Post-Doctorate Research Fellow in the Centre for Service Excellence (CenSE) at the University of Edinburgh.

# Routledge Critical Studies in Public Management

Edited by Stephen Osborne

The study and practice of public management has undergone profound changes across the world. Over the last quarter century, we have seen

- increasing criticism of public administration as the over-arching framework for the provision of public services,
- the rise (and critical appraisal) of the 'New Public Management' as an emergent paradigm for the provision of public services,
- the transformation of the 'public sector' into the cross-sectoral provision of public services, and
- the growth of the governance of inter-organizational relationships as an essential element in the provision of public services.

In reality these trends have not so much replaced each other as elided or co-existed together—the public policy process has not gone away as a legitimate topic of study, intra-organizational management continues to be essential to the efficient provision of public services, whist the governance of inter-organizational and inter-sectoral relationships is now essential to the effective provision of these services.

Further, whilst the study of public management has been enriched by contribution of a range of insights from the 'mainstream' management literature it has also contributed to this literature in such areas as networks and inter-organizational collaboration, innovation and stakeholder theory.

This series is dedicated to presenting and critiquing this important body of theory and empirical study. It will publish books that both explore and evaluate the emergent and developing nature of public administration, management and governance (in theory and practice) and examine the relationship with and contribution to the over-arching disciplines of management and organizational sociology.

Books in the series will be of interest to academics and researchers in this field, students undertaking advanced studies of it as part of their undergraduate or postgraduate degree and reflective policy makers and practitioners.

**Public Service Management and Asylum**
Co-production, Inclusion and Citizenship
*Kirsty Strokosch*

For a full list of titles in this series, please visit www.routledge.com

# Public Service Management and Asylum

Co-production, Inclusion and Citizenship

**Kirsty Strokosch**

 Routledge
Taylor & Francis Group

NEW YORK AND LONDON

First published 2019
by Routledge
605 Third Avenue, New York, NY 10017

and by Routledge
2 Park Square, Milton Park, Abingdon, Oxon, OX14 4RN

First issued in paperback 2021

*Routledge is an imprint of the Taylor & Francis Group, an informa business*

*Library of Congress Cataloging-in-Publication Data*
A catalog record for this book has been requested

ISBN 13: 978-0-367-78614-4 (pbk)
ISBN 13: 978-1-138-33314-7 (hbk)

Typeset in Sabon
by Apex CoVantage, LLC

For Alasdair, Laila, Aaron and Cal.

# Contents

# Figures

# Tables

# Acknowledgements

First, I would like to thank Stephen Osborne for his continued support, guidance and encouragement throughout my doctoral studies and beyond. In writing this book, I would also like to express thanks to Maria Røhnebæk and Paula Rossi for their valuable suggestions and comments on earlier versions of chapters. Last, I would like to thank my family for their support and help caring for my three young children which enabled me to focus on this work.

# 1    Introduction

## Abstract

This chapter introduces co-production in a public sector setting. It argues that there has been a surge in interest in co-production in both academic research and practice over the last fifteen years, with the concept undergoing notable conceptual developments during this time. The debate on co-production is framed with reference to the role of individual or groups of service users in the planning and delivery of public services and also co-production at an organisational level. This chapter suggests that by developing an integrated and multi-dimensional model of co-production that draws on two streams of literature from public administration and service management, the co-production of public services can be better conceptualised and understood. The chapter concludes by detailing the structure of the book.

## The Co-production of Public Services

Co-production has a high profile in the UK, Europe and around the world, occupying a prominent place for policymakers, public service managers and academics alike. It has been described as a revolutionary solution to public service reform, offering both a means for service improvement, increased efficiency and innovation (Parks et al., 1981; Meijer, 2011; Bovaird and Loeffler, 2012; Clark et al., 2013; Sicilia et al., 2016; Thomsen, 2017) as well as more normative benefits such as active citizenship and greater participation (Dunston et al., 2009; Denhardt and Denhardt, 2015). The focus of this book will emphasise the significance of co-production, which 'goes to the heart both of effective public service delivery and of the role of public services in achieving other societal ends—such as social inclusion or citizen engagement'. (Osborne et al., 2013, p. 145), but significantly will subscribe to a different starting point for theorising about co-production that has only recently started to be discussed in relation to public service design, delivery and reform (see for example, Osborne and Strokosch, 2013; Osborne et al., 2016).

Sicilia et al. (2016), describe co-production as a heterogeneous concept, with both an individual and organisational dimension, which can refer specifically to service delivery (Alford, 2009) or to the complete cycle of public services encompassing planning through to evaluation (Bovaird, 2005). However, it is a concept that is still evolving both in theory and practice (Verschuere et al., 2012) and, as such, the processes that support and facilitate co-production and its impact on service users, service systems and society at large require further examination and understanding. Historically, co-production has also held an important place in the study and understanding of social welfare services (Pestoff, 2005; Evers, 2006) particularly because of the intricate nature of the relationship between the needs of, often vulnerable, service users and the service delivery system. Equally though, co-production is important across a whole range of public services—including education, policing, community development, care for the elderly and sports and leisure services.

The interest in co-production has been highlighted by the increase in academic research conducted in the area over the past few years (Osborne and Strokosch, 2013; Fledderus et al., 2015; Voorberg et al., 2015; Nabatchi et al., 2017), evolving within the literature on public service reform, through various narratives starting with the classical public administration view of co-production, which has over the past forty years been shaped by the hegemonic influence of the New Public Management movement and also by the New Public Governance and more recently, the Public Service Logic (Osborne et al., 2015). Latterly, from being a marginal concern of public administration, co-production has moved to occupy a central position in it (Alford, 2002; Bovaird, 2007; Osborne et al., 2015). This evolution has had implications for the expectations, and conceptualisation, of service users in public service management. Their role has also evolved, with public service users being portrayed variously as citizens/clients, consumers, customers—and *co-producers*. The negotiation of these differing narratives is at the heart of this book.

The discussion on co-production as a core process of public service production is introduced in order to consider the specific relational nature of public services, both at the individual level of service delivery and the organisational level of public service production. The public administration perspective on co-production includes developments under the New Public Management narrative, which will be drawn on to present an overview of co-production between public service organisations and individual service users, while the New Public Governance narrative will be reviewed mainly to inform the discussion around inter-organisational relationships. Insight from the service management literature will be drawn on to develop a more comprehensive conceptualisation of co-production both during individual relationships between service users and the organisations (and their staff) delivering public services through inter-organisational relationships.

It is important to note from the outset that the focus here is not concerned with the literature that explores 'upstream' public policy formulation, with a focus on the work of government ministers and civil servants and their interactions with citizens during the process of policymaking (e.g. Scott and Baehler, 2010; Trischler and Charles, 2019). Rather it is concerned with the implementation of public policy and most specifically with the delivery, design and reform of public services. The concept of co-production will be examined specifically through the case of asylum seekers living in Glasgow and in receipt of social care services. Asylum seekers are positioned as a marginalised and disadvantaged group, having exercised their legal right under the Geneva Convention (1951) to apply for asylum but remaining non-citizens while they await the outcome of their case. Their lives are regulated and constrained by strict immigration laws, which are rooted within and built upon 'policies of deterrence' (Williams, 2006). The legislation has built a very much stratified system of social rights which limits asylum seekers' access to public services and singles them out as a visibly in-need group distinct from mainstream society (Sales, 2002). Given the position of asylum seekers as a disenfranchised group who do not share the rights bestowed on the indigenous population at birth, such as citizenship, the case used in this text to explore the actuality of co-production sharpens the focus on the concept. These considerations have important implications for public service planning and delivery and will provide the context through which the conceptual models of co-production can be examined and explained, while also raising pertinent questions around co-production and its implications for citizenship and social inclusion.

## Evolution of the Concept of Co-production

The co-production of public services has been in receipt of varying degrees of interest over the last five decades, with understandings evolving in theory and practice in line with public service reform. Although the concept of co-production can be traced back to the 1920s, there was a renewed interest in the idea in the late 1970s and early 1980s, which can be traced to the seminal work of Ostrom and her colleagues (Ostrom, 1978; Parks et al., 1981). Ostrom subscribed to a classical public administration perspective, referring to the role of citizens and communities in the production of public services. Following this approach, the examination of co-production has been aligned closely to the scholarly work on citizen participation, with service users being conceptualised as playing a potentially active role in service planning and delivery as co-producers (see, for example, Brudney, 1987; Ostrom, 1999; Pestoff, 2006; Alford, 2002, 2009; Bovaird, 2007; Benington, 2011; Denhardt and Denhardt, 2015).

The concept of co-production has continued to be aligned with this classical perspective, but its emphasis has shifted in line with emerging narratives of public service reform. The New Public Management movement of the 1980s and 1990s, for instance, brought with it a different landscape upon which co-production operated. While the New Public Management narrative on co-production confirms the idea of partnership that is espoused under the classical public administration view, it shifts attention from the citizen to the individual, self-interested consumer (Aberbach and Christensen, 2005). The focus here was improving service effectiveness and efficiency usually by shifting costs to consumer co-producers (Fotaki, 2011; Sicilia et al., 2016). The emergence of New Public Governance in the mid-2000s (Osborne, 2006), by contrast, emphasised the increasingly fragmented nature of public service design and delivery, with services being produced by networks of organisations from the public, for-profit and non-profit sectors. Here, co-production has re-entered the debate, with service users being described as co-producers working in a horizontal relationship with government (Pestoff, 2006; Pestoff and Brandsen, 2010; Meijer, 2016).

Over the last decade, the conceptualisation of co-production has developed under the work of Osborne and colleagues (2013, 2015, 2016) who have developed the Public Service Logic which draws on the service management literature and the unique insights it offers to the understanding of public service management (Osborne, 2010; Osborne and Strokosch, 2013). The Public Service Logic is in its infancy and as such is continuing to develop and evolve. In particular, this body of work has started to direct a strong focus on value, how it is created during public service design and delivery and which actors are involved in these processes, but this discussion is beyond the reach of this book. Within this broader debate, however, it is important to state from the outset that the conceptualisation and understanding of co-production (and the associated implications for public service management) are continuing to develop and evolve. Originally, this literature defined co-production as an integral part of service delivery, which it situated as an essential and intrinsic process of interaction, recognising the intangible nature of the service and the inherent role played by the consumer during the service interaction—what Normann (1991) has termed the 'moment of truth' (Osborne and Strokosch, 2013). However, following theoretical progress and developments in practice, there has been a movement within the Public Service Logic to use co-production as one of the distinct (and extrinsic) processes through which citizens can participate in public service production. This book follows that approach, suggesting that 'participative co-production' is one of three discrete processes of involvement through which service users can be involved, which are further complemented by two organisational forms of co-production. This position is in response to Osborne et al's (2013) call for more conceptualisation around public services as *services* and their recommendation that the theory around co-production at the individual and organisational levels be developed. This work offers a core contribution to that debate.

## Co-production Between Organisations

A core aim of this work will also investigate the relationships across organisational boundaries, with a view to exploring whether asylum seeker integration is fostered through such inter-organisational connections between third sector organisations and government agencies/public sector organisations. As mentioned earlier, the New Public Governance has emphasised the fragmentation of public services that are produced across organisational boundaries through collaboration and partnership (Osborne, 2010; Osborne et al., 2013). These developments have revived the focus on the concept with the development of a more pluralistic and fragmented model of governance and service provision (Pestoff, 2012; Osborne et al., 2015). Conceptualisation around public service production can no longer be restricted solely to public service organisations, as the lines between roles and responsibilities become more blurred and must now take into account various partners across organisational boundaries and sectors.

To develop a comprehensive understanding of co-production then, account must also be taken of the way organisations work together to plan and deliver services. The work of Pestoff and colleagues is of particular importance here and has typically focused on the co-productive role of third sector organisations during public service production (Pestoff, 2006; Vidal, 2006; Brandsen and van Hout, 2006). Pestoff and Brandsen (2009) differentiate the inter-organisational role in two ways: as *co-management*, where a third sector organisation co-produces, together with the service planners, the delivery of a public service on behalf of its service users; and as *co-governance*, where it co-produces during both the planning and delivery of a service. Although such inter-organisational relationships are possible between a range of actors from across the range of public, for-profit and non-profit sectors, for the purposes of this work, focus will be placed on the role of third sector organisations, given the critical role played by the third sector in the production of social welfare services for asylum seekers in Scotland (Wren, 2007), drawing on Berger and Neuhaus' (1978) conception of third sector organisations as *mediating structures* that enable people to express their needs against the 'mega-institutions' of society. Again, the service management literature will be explored to better understand how these inter-organisational relationships function and ultimately how they might be better managed.

## Moving Forward: Developing an Integrated Approach to Co-production

The discussion in this book integrates theory from two broad schools of literature on co-production from the public administration and service management perspectives. It will be argued that the integration of these perspectives offers a more holistic understanding and conceptualisation of co-production, an area which has been described by Osborne et al. (2016) as lacking. In particular, it argues that the service management literature offers a better starting point for theorising about the co-production of public services and its management than does the public administration literature because of its greater clarity about the nature of services and the service delivery process (e.g. Normann, 1991; Gronroos, 2007; Vargo and Lusch, 2008), moving away from the product-dominant logic which has traditionally been the basis for understanding public service production.

This does not devalue the offerings of the broader public administration theory which by contrast provides valuable insight around how co-production can be extended through various participative mechanisms (e.g. Ostrom, 1972; Parks et al., 1981; Pestoff and Brandsen, 2006; Bovaird, 2007; Alford, 2009). Taken together, these two literatures provide a more comprehensive view of the co-production of public services, suggesting that different levels of co-production can be achieved. Using this revised theoretical basis, two conceptual models are developed that explore and differentiate a whole range of dimensions of co-production. This is important not only for focused research upon public service reform but also as a guide for policy and practice in understanding how public services are produced and, therefore, how they might be more effectively managed.

The first model categorises service user co-production into three types according to the mechanisms used and the goals aspired to, while the second combines these three individual types with the two organisational forms of co-production, providing a more holistic view of the concept, in line with the idea that public services are produced within complex environments or service systems (Osborne et al., 2015) where multiple actors contribute during every point of the public service cycle.

These models will be used during the empirical element of the study, in order to differentiate the various types of co-production that exist in practice. The discussion will focus particularly on whether asylum seekers, as non-citizens, can co-produce the public services they receive and, if so, what forms co-production takes. It will then consider the implications of this enactment of co-production for social inclusion and as a potential route to citizenship. Although the focus of the empirical work is Scotland, co-production is a global issue (Ostrom, 1999; Alford, 2002, 2009; Pestoff, 2006; Osborne et al., 2013) and this work therefore has wider relevance to public service design and delivery across various public services and within different nation states.

The case of asylum seekers is particularly interesting, given that they are a group that exists at the nexus of the policy narratives both about the consumption of public services and about the nature of citizenship. They have limited access to services having to contend with, for example, complicated bureaucratic procedures to apply for benefits and are placed in housing on a 'no-choice' dispersal policy (Sales, 2002). In addition, their identity as non-citizens, whose lives are regulated and constrained by immigration laws, arguably impedes their potential to integrate into society and their ability to involve themselves through the participative mechanisms used with the indigenous population. Their status has a negative impact on their potential to engage politically, prohibiting them from participating in democratic structures. The different modes of co-production presented here, by consequence, potentially offer an important route through which asylum seekers can engage around public service design and delivery and may also have a more normative dimension that supports social inclusion and citizenship.

## Book Structure

This book is split into three parts. The first will analyse the different types of co-production which exist between service users and public service organisations and between organisations that are planning and delivering services, drawing on two distinct streams of literature from the public administration and service management perspectives. A coherent body of literature on co-production, from the public administration perspective already exists and Chapter 2 will provide a critical review of this work. This literature has been shaped by the hegemonic influence of the New Public Management and has been applied in various contexts and for different phenomena that have made the theory on co-production difficult to untangle and clarify. Chapter 2 will seek to rectify this by providing a coherent examination of the different narratives that have evolved in the public service management literature, in order to formulate an understanding of how co-production has been applied in the public service setting. It will start with a discussion of co-production from a classical public administration perspective, focusing on its participative dimensions and also the constraints preventing the achievement of its associated benefits. The chapter will then discuss the formulation of co-production under the New Public Management, considering specifically the influence of consumerism, before considering the challenges and limitations of such an approach. It will conclude by considering the role of the co-producer in public services, which has implications for the nature, extent and ultimately the impact of co-production.

Chapter 3 introduces the service management literature, an area which until recently has been largely neglected from theorising about public service co-production (Osborne and Strokosch, 2013). The focus here moves beyond the management theory derived from the manufacturing sector, which suggests that services are produced and consumed as discrete processes and focuses on the inseparability of production and consumption, therefore positioning the service user at the heart of production. Chapter 3 also introduces the contrast between the product-dominant logic—which has formed that basis of conceptualising co-production from a public service management perspective—and the service-dominant logic, which introduces the idea of value co-creation. It is the inclusion of this theory which, it will be argued, offers a stronger base from which to theorise about the co-production of public services, although the chapter also discusses the more recent criticisms of the service-dominant logic, which are significant for understanding the operationalisation of co-production within the public service context. The chapter concludes with a discussion of service relationship management, which is described as a central element in the effective management of co-production.

Chapter 4 combines the two theories on co-production, from the public administration and service management perspectives, to develop an integrated model of co-production. The model differentiates and explains co-production at the level of individual or groups of public service users into three broad modes: co-construction; participative co-production and co-design. The chapter offers examples of each of the modes and also suggests some challenges of this conceptualisation of co-production.

Developing an understanding of co-production will continue in Chapter 5 with a focus on inter-organisational relationships. First, the chapter will introduce the third sector which has been understood as playing an indispensable role in public service production in the UK. Inter-organisational relationships will be discussed, considering both their potential and their constraints. The concepts of co-management and co-governance will then be introduced to differentiate the role played by third sector organisations in public service production. Using the theory around governance and networks, the two modes of organisational co-production and their associated challenges are developed and understood. Finally, the service management literature and its valuable insight into the management of inter-organisational relationships will be discussed. Chapter 5 concludes with an integrated presentation of two organisational modes of co-production alongside the three modes presented in Chapter 4.

The second part will examine the case of asylum seekers and the social welfare services they receive in a Scottish context. Chapter 6 introduces the situation of asylum seekers in Scotland by presenting a discussion of the immigration policies operating at a national level and the rights and entitlements afforded to those seeking asylum while they await the outcome of their application. The chapter focuses specifically on the devolved Scottish context, concentrating on the policies of integration and the role of the third sector in Scotland in planning and delivering social welfare services. Importantly, it also examines the challenges of integration, citizenship and rights in the case of asylum seekers, with a view to later exploring whether co-production may have any influence over these dimensions. The latter part of the chapter will then provide a brief discussion of the methods used to conduct the empirical research.

The following two chapters present the evidence from an empirical case study on asylum seekers and the social welfare services they receive in Glasgow. The purpose of this part of the work is to examine the ideas of co-production, at the level of service users and organisations, presented during part one of this book. Chapter 7 will explore the existence of the three modes of co-production (co-construction, participative co-production and co-design) in the empirical case, while also investigating the challenges that impede each type. Chapter 8 will discuss the case of asylum seekers with reference to the role of the third sector and evidence of inter-organisational relationships.

The concluding third part of the book will position co-production in a complex system of public service production and will discuss the implication of co-production, in its various dimensions, for social inclusion and citizenship. Chapter 9 discusses the fact that although asylum seekers were introduced as occupying a powerless position in society, they are public service users and, as such, they do co-produce. It will be argued that their marginalised position sharpens the focus on co-production during the service relationship, highlighting the prominence of service interactions. The discussion will frame co-production as a fundamental component within a complex service system, existing through various individual relationships with public service users and also through inter-organisational relationships. Chapter 9 continues with an examination of the implications of co-production for asylum seeker integration and citizenship, suggesting that while co-production—unlike political forms of participation—is not predicated on citizenship, it may in fact offer a partial route towards citizenship for asylum seekers. It argues that the various dimensions of co-production on the individual and organisational levels have supported the inclusion of asylum seekers in Scotland, with integration forming a core policy goal that has been translated and operationalised through social welfare service production.

The final chapter will conclude the discussion of co-production from this integrated perspective, arguing that it has important consequences for the nature and actuality of co-production in a public service setting. It will revisit the discussion on the various modes of co-production at the service user and organisational level, emphasising the implications for social inclusion and citizenship before finally considering the implications for public service management in practice.

## References

Aberbach, J. D. and Christensen, T. (2005). Citizens and consumers: an new public management dilemma. *Public Management Review*. (7,2), 225–245.
Alford, J. (2002). Why do public-sector clients coproduce? *Administration and Society*. (34,1), 32–56.

Alford, J. (2009). *Engaging public sector clients: from service-delivery to co-production*. Basingstoke: Palgrave Macmillan.

Benington, J. (2011). From private choice to public value. In Benington, J. and Moore, M. (eds.), *Public value: theory and practice*. Basingstoke: Palgrave Macmillan.

Berger, P. L. and Neuhaus, R. J. (1978). *To empower people: the role of mediating structures in public policy*. Washington, DC: American Enterprise for Public Policy Research.

Bovaird, T. (2005). Public governance: balancing stakeholder power in a network society. *International Review of Administrative Sciences*. (7,12), 217–228.

Bovaird, T. (2007). Beyond engagement and participation—user and community co-production of public services. *Public Administration Review*. (67), 846–860.

Bovaird, T. and Loeffler, E. (2012). From engagement to co-production: how users and communities contribute to public services. In Pestoff, V., Brandsen, T. and Verschuere, B. (eds.), *New public governance, the third sector and co-production*. New York: Routledge.

Brandsen, T. and van Hout, E. (2006). Co-management in public service networks: the organizational effects. *Public Management Review*. (8,4), 537–549.

Brudney, J. (1987). Coproduction and privatization: exploring the relationship and its implications. *Nonprofit and Voluntary Sector Quarterly*. (16), 11–21.

Clark, B. Y., Brudney, J. L. and Jang, S. G. (2013). Coproduction of government services and the new information technology: investigating the distributional biases. *Public Administration Review*. (73,5), 687–701.

Denhardt, J. V. and Denhardt, R. B. (2015). *New public service: serving, not steering* (4th ed.). New York: Routledge.

Dunston, R., Lee, A., Boud, D., Brodie, P. and Chiarella, M. (2009). Co-production and health system reform—from re-imagining to re-making. *The Australian Journal of Public Administration*. (68,1), 39–52.

Evers, A. (2006). *Current strands in debating user involvement in social services*. Strasbourg: Council of Europe.

Fledderus, J., Brandsen, T. and Honingh, M. E. (2015). User co-production of public service delivery: an uncertainty approach. *Public Policy and Administration*. (30,2), 145–164.

Fotaki, M. (2011). Towards developing new partnerships in public services: users as consumers, citizens and/or co-producers in health and social care in England and Sweden. *Public Administration*. (89,3), 933–955.

Gronroos, C. (2007). *Service management and marketing: customer management in service competition* (3rd ed.). Chichester: John Wiley & Sons.

Meijer, A. J. (2011). Networked coproduction of public services in virtual communities: from a government-centric to a community approach to public service support. *Public Administration Review*. (July–August), 598–607.

Meijer, A. J. (2016). Coproduction as a structural transformation of the public sector. *International Journal of Public Sector Management*. (29,6), 596–611.

Nabatchi, T., Sancino, A. and Sicilia, M. (2017). Varieties of participation in public services: the who, when and what of co-production. *Public Administration Review*. (77,5), 766–776.

Normann, R. (1991). *Service management: strategy and leadership in service business* (2nd ed.). West Sussex: John Wiley & Sons.

Osborne, S. P. (2006). Editorial: the new public governance? *Public Management Review*. (8,3), 377–387.

Osborne, S. P. (2010). Delivering public services: time for a new theory? *Public Management Review*. (12,1), 1–10.

Osborne, S. P., Radnor, Z., Kinder, T. and Vidal, I. (2015). The SERVICE framework: a public-service-dominant approach to sustainable public services. *British Journal of Management*. (26,3), 424–438.

Osborne, S. P., Radnor, Z. and Nasi, G. (2013). A new theory for public service management? Toward a (Public) service dominant approach. *American Review of Public Administration*. (43,2), 135–158.

Osborne, S. P., Radnor, Z. and Strokosch, K. (2016). Co-production and the co-creation of value in public service: a suitable case for treatment? *Public Management Review*. (18,5), 639–653.

Osborne, S. P. and Strokosch, K. (2013). It takes two to tango? Understanding the co-production of public services by integrating the service management and public administration perspectives. *British Journal of Management*. (24), S31–S47.

Ostrom, E. (1972). Metropolitan reform: propositions derived from two traditions. *Social Science Quarterly*. (53), 474–493.

Ostrom, E. (1978). The public service production process: a framework for analysing police services. *Policy Studies Journal*. (7), 381–389.

Ostrom, E. (1999). Coping with tragedies of the commons. *Annual Review of Political Science*. (2), 493–535.

Parks, R. B., Baker, P. C., Kiser, L., Oakerson, R., Ostrom, E., Ostrom, V., Percy, S. L., Vandivort, M. B., Whitaker, G. P. and Wilson, R. (1981). Consumers as co-producers of public services: some economic and institutional considerations. *Policy Studies Journal*, (9,7), 1001–1011.

Pestoff, V. (2005). *Beyond the market and state: civil democracy & social enterprises in a welfare society*. Aldershot: Brookfield.

Pestoff, V. (2006). Citizens and co-production of welfare services. *Public Management Review*. (8,4), 503–519.

Pestoff, V. (2012). Co-production and third sector services in Europe: some critical conceptual issues. In Pestoff, V., Brandsen, T. and Verschuere, B. (eds.), *New public governance, the third sector and co-production*. New York: Routledge.

Pestoff, V. and Brandsen, T. (2006). Co-production, the third sector and the delivery of public services. *Public Management Review*. (8,4), 493–501.

Pestoff, V. and Brandsen, T. (2009). *The governance of co-production*. Paper Presented at the 13th Annual Conference of the International Research Society for Public Management, Copenhagen.

Pestoff, V. and Brandsen, T. (2010). Public sector governance and the third sector: opportunities for co-production and innovation? In Osborne, S. P. (ed.), *The new public governance?* Oxon: Routledge.

Sales, R. (2002). The deserving and undeserving? Refugees, asylum seekers and welfare in Britain. *Critical Social Policy*. (22), 456–478.

Scott, C. and Baehler, K. (2010). *Adding value to policy analysis and advice*. Sydney: University of New South Wales Press Ltd.

Sicilia, M., Guarini, E., Sancino, A., Adreani, M. and Ruffini, R. (2016). Public service management and co-production in multi-level governance settings. *International Review of Administrative Sciences*. (82,1), 8–27.

Thomsen, M. K. (2017). Citizen co-production: the influence of self-efficacy perception and knowledge of how to co-produce. *American Review of Public Administration*. (47,3), 340–353.

Trischler, J. and Charles, M. (2019). The application of service ecosystems lens to public policy analysis and design: exploring the frontiers. *Journal of Public Policy and Marketing*. (38,1), 19–35.

Vargo, S. L. and Lusch, R. F. (2008). Service-dominant logic: continuing the evolution. *Journey of the Academy of Marketing Science*. (36), 1–10.

Verschuere, B., Brandsen, T. and Pestoff, V. (2012). Co-production: the state of the art in research and the future agenda. *Voluntas*. (23,4), 1083–1101.

Vidal, I. (2006). Reflections on the market, networking and trust. *Public Management Review*. (8,4), 583–589.

Voorberg, W. H., Bekkers, V. J. J. M. and Tummers, L. G. (2015). A systematic review of co-creation and co-production: embarking on the social innovation journey. *Public Management Review*. (17,9), 1333–1357.

Williams, L. (2006). Social networks of refuges in the United Kingdom: tradition, tactics and new community spaces. *Journal of Ethnic and Migration Studies*. (32,5), 865–879.

Wren, K. (2007). Supporting asylum seekers and refugees in Glasgow: the role of multi-agency networks. *Journal of Refugee Studies*. (20,3), 391–413.

# Part 1
# Differentiating Co-production

# 2 The Co-production of Public Services

## The Public Administration Perspective

### Abstract

In the public administration literature, the concept of co-production has developed under the influence of the participatory democracy narrative and has also been strongly influenced by the New Public Management. This chapter discusses the important conceptual developments made within this broad literature and argues that co-production has been positioned mainly as an optional extension of the public service production process. Here, the emphasis is on the voluntary and active partnership of citizens (as individuals or in groups) during the design and delivery of public services. The rationale for co-production, from this perspective, is around its potential to create value by increasing the number of actors who can contribute to tackling difficult and cross-cutting social problems. Importantly, co-production is also forwarded as a means of improving democracy through increased participation. However, this chapter also considers the various barriers and challenges to co-production, such as tokenistic involvement and unequal power relations.

## Introduction

Although a coherent body of literature exists on the co-production of public services, co-production has been used in various contexts for different phenomena, making it difficult to untangle and clarify (Pestoff, 2012a). Indeed, recent analysis has described co-production as an imprecise concept that lacks clarity and definition (Voorberg et al., 2015; Nabatchi et al., 2017). This chapter starts with a brief discussion of the rationale for co-production, detailing the normative ('the right') and instrumental ('the smart') reasons that have been presented across the literature in support of the operationalisation of co-production in the design and delivery of public services. It then seeks to unpack and differentiate co-production, drawing on the different narratives that have evolved within the public administration literature. It starts with a discussion of co-production from the public administration perspective, which has its roots in the seminal work of Ostrom (1972, 1978).

In doing so, it presents an analysis of the participative roots that are the bedrock of the concept, before examining the associated challenges that have resulted. It also discusses how the classical view of co-production has been shaped over time and particularly how it has been influenced by the New Public Governance narrative. The chapter then moves on to focus on the concept of co-production that has developed under the hegemonic influence of the New Public Management. Here, the discussion introduces co-production against an economic rationale that focuses on the implications of positioning service users as self-interested consumers. Finally, the chapter discusses who the co-producer is, examining specifically the roles of the client, citizen and consumer, again linking both the classical public administration view of co-production and the New Public Management narrative.

## The Rationale for the Co-production of Public Services

Normative and instrumental reasons have been forwarded in defence of co-production, which respectively mean 'the right thing' or 'the smart thing' to do (Mayer et al., 2005; Denhardt and Denhardt, 2015). The achievement of normative goals particularly around the achievement of broad public policy objectives and efforts to improve democracy by placing service users and communities at the heart of service delivery decision-making processes have been used in support of co-production (Ostrom, 2000; Alford, 2002a; Bovaird, 2007; Bovaird and Loeffler, 2009; Dunston et al., 2009; Denhardt and Denhardt, 2015). Pestoff (2006, p. 504), for instance, argues that co-production 'provides a missing piece of the puzzle for reforming democracy and the welfare state'. The assumption of such arguments is that offering opportunities for citizens to contribute to the design and delivery of public services through a partnership approach is good in itself, as it provides an opportunity for participation through which citizens can generate personal benefit, such as self-worth, while also sharing responsibility for service production (Denhardt and Denhardt, 2015).

Instrumental justifications have also been used in support of co-production and have been tied to objectives of service improvement and the achievement of wider social ambitions (see, for example, Thomsen, 2017). In terms of service improvement, co-production has been associated with increased efficiency and effectiveness (Joshi and Moore, 2004, Pestoff, 2014). Linked to this, co-production has been praised for mobilising community resources that would not otherwise have been accessed (Bovaird, 2007). It has also been promoted as a means of tackling challenging social or so-called wicked issues. This argument suggests that social inclusion might be tackled more effectively where services are controlled and tailored at the grassroots level by service users and/or organisations that represent or work closely with them and therefore understand their needs

(Sicilia et al., 2016). Pestoff (2014), for example, defines co-production as an 'innovation' in public service provision 'that promotes a mix of public service agents and citizens/users who contribute to the provision of public services' (2014, p. 384). Joshi and Moore (2004) suggest that co-production can also be justified in cases where public service provision is deemed ineffective or inefficient. Arguments in favour of co-production might, for example, contend that public officials are overly self-interested or that statutory organisations are too big and bureaucratic to provide efficient services alone. Citizens, as co-producers, can therefore replace the roles of public service staff at certain points in production, which the literature suggests may result in service improvement and increased efficiency. Others have also pointed to the potential for co-production to add value as an extension to the process of service production (Brudney and England, 1983; Brudney, 1987). Wilson (1981, p. 43) argues that co-production 'involves a direct transformation of a product' through the joint action of the service provider and user, while Whitaker (1980, p. 240) argues that the service user is 'a vital "coproducer" of any personal transformation that occurs'.

Alford (2002a, 2009) discusses the rationale for co-production from the service user perspective. Drawing on public choice theory, he argues that individuals may co-produce out of self-interest, but that the motivations to co-produce are complex and may be shaped by social values such as altruism. However, he also notes that those who play different roles are likely to have different motivations; while customers might be self-interested and seek to maximise material rewards for themselves, citizens might be encouraged to produce more complex reasons such as intrinsic rewards. Alford and Yates (2016) also examined the reasons why service users might co-produce and found that individual activities with high levels of private value are more likely, while group activities that invoke public value are less frequent. Along similar lines, Pestoff (2012a) argues that individuals are more likely to be involved if service is important to themselves or family, while Verschuere et al. (2012) expand the proposal, suggesting that individual participation in co-production will depend upon the ease at which people can be involved and the time and effort they need to expend to participate. In their empirical study on healthcare, Van Eijk and Steen (2014) theorise motivation for co-production among service users under four perspectives, each of which was found to adhere to community-centred rather than self-centred motivations: the 'semi-professional' who aims to make a material contribution to the public service organisation, the 'passive socialiser' who seeks to build trust and an open relationship, the 'network professional' who seeks to improve the operations of the service organisation for the benefit of its clients and the 'aware co-producer' who resists motives of self-interest.

# The Evolution of Co-production From a Public Administration Perspective

## Origins of Co-production

Prior to 1979, public service production centred around notions of professional autonomy and the dependency of clients (Clarke and Newman, 1997) who Fotaki (2011) describes as the 'passive beneficiaries' of the welfare state as they exercise no control over bureaucratically produced public services. Debate has generally set the co-production of public services apart as a variation on the 'traditional' model of public service production (e.g. Ferris, 1988; Brudney, 1987), where 'public officials are exclusively charged with responsibility for designing and providing services to citizens, who in turn *only* demand, consume and evaluate them' (Pestoff, 2006, p. 506, my emphasis). Instead, responsibility for the design and delivery of services was placed predominantly in the hands of public officials and professionals, while the role of the service user was largely passive (Ostrom, 1978; Brudney and England, 1983); any contribution made by individual service users was typically received as an insignificant or supplementary role (Parks et al., 1981).

Although the term 'co-production' can be traced back to the 1920s, a pivotal point in the debate was the seminal work of Ostrom (1972, 1978), who subscribed to a classical public administration narrative. Alford (2014) offers a comprehensive account of Ostrom's work, so the discussion here will be brief. Ostrom studied urban reform in major cities in the United States and her findings suggested that most public services were not delivered by an organisation working alone, but by various public and private actors, and particularly that many public services are dependent upon the efforts and contributions of those who consume them. She defines co-production broadly as a 'process through which inputs are used to provide a good or service that are contributed by individuals who are not in the same organisation' (1996, p. 1073) and argued that citizens play an active role in the production of public services that are of consequence to them. She concluded that organisations providing public services depend as much upon the community for policy implementation and service delivery as the community depends upon them (Ostrom, 1972, 1978). This was the genesis of the concept of co-production within the public administration literature.

According to Porter (2012), Ostrom's work developed two distinct streams of focus on co-production. Her initial work focused on co-production as combined effort from consumer and regular producer: 'the mix of activities that both public service agents and citizens contribute to the provision of public services' (Pestoff, 2006, p. 506). The former is involved as professionals, or 'regular producers'. After reviewing the public administration conceptualisation of co-production,

Nabatchi et al. (2017, p. 769) offer a useful distinction of the two actors who are involved in co-production: '(1) state actors who are (direct or indirect) agents of government serving in a professional capacity (i.e. "regular producers"), and (2) lay actors who are members of the public serving voluntarily as citizens, clients, and/or consumers (i.e., the "citizen producers")'. This definition is helpful in clarifying that any type of organisation delivering public services can co-produce, with public service users operating in various roles depending on what type of co-productive activities they are engaged in. 'Citizen production' refers to the voluntary efforts by individuals and groups to enhance the quality and/or quantity of the services they use (Parks et al., 1981). The inference here is that co-production is voluntary and citizens are drawn upon by professionals to improve service quality or quantity. However, by using examples from education and policing, Ostrom argued that the quality of public services is typically framed not only by the public service organisation but depends also on the contributions of those using the services: 'users of many public services are themselves essential co-producers. . . . Public servants help to accomplish these tasks, they rarely produce the results themselves' (Ostrom, 1989, p. 148). However, Ostrom's work latterly emphasised co-production as an alternative to institutional rule that may or may not be used to create a service: 'co-production adds qualities to a service even if the service could be created without inputs from the consumer producer. Co-production becomes an alternative institutional rule through which decentralised institutions may contribute to the creation of a public service' (Ostrom, 1996, p. 149). This latter, more normative view of co-production has become the main focus of the public administration literature, with co-production typically being seen to promote participative democracy (Ostrom, 2000; Fung, 2006).

Ostrom's early writings led to the subsequent development of a highly influential implementation literature on co-production, predominantly in the United States, Europe and Australia (Sharp, 1980; Whitaker, 1980; Levine and Fisher, 1984; Rosentraub, 1981; Brudney and England, 1983; Bovaird, 2007; Alford, 2002a, 2009). However, the conceptualisation of co-production in the public sector setting has been criticised for its lack of clarity (Osborne et al., 2016) with debate continuing around its definition and potential impact (Verschuere et al., 2012; Voorberg et al., 2015).

### The Classical View of Public Service Co-production

In line with Ostrom (1996), a strong participatory narrative of co-production has evolved in the public administration literature, which has generally espoused a partnership approach (Parks et al., 1981; Alford, 2002a; Pestoff, 2006; Denhardt and Denhardt, 2015; Nabatchi et al., 2017) where service users (as individuals or in groups) actively and voluntarily cooperate with public service organisations and contribute to the processes of service design and delivery (Brudney and England, 1983; Whitaker, 1980; Pestoff, 2006). Co-production has been employed to refer specifically to the relationship that exists during service delivery (Alford, 2009) and also to the complete cycle of public services encompassing planning through to evaluation (Bovaird, 2005).

Partnership and the voluntary and active participation of service users have been emphasised as the key components of co-production throughout the evolution of the concept. In the early theory, co-production manifested through an economic perspective that recognised an overlap between the consumer and producer spheres (Brudney and England, 1983). The combined efforts of the consumer and front-line service providers to determine the quality and quantity of services draws on Parks et al. (1981, p. 1002) who refer to this as the 'mixing of the productive efforts of regular and consumer producers'. The Figure 2.1 highlights this overlap, which is typically described as the site of co-production. The economic desirability of co-production, according to Parks et al. (1981), was dependent upon whether mixing the productive efforts of the public service organisation and service user was efficient. They argued that 'consumer producers' can substitute public service staff where the necessary conditions for co-production are present, arguing that co-production must be technically feasible, economically viable and institutionally achievable for an organisation.

The emphasis here is on the partnership of two parties that operate from different places in the production process (i.e. service provider and consumer) and whose productive efforts are combined to increase efficiency and effectiveness (Parks et al., 1981; Brudney and England, 1983). One party is the public service organisation or the professional staff of such an organisation, which/who would have traditionally planned and produced a public service in its own right (Parks et al., 1981). The other is the individual service user who subsequently consumes the public service and through co-production contributes through consumer mechanisms.

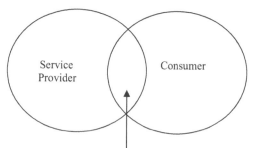

Co-production: 'the critical mix' where the two actors overlap

*Figure 2.1*  Mixing productive efforts

Source: Adapted from Brudney and England (1983, p. 61)

From the public administration perspective, Bovaird (2007) has built and refined the idea of co-production, extending the idea of partnership. He defines co-production as 'regular, long-term relationships between professionalised service providers (in any sector) and service users or other members of the community, where all parties make substantial resource contributions' (Bovaird, 2007, p. 847). Bovaird argues that various relationships between service users and public service organisations can exist, depending upon the respective roles of each in the planning and delivery of public services. This is a significant conceptual development for co-production within public administration for it comprehensively details the range of roles and experiences service users might play. Pestoff (2014) contends that such a partnership can operate on an individual or collective level, between public service providers and citizens as individuals or groups of citizens. He argues that collective action among small formally organised groups, mixed with individual acts of co-production, is critical to the viability and sustainability of co-production because the collective or group co-production overcomes the risk of disparity in services where individual co-producers might 'do their own thing'. Furthermore, Bovaird et al. (2016) argue that, through group-based activities, collective co-production can achieve greater value than individual forms.

An underpinning element of partnership in co-production is dialogue and interaction (Sharp, 1980). Dunston et al. (2009) differentiate co-production from the traditional participative approach of voice or choice that is espoused by the New Public Management literature (e.g. Hirschman, 1970), and will be discussed later, as a form of partnership that is rooted within dialogue and learning. They describe co-productive services as relational, involving dialogue, empathy and understanding. Bovaird (2007) also emphasises reciprocity and mutuality in co-production. Bovaird and Loeffler (2012) expand this argument, emphasising that service users are not passive and often have knowledge that the public service organisation does not, and therefore have an essential role to play in service production. They can thus engage in a collaborative way rather than through the more traditional paternalistic relationship with public service providers.

The focus on partnership has continued within the New Public Governance narrative that has more recently dominated the debate on co-production and has also developed the classical formulation of the concept. Within this narrative, the emphasis on collaboration has sought to transform traditional roles, with citizens typically conceptualised as co-producers working within a horizontal relationship with government (Pestoff, 2006, 2014; Pestoff and Brandsen, 2010; Meijer, 2016). In this context, co-production describes a cooperative relationship between citizens and government during public service planning and delivery (Meijer, 2016) where citizens possess valuable knowledge, skills and resources to make effective contributions (Thomsen, 2017). Verschuere et al. (2012)

describe this collaborative approach as adhering to a transactional model that shapes a relationship of agreement between partners who both cooperate and compensate for one another's shortcomings. The suggestion implicit here is that co-production potentially blocks a gap on either side of the relationship to achieve service improvement. However, the arguments made relating to service user potential to add knowledge and skills is problematic as the narrative on co-production has referred to service users as 'lay people' (see, for example, Nabatchi et al., 2017), which has significant implications for how their part is played out in practice. These will be discussed in greater detail in the section on the limitations and challenges of co-production.

The active role of the citizen is also a key dimension of co-production from this perspective, with Brandsen and Honingh (2016, p. 431) forwarding the following definition: 'Co-production is a relationship between a paid employee of an organisation and (groups of) individual citizens that requires direct and active contribution from these citizens to the work of the organisation'. Nevertheless, their level of activeness is likely to sit on a continuum and depend upon the mechanisms through which they co-produce. In other words, those citizens who regularly sit on the board of a service organisation are likely to play a more direct and active role in the operations of the organisation than those whose opinions are gathered through a one-off consultation event. Ultimately, citizen activeness in co-production depends upon two factors: the extent to which the public service organisation facilitates their genuine involvement (and the mechanisms it utilises to facilitate this) and, perhaps more crucially, the propensity for each party to engage in and support the co-productive activity. Indeed, the output of both examples of co-production is likely to be regulated by public managers who can control the extent to which a citizen's contribution is reflected in and shapes public service planning and delivery. The second point also suggests that citizens need to be motivated to co-produce and this further reflects the voluntary dimension of co-production, which is also key to understanding the concept from this perspective, because it suggests cooperative action that is not in any way coerced or obligated (Nabatchi et al., 2017). According to Pestoff (2014), co-production emphasises the existence of a synergy between the activities of public service providers and citizens/service users, and also a partnership relationship among services users and between service users and public service staff. Taking a different perspective from Bovaird (2007), Pestoff (2009) recognises that while co-production forwards a shift in relations between public service organisations and citizens, the strength of that new relationship is variable; co-production can be through intense and persistent citizen participation or can take the form of short-lived and sporadic involvement, depending upon the choices made by public service staff and the co-producers they invite into the process of service design or delivery.

The central point in this argument is that co-production is something external to the delivery of a public service that needs to be designed into these services in order to achieve specified desired outcomes. The implementation, application and impact of co-production ultimately then relies upon the commitment of managers, professionals and service users (Boyle et al., 2006; Crowley et al., 2002). Gaster and Rutqvist (2000) argue that in order to understand local needs and uphold their accountability, delivery organisations rely on front-line service staff to implement ideas in their local setting. According to Gaster and Rutqvist, the role of the front-line staff in a public service organisation is essential if public services are to be successfully re-designed to meet need. This confers a high degree of responsibility and discretion over the execution of policies on the ground to those organisations delivering the services and particularly to their staff who have personal contact with the service users.

### Co-production Through Participation

Within the classical formulation, co-production has been closely aligned with participation, with the terms often being used interchangeably (Percy, 1983; Whitaker, 1980; Wilson, 1981; Brudney and England, 1983). Indeed, the literature from the 1980s, largely from the United States, equates co-production with citizen participation but focuses on service delivery, where the ultimate goal of public service staff is to 'transform' those using services (Whitaker, 1980, p. 240).

The participation literature is vast and complex, with participation being captured by a multitude of terms including involvement, engagement, volunteering and empowerment—each of which has its own distinct nuances. Participation can be broadly defined as the process by which citizens can share power with public officials in taking substantive decisions or actions related to the community (Roberts, 2004). It can also take two broad forms, involving individual or collective actions (Box, 1999). At both levels, participation has been strongly associated with the concept of citizenship. For individual participation, the focus is typically around personal gains, while collective forms of participation such as lobbying and membership of interest groups are likely to strive for values of shared interest.

Various models of participation have been developed to provide an understanding of the democratic input people can have individually or collectively. Although dated, and not without its critics (e.g. Fung, 2006; Tritter and McCallum, 2006), Arnstein's (1969) ladder of civic engagement, for example, continues to feature in the academic literature as a means of describing and understanding the extent to which individuals co-produce services (e.g. Havassy and Yanay, 1990; Bovaird, 2007; Farrell, 2010; Denhardt and Denhardt, 2015; Boyer et al., 2016; Jun and

Bryer, 2017). Arnstein's model presents participation in a hierarchical model, which depicts eight levels of participation that denote the degree of power participants may exercise from low to high. 'Non-participation' (manipulation and therapy) is therefore situated at the bottom of the ladder, in the middle 'tokenistic forms' of participation are included (information, consultation, placation) and at the top, 'citizen control' (partnership, delegation, citizen control) forms the greatest degree to which citizens might be empowered.

The model is helpful in exploring the actuality of co-production from the participatory democracy narrative that underpins the classical formulation of the concept of co-production. It recognises that participation in service planning and delivery can, in reality, range from cosmetic and limited forms of co-production to a higher degree of service user empowerment. At the lower rungs of the ladder, co-production may take the form of public consultations where there is no commitment to act. Although these terms are often used interchangeably in policy documents (Martin and Boaz, 2000), consultation and co-production are unalike in process and output. Needham (2007), for example, argues that consultation typically reaffirms traditional roles and divisions between service users and officials due to their one-off nature and the output of wish-lists, while co-production stresses dialogue, interaction and negotiation. At the higher end of the ladder, where much of the classical work points to as the locus of co-production, the service user is an active member of a service partnership. Indeed, as the earlier discussion indicated, partnership is a core element of co-production in the early public administration literature and more recently within the New Public Governance narrative (Brudney and England, 1983; Levine and Fisher, 1984; Sundeen, 1988; Marschall, 2004; Pestoff, 2006). Referring again to Arnstein's ladder of participation, public service users might also exercise greater power where they have a direct effect upon the direction of service development through devolved service planning/delivery (e.g. Levine and Fisher, 1984; Parks et al., 1981). For example, in health and social care provision, there is a strong impetus towards self-directed support or self-management, where the service users or their guardians/carers control their care budget and plan their care package according to their needs.

In his analysis, Ferris (1988) describes *volunteers* as co-producers, suggesting less power for the citizen than through completely devolved provision, but perhaps delegated forms of power in Arnstein's model. Ferris argues that although the focus upon citizen participation has been helpful in understanding co-production, it can overlook and misrepresent the role of volunteers in public service delivery. Rather, Ferris argues that voluntary action can reduce the efforts and resources required from public service organisations to produce or improve services (see also Sundeen, 1988). Others have taken a similar stance. Brudney (1987) contends that co-production includes the self-help and voluntary activities of individuals and organisations and Bovaird (2007) uses the number of active volunteers as a proxy for co-production in UK public services. Nevertheless, other scholars such as Alford (2009) and Verschuere et al. (2012) make a distinction between volunteering and co-production, suggesting that citizens contribute resources when they volunteer, but co-production requires both the contribution of resources and also consumption of the service. This argument suggests a narrower interpretation of co-production, which implies that only service users can co-produce, and thereby neglects the potential co-production of friends, families or the wider community.

### Limitations and Challenges of Co-production: The Public Administration Perspective

There is an assumption in much of the co-production literature that co-production itself, like public engagement, is a good thing. Indeed, co-production has generally been positioned normatively in the literature as a means of reducing costs, improving services and building social capital through the participation of service users, but the literature emphasises that co-production is not a panacea to all challenges within public service production (Percy, 1983; Levine and Fisher, 1984; Pammer, 1992; Bovaird, 2007). Williams et al. (2016) for example warn that implicit in the narrative around co-production is the potential for active service user involvement to result in various benefits for individual service users and wider society, but that co-production can also serve to destroy public value.

Six clear challenges for co-production from the public administration perspective have been identified in the review of the literature. First, the idea of partnership that is espoused through co-production is problematic on two levels. On one level, partnerships can lead to methods of working that may preclude co-production, as resources may be diverted predominantly to the facilitation of the partnership and may also lead to 'organised tribalism' where professionals become more protective of their expertise and less open to outside involvement (Rummery, 2006). The other level concerns the issue of sharing power that is implied through the partnership approach. The discussion so far suggests that the power relations between public service staff and service user co-producers are far from equal. The conceptualisation of co-production within classical public administration narrative suggests that the balance of power is tipped strongly in favour of the public service organisation, particularly in certain public services where front-line staff not only promote and facilitate co-production, but also 'refuse treatment, commit users to mental hospital or take children into care' (Wilson, 1994, p. 247). Evers et al. (2005, p. 744) note that professionals might be overly concerned with 'defending their power and privileges', which could limit scope for co-production at this level. Indeed, the conceptualisation of empowerment, which has often been central to co-production, from this perspective necessitates that those in power share power, but because traditional power holders (e.g. professionals or managers) control the dispersal of power, they ultimately control the extent to which various outside stakeholders might influence decision-making processes: the 'language of empowerment can provide a cloak under which powerful actors obscure their continuing exercise of power' (Callaghan and Wistow, 2006, p. 596). Verschuere et al. (2012) also argue that professionals potentially value their own education and experience above that of 'lay people'. In comparison to healthcare professionals, who hold expert knowledge and a strong professionalism, for example, service users may always be positioned as second-class experts or 'lay people' (Dunston et al., 2009; Ewert and Evers, 2012). Nabatchi et al. (2017), for instance, describe co-production as the cooperative action of 'lay actors' with public service staff. The focus on the empowerment of service users arguably maintains dominant power asymmetries and potentially therefore limits the transformative potential of co-production.

Second, the structural positioning of co-production within the public administration narrative has significant challenges for its application and impact. By conceptualising co-production as an alternative to the traditional model, the literature discusses the ways in which the service user—as co-producer—might be 'added into' the process of service production to improve the quality of these services. Co-production does change the nature of public administration, or at least reframes it, but this can only occur at the behest of, and is controlled by, service professionals (Brandsen and Pestoff, 2006). Co-production is positioned as an option for public service organisations, being introduced by public managers and thereafter embedded into organisational processes (Nabatchi et al., 2017). Ostrom (1996) argues, for instance, that public service staff—and particularly the 'street level bureaucrats' working on the front line—play a significant role in the facilitation of co-production, exercising the power to encourage or discourage participation. The implication is that co-production, like traditional methods of participation, is appended to service design and delivery; the implementation of the process and the associated outcomes are therefore controlled to a large extent by the public service organisations and the staff within them.

Third, because co-production exists through relationships between public service staff and service users, there is a challenge for public service organisations to effectively manage co-production to ensure the intended aims. Jaspers and Steen (2018) argue that the process of co-production is expected to enhance the relationship between service users and public service organisations, but Williams et al. (2016) argue that the misuse of resources by either partner during the processes and interactions of co-production can result in the contamination of value: 'Acknowledging the potential for value co-contamination by regular and user producers is the first step in the dance to enhance co-production' (Williams et al., 2016, p. 710).

From the conceptualisation of co-production depicted so far, service users need an appetite or motivation to co-produce given that co-production is voluntary and 'added on', which requires that they dedicate personal time and energy to service production; this forms the fourth challenge. A debate exists as to whether they have either the time or inclination for this (Williams et al., 2016). Pestoff argues, for instance, that 'citizens are not like a jack-in-the-box, just waiting for someone to push a lever or remove a latch that will immediately release their energies and result in their engagement in social service co-production' (2012a, p. 25). Alford (2002a, 2009, 2014) has usefully explored the possibilities of co-production in public services, in terms of the inducements and sanctions used by public service professionals, to enable the process. He discusses co-production, using a social exchange perspective that he differentiates from customer transactions in the private sector, given that it is founded upon trust, co-operation and compliance whereby public service clients not only consume services but can also contribute to and influence 'positive actions to collective purposes' (Alford, 2002b, p. 344). Alford argues that without the contribution of clients, the service can fail, but further contends that collectively citizens can exert greater power (Alford, 2009). Denhardt and Denhardt (2015) uphold this argument, reasoning that the justification for co-production should not be narrow economic or political criteria, but the potential for enhanced citizenship through increased citizen responsibility and a shared conception of the common good. Nevertheless, the assumption here is that there is a latent desire among the citizenry to co-produce.

The fifth challenge concerns the disconnect between the definition of co-production presented within the public administration narrative and the reality (and limitations) of co-production in practice. Bovaird (2007) and others (e.g. Verschuere et al., 2012) question who is likely to participate in co-production, which is likely to fall disproportionately to more well-off sections of society. The leading narrative of co-production places citizens at the heart of the process of service production (Ostrom, 1996), but the reality is that, like traditional forms of participation, the nature and reach of co-production and the role of citizens is on the periphery of service delivery and design, being open predominantly to those with the necessary skills and resources. In her study of stakeholder experiences of co-production, for example, Crompton (2018) found that inclusivity was not an overriding feature of co-production and typically favoured those stakeholders with an understanding of the purpose and process of co-production who could therefore use co-production to pursue their own agenda or deter change. Indeed, Pestoff (2014) defines co-production as various collaborative tasks that involve close interdependence. Within the examples, he includes the installation of burglar alarms to support policing, eating healthily and exercise to support effective healthcare and fundraising for schools. However, such a description of co-production focuses on those citizens who possess the social and economic means to co-produce (i.e. those who can afford to eat healthily or install burglar alarms, or who have the requisite skills, motivation and feelings of civic responsibility to raise funds for the local school).

Finally, there are challenges around the empirical analysis of co-production in the public sector setting. Nabatchi et al. (2017, p. 766) argue that 'the normative appeal and orthodoxy surrounding coproduction may be hindering needed empirical scrutiny', which suggests that the focus on co-production as an inherently good thing, overlooks its destructive potential (Alford, 2016). The terms co-creation and co-production have also been used interchangeably in much of the literature (Voorberg et al., 2015) which adds to this conceptual confusion. Furthermore, the broad application of co-production as an 'umbrella' concept makes meaningful analytical examination difficult (Verschuere et al., 2012; Nabatchi et al., 2017).

## The Influence of the New Public Management on Co-production

The concept of co-production has been shaped and influenced by different narratives: 'Perspectives on co-production relationships are coloured by various background narratives such as consumerism or participatory governance' (Ewert and Evers, 2012, p. 6). The discussion has already noted the participatory underpinnings of the concept detailed in the public administration literature. The discussion will now focus on the substantial influence the New Public Management has had on the evolution of co-production in theory and practice.

As discussed earlier in this chapter, co-production emerged in scholarly debates and in practice in the late 1970s and early 1980s, but the concept lost resonance when focus shifted towards the managerialist agenda of efficiency through privatisation and marketisation (Alford, 1998) under the hegemonic influence of the New Public Management, which traditionally drew upon management theory derived primarily from the manufacturing sector. The New Public Management is strongly linked to a political agenda that involved the privatisation of public service provision in order to 'roll back the state' (Hood et al., 1988; Aberbach and Christensen, 2005). It is underpinned by public choice theory (Hood, 1991), which, in its simplest form, positions the market as the optimal structure for the production of measurable outputs and advocates the relevance of private management experience (Pollitt and Bouckaert, 2004). The economic rationale presented earlier that situates co-production as a way of increasing efficiency and effectiveness (Parks et al., 1981; Brudney and England, 1983) and has developed and extended over the last forty years (devolving responsibility for service production to service users, where consumers as co-producers can substitute the efforts of service providers) has been associated for example with reduced costs (Parks et al., 1981; Levine and Fisher, 1984; Fotaki, 2011, 2015). The managerialist focus of New Public Management, which implies closed decision-making by experts (Ansell and Gash, 2007) through the application of private management techniques, has nevertheless been criticised by adherents of co-production for overlooking the potential of co-production (Pestoff, 2006; Christensen and Laegreid, 2011). Instead, consumerism has characterised the New Public Management, where citizens are re-conceptualised as consumers who are empowered in the market through information and choice or redress through complaints' procedures (Hirschman, 1970; Jung, 2010).

The managerialist offshoots and related performance measurement focus of the New Public Management have implications for how co-production has been constructed and what benefits it is seen to accrue. Co-production has been framed as a means of service improvement through evaluation (Fotaki, 2011; Sicilia, 2016), but is more generally viewed by New Public Management adherents as a means of reducing costs and making efficiency savings, by offering opportunities through which the service user can substitute the efforts of public service staff (Levine and Fisher, 1984; Sundeen, 1988; Clark et al., 2013). Sundeen (1988), for example, recognises that the co-production of public services garnered heightened attention since the late 1970s given budgetary constraints and the associated view that citizen participation may shift the costs of public service production away from public service organisations. Such a rationale is a significant departure from that associated with the more classical view of co-production and the strong focus on normative goals such as improving democracy (e.g. Ostrom, 2000; Pestoff, 2006; Bovaird, 2007).

A defining feature of reforms in the 1990s, for example, was for the revival of participation across nations. In the UK, for example, under the Blair government there was a strong rhetoric around to the potential for participation (of which co-production was described as one mechanism) to catalyse a 'shift of power and influence away from bureau-professionals and front-line staff towards citizens and service users' (Martin and Boaz, 2000, p. 47). Service users were asked to participate in planning, provision and evaluation of services in order to increase the legitimacy and responsiveness of local government (Martin and Boaz, 2000). This took place through various forms of participative mechanisms including consumer councils, customer relations through a two-way flow of information, tenant groups, consultation, consumer/citizen panels and co-production (Martin and Boaz, 2000; Lowndes et al., 2001; Barnes et al., 2003; Simmons and Birchall, 2005). These mechanisms were used to engender information-sharing between public service organisations and their customers, to make services more responsive and user-focused and to encourage user-led services, namely co-production (Martin and Boaz, 2000). However, these developments were largely criticised as shallow attempts at reform with government more likely to implement cosmetic forms of participation such as communication and consultation, rather than embedding participative forms of co-production to foster service improvement or innovation (Ross, 1995; Martin and Boaz, 2000; Lowndes et al., 2001).

### Consumerism and Co-production

Under the managerialist narrative, citizens have generally been re-conceptualised as either consumers or customers (Parkinson, 2004; Aberbach and Christensen, 2005), with the terms being used interchangeably throughout much of the literature (Powell et al., 2010). The application of consumerism to public services was intended to shift the power relations away from service producers and toward service users with public services being provided *for* rather than *to* service users (Jung, 2010). Consumerism also had significant implications for the role of service users in co-production. Within the New Public Management narrative, the emphasis was on self-interested consumers and their satisfaction with public services (Hood, 1991; Osborne and Gaebler, 1992). The resulting focus for co-production was on empowering sovereign consumers who exercise individual preferences (Aberbach and Christenson, 2005), but who play a passive role, limited to demanding, consuming and evaluating public services. A key argument of Osborne and Gaebler (1992), for instance, was that public services should focus on steering rather than rowing, thus opening up an opportunity for the increased involvement of individuals and organisations in service production. However, the ways that individuals and organisations were involved were specific to the parameters of the movement.

By reconceptualising service users as consumers, the New Public Management has been argued to have created more responsive and inclusive services, removing barriers to access and encouraging producers to predict preferences, listen to consumers (through choice) and involve them (through redress) (Jones and Needham, 2008). There is an assumption in the New Public Management literature that consumers, as the 'perfect cog' in the public management machinery, will become more engaged and responsible citizens (Ventriss, 1998). However, their role and impact are mediated by public managers who are cast as powerful protagonists with the capacity to catalyse deep transformations and innovations in public service delivery through managerial actions and discretion (Terry, 1993). Sicilia et al. (2016) argue that public managers support co-production when it serves normative goals, such as the identification and channelling of people's skills.

One framework which can be drawn on to understand the mechanisms through which individuals can co-produce as consumers is that of Hirschman (1970), who suggests that individuals who seek service improvements have two central strategies: exit or voice. Consumers are then empowered through their access to information and through their associated capacity to make choices or seek redress through complaints' procedures (i.e. voice). With the New Public Management came an expectation that consumers would become more active, with the capacity to make choices, leading Gabriel and Lang (2006) to argue that the idea of the 'consumer as chooser' has monopolised the debate about public services. This is embedded in the idea of individualisation, where self-interested individuals make choices to meet their own specific needs. The aim of choice was to promote independent advocacy by shifting some power away from the service provider and towards the individual consumer who was empowered through his/her ability to make choices in the marketplace (Osborne, 1994). Perri 6 (2003) describes some choices consumers might have, including over the content of the service, its level/quantity, the manner of access and the identity of the service provider.

Although Dunston et al. (2009) differentiate co-production from voice or exit, arguing that co-production places the consumer in the central position of an 'insider'—who works with service providers, within the production process—other commentators such as Greener (2007) argue that co-production combines exit and voice. Indeed, Clarke (2007) found that voice and exit were two of the most prominent modes of exercising influence over the behaviour and output of service providers, with the service users wanting to be heard and recognised and the service providers wanting to learn from service users. Thus, it is important to consider the implications these mechanisms have for co-production. Choice is therefore invariably limited to expressing a preference within a predetermined set of options rather than the exercise of free decision-making capabilities. Voice, by contrast, refers to the capacity of consumers to make complaints, suggestions or provide feedback on the services they receive and this narrative is focused on an individualised notion of voice as opposed to collective action.

## Challenges of Co-production Within the New Public Management Narrative

The reformulation of co-production within the New Public Management narrative, faces various challenges not least because of the managerialist agenda and related closed nature of decision-making which have resulted in the subsequent exclusion of co-production and other forms of participation. Seven key challenges have been identified in the literature.

First, there is an underlying assumption within the managerialist narrative, that public service staff and professionals exercise the necessary expertise and knowledge to design and deliver services (Jones and Needham, 2008). By contrast, service users are viewed as 'lay people' who lack the skills and expertise that would permit their substitution into the role of professionals during service design and delivery (Percy, 1983; Timney, 1998; Pollitt and Bouckaert, 2004). Service users may, as a result, require specialised training, making the facilitation of co-production time-consuming and resource-intensive for public service organisations and potentially diverting attention from the 'real' task of effective and efficient service production and therefore not worthwhile or potentially disruptive to effective managerial practice (King et al., 1998; Martin and Boaz, 2000; Barnes et al., 2003; Lowndes et al., 2006; Bovaird, 2007). This juxtaposition of expertise and roles serves to maintain and strengthen power relations that favour public service staff (Potter, 1988).

Second, citizens are positioned as 'consumers' with limited scope (through choice or redress) to participate or influence closed systems of decision-making. By facilitating the exercise of individual preferences (Aberbach and Christensen, 2005) choice has been argued to empower consumers by increasing the responsiveness of public services (Clarke, 2007). Indeed, the idea of empowering the consumer has become a core theme of public management reform across the globe (Hood et al., 1996). However, the extent to which consumerism has empowered service users is contested (see, for example, Havassy and Yanay, 1990; Jung, 2010; Haikio, 2010): 'the passive user "pawn" of the hierarchically planned and delivered welfare systems is yet to be replaced by the empowered user-consumer with the freedom of movement of a "queen" in the chess board' (Fotaki, 2011, p. 944). Havassy and Yanay (1990) question whether co-production actually seeks to empower service users or co-opt them into the service delivery system, effectively neutralising their voice. Information provision, complaints' procedures and market research do not promote empowerment in the sense of user involvement in planning services (Locke et al., 2003). It does not involve a transfer of power from the public service professional to the individual, which has been a fundamental condition of co-production from the public administration perspective (Bovaird, 2007). Choice can also be disempowering (Locke et al., 2003; Jung, 2010). Bolzan and Gale (2002) argue, for example, that although consumers have power to influence the parameters of competition between service providers and can make demands and complaints, they cannot negotiate unacknowledged needs. Furthermore, in her study of health and social care services, Fotaki (2011) found that in reality consumers have little power and willingness to choose alternate public services, which are often limited by postcode, few alternatives, insufficient information and inadequate or no influence over the content of services. Pestoff (2009) also argues that some public service users are locked into services, providing no option of exit, while the New Public Management narrative offers limited space for participation. The market mechanisms articulated under New Public Management have therefore been criticised for their failure to shift the power balance towards public service users or citizens (Lowndes et al., 2001; Simmons and Birchall, 2005).

Third, but still on the theme of empowerment (or lack of it), the closed nature of managerialist decision-making serves to exclude consumers, with public managers controlling the applications and impact of consumer mechanisms (Timney, 1998). When co-production has taken place, it has been criticised as a mechanism of control (Parkinson, 2004) and as a way of rubber stamping pre-made decisions for the benefit of public officials rather than influencing service delivery or design (Timney, 1998). Dunston et al. (2009) argue that although voice and choice offer important means of participation, such mechanisms do not modify the dominant culture and practices in the health service that are based on an inside-out, professionally designed and delivered approach. They suggest that such an approach does not support a truly interactive and learning partnership that is implicit in the classical formulation of co-production. The implication here is that public service staff control whether to append co-production, which form it will take, its impact and, importantly, therefore the extent to which consumers are empowered. The challenge here is that power is transferred to service users at the whim of traditional power holders (e.g. professionals), which essentially maintains a paternalistic relationship where the power holder controls the extent to which service users might influence decision-making processes. Professionals may therefore resent and even resist the inclusion of untrained and inexperienced service users into the production process, particularly when they fear losing control or authority over their role and professional expertise (Pestoff, 2006; Bovaird, 2007).

Fourth, and related to the New Public Management focus on consumers, are the various challenges associated with consumer mechanisms. Similar to traditional participative mechanisms described with reference to the classical view of co-production, the mechanisms of involvement offered by the New Public Management are challenging in a public service context due to their inequitable use and application. Accessing information to enable consumers to make informed choices, for example, is likely to fall disproportionately to well-educated sections of society, exacerbating inequalities (Fountain, 2001; Bochel et al., 2007; Haikio, 2010; Christensen and Laegreid, 2011). Haikio (2010) argues that the narrative on voice and exit fails to contend with the issue that such mechanisms are open to only certain parts of society and generally 'the people who are most in need of public services have the weakest capacity to identify themselves as having political agency to take action' (Haikio, 2010, p. 377). Choice and voice may therefore result in an inequitable distribution of services, disadvantaging those who are most in need of the services (Langan, 2000). Jakobsen and Andersen (2013) also argue that co-production is open to certain sections of society and typically closed to more disadvantaged groups who lack the necessary knowledge and resources that would support their participation; the authors found that this may increase inequity in service outcomes. This raises important questions, particularly in the case of marginalised groups, such as asylum seekers, who may not have the capacity to make choices and voice their opinions or complaints. Choice, for instance, is dependent on the availability of necessary information and also the ability to understand this information in order to make informed choices (Jones and Needham, 2008). Concerns over the depth and applicability of voice, and whether some voices will be heard over or will delegitimise others, have also been raised (Clarke, 2005, 2007; Jones and Needham, 2008).

Within the New Public Management, consumers act as economically rational individuals and by consequence, the values of reciprocity, collective action and co-production are of less significance (Pestoff, 2012b). The New Public Management's individualistic ontology has thus been criticised for focusing on individual consumers rather than on the collective (Powell et al., 2010) and this forms the fifth challenge for co-production within this narrative. The focus on self-interested consumers has been argued to misrepresent the collective experience of public services by corroding the collaborative relationships and trust that are essential to effective public services in contemporary fragmented societies (Farrell, 2000; Jones and Needham, 2008; Dougherty and Easton, 2011). The individualistic focus has been further condemned for its disregard of democratic principles, such as equity and fairness (Frederickson, 1996; Terry, 1993; Box, 1999; Martin and Boaz, 2000; Christensen and Laegreid, 2002; Goodsell, 2006; Moynihan, 2010).

The sixth challenge concerns the reasoning behind co-production in relation to reducing costs and making efficiency savings. Critics have argued that the goal of co-production has not been to improve services but to shift costs and risk to service users who share the burden of production, including its monetary costs, time and effort (Needham, 2007; Levine and Fisher, 1984).

Finally, the New Public Management has been criticised for embracing a 'product-dominant logic', likening public services to manufactured goods that are designed and produced by service professionals in isolation (Dunston et al., 2009; Osborne et al., 2013). Production and consumption are therefore conceptualised as discrete processes and consumers are passive players who may only contribute, by invitation, to the process of service production (Alford, 2016; Osborne et al., 2016). This has implications for how participation is understood, suggesting that it is a process that is added on and that power then rests with public service staff to implement, facilitate and sustain co-production.

## Who Is the Co-producer: Clients, Consumers and Citizens

Early literature on co-production focused on two sets of actors. First, 'regular producers' such as public service staff or professionals and second, 'citizen producers' who were generally described as lay people who voluntarily participate in service design or delivery as either individuals or groups (Parks et al., 1981; Ostrom, 1996). The idea of who co-produces has developed and expanded over time, with regular producers including any organisations that deliver public services, including the third and for-profit sectors, and the other party of the relationship being expanded to include not only citizens, but also consumers, service users, communities and family members (Pestoff, 2006; Bovaird, 2007; Alford, 2014). The role of the 'citizen co-producer' has advanced concurrently with the theoretical developments. While traditional public administration emphasises the separation of politics and administration, with the latter focusing upon the relationship between citizens and public services and their mediation through professionals, the New Public Management, by contrast, has emphasised the resource constraints of public service delivery and the need for a managerial approach to their delivery, recasting citizens as the 'consumers' rather than 'clients' of public services (Hood, 1991). Its focus on consumers has been criticised for overlooking the role of co-producers in public service production (Bovaird, 2007; Meijer, 2011).

The terminology used to describe the role played by those using public services is nevertheless disorderly and, at times, confusing. Jung (2010) argues that, under the vague concept of consumerism, disagreement exists over what public service users should be called. He notes that various descriptions have been used, including consumers, citizens, clients and customers, coupled with more specific terms relating to the type of service being provided (e.g. patients, pupils, parents, tenants and prisoners). This variety leads to a lack of clarity about respective roles. Likewise, in the co-production literature, developing clear categorisations of who co-produces is challenging given that terms are used interchangeably. For example, Rosentraub and Warren (1987) argue that 'coproduction involves the participation of citizen-consumers in the production of services' and Brudney and England (1983, p. 63) refer to 'consumers (e.g. citizens)'. Each term suggests different connotations and implications for co-production, but Fotaki (2011) questions whether these terms are appropriate given that public service users themselves are unlikely to think of themselves using these categorisations. However, the casting of the role played by those co-producing public services is of particular importance here given the focus of the empirical work is on asylum seekers who occupy a challenging position as non-citizens and, as such, typically have limited or no capacity to participate fully in society (Chapter 6 will discuss this in depth).

The wider literature on public management has often compared and contrasted the role of the citizen and consumer. Needham (2007) for example discusses the various categories of the citizen (public, collectivist, common culture, active production and creativity, rights and obligations, political accountability) vs the consumer (private, individualistic, diversity, passive recipient, choice and market accountability). However, she caveats this distinction arguing that both citizens and consumers can step outside their conventional depictions.

A *citizen*, according to Alford (2002b), is part of a collective who express themselves through voice as opposed to choice, but they can also be viewed as individuals: 'citizens are often seen as the quintessential welfare state user. Control is exercised through political voice' (Powell et al., 2010, p. 326). Citizenship has traditionally offered an alternative path towards empowerment, typically through collectivism, but as the preceding discussion has suggested, the methods through which empowerment can be achieved range from tokenistic to control (Fotaki, 2011). Pickard (1998) makes some interesting distinctions between service users and citizens. Only citizens confer legitimacy upon political structures and increasing the involvement of citizens would strive towards creating greater active citizenship and trust in service providers. *Service users*, by contrast, are described as being more sensitive to issues of responsiveness, but like citizens have a stake in accountability. Gilliatt et al. (2000, p. 335) recommend that to involve service users in the planning and delivery of services, there is a need to move away from the narrow concept of the consumer towards 'a wider idea of citizenship which would empower users, giving them policy-making rather than policy-taking roles'. It is questionable whether all public service users can fully embrace the role of either consumers or citizens in order to engage in the types of co-production described earlier, each of which is dependent upon access to consumer or participative mechanisms. As will be discussed in the next chapter, it is around this issue that the service management literature becomes of import, as it suggests that co-production exists through the process of service production and is therefore not attached to a specific persona or mechanisms of involvement, but the relationship between the individuals using the service and those providing it.

The term 'client' has traditionally been associated with the public administration era (before Ostrom and co-production) when service users were treated as passive and dependent (Christensen and Laegreid, 2002). Among Ostrom and her colleagues, there was some agreement that referring to a client co-producer was inappropriate. Ostrom (1996) notes, for example, that the term 'client' is passive in the sense that clients are acted upon, while both Whitaker (1980) and Levine and Fisher (1984) argue that 'client' wrongly infers that an individual is seeking the favour of the service provider. Thus, the term 'citizen' was favoured because it implied a more active role through participative mechanisms (Ostrom, 1990, 1999). More recently, the term 'client' has emerged in the co-production literature to suggest an active role for service users. It has, nevertheless, been subject to different responses. Alford (1998, 2002a, 2009) discusses various co-producers, including clients, citizens, volunteers, service users and third sector organisations, but his primary focus is the client. In co-productive relationships, clients are said to be comparable to buyers, taking on a dual role as recipient of the service and contributory producer. Clients receive private value from services, exercise choice through market mechanisms and have a direct interest in their relationship with the service provider because they receive material benefit from the service (Alford, 2002a).

Nabatchi et al. (2017) further clarify the roles of the citizen, client and customer, arguing that the citizen is a member of a geographical or political community, a client is a recipient of a public service to which he/she is legally entitled to and a customer pays for the public service. As suggested previously, the non-citizenship status of asylum seekers makes it difficult to view them as citizen co-producers and, as such, the case study investigates whether they can co-produce under the other two guises. However, an important consistency that has formed a key thread of the narrative on who co-produces has been the depiction of the client, citizen or consumer *'lay people'* who, by consequence of this categorisation, are unqualified and do not possess the requisite knowledge and expertise to be involved in the complex processes of service design and delivery (Fischer, 2006; Wagenaar, 2007; Meijer, 2014). Their participation may, as a result, be considered by skilled public service staff as an uninformed intrusion on their professional decision-making capacity (Kweit and Kweit, 2004; Bryer and Cooper, 2012). However, an alternative perspective has been forwarded in relation to participatory budgeting, where citizens are viewed as possessing the necessary local knowledge and understanding of their communities that supplements that of professionals and results in the production of more effective public services (Guo and Neshkova, 2012). Others have argued along similar lines. Boyer et al. (2016) suggest, for instance, that, as non-experts, citizens can offer a nuanced perspective on the local context and needs, while professionals offer technical skill and knowledge, and in the healthcare context Dunston et al. (2009) argue that consumers are increasingly viewed as assets. The knowledge and skills that service users possess and potentially benefit the process of service production will be discussed in greater depth in Chapter 3 which explores the service management theory.

## Summary: Co-production From a Public Service Management Perspective

Although Ostrom's early work concluded that most public services are not delivered by a single public authority alone but several different actors working together including individual co-producers, the normative development of the concept, its alignment with participatory democracy and the dominance of the New Public Management in many countries across the world has meant that public service production has neither been conceptualised or managed in the way that Ostrom's (1989) early work signified (i.e. with the service user playing a central role in co-production).

There have nevertheless been important conceptual developments of co-production, notably through the work of Bovaird (2007, 2009) and Alford (2009), who have moved the debate considerably from initial concerns of writers in the late 1970s and 1980s.

While the concept of co-production has evolved under different narratives of public service reform, the literature shares the general assumption that public service users are not only passive consumers but also *potential* producers of services, who can be enacted when required. Co-production, from this perspective, is an extension of the service production process; it is voluntary on the part of the individual or groups who can play various roles, including citizens, clients and consumers and is applied at the behest of public service organisations and their employees. The emphasis here is a partnership relationship between individuals or groups of citizens/consumers and public service organisations, which is rooted in dialogue, reciprocity and mutuality, but the challenges surrounding co-production, such as professional dominance and tokenistic forms of involvement, raise questions as to whether these qualities do in fact exist. Co-production has generally been upheld as a means of creating value, helping to achieve broad policy goals or improve democracy by increasing the number of actors involved, but it has been suggested that using categorisations such as 'consumer' and 'citizen' and their associated mechanisms of involvement may restrict the involvement of certain parts of society.

A key dimension of co-production which has characterised the literature is that the public service user's contribution over the past four decades is its operationalisation as *an optional extension* of 'traditional' service production, rather than as a core component of it. The discussion has suggested the various ways in which the service user (as a consumer or citizen) can be 'added into' the process of service production and that co-production can only occur at the behest of, and controlled by, service professionals. The public service organisation—which is defined throughout the literature as the locus of power, knowledge and capability—controls the extent to which public service users can actively co-produce their services through the facilitation of various mechanisms. The public administration literature aligns co-production with the citizen and the use of participative mechanisms, such as partnership and volunteering, while the New Public Management promotes the consumer with mechanisms of voice and choice. At the service planning stage, a public service organisation might, for example, introduce opportunities for service users to contribute to decisions over which services are produced, and the format that they take, by consulting them. An alternative mode of engagement at the service delivery stage might be through a service user's involvement in service provision as a volunteer—though invariably as an add-on to another service user's service experience. In neither formulation, though, is co-production seen as inherent to service delivery.

## References

Aberbach, J. D. and Christensen, T. (2005). Citizens and consumers: an new public management dilemma. *Public Management Review.* (7,2), 225–245.

Alford, J. (1998). A public management road less travelled: clients as co-producers of public services. *Australian Journal of Public Administration.* (57,4), 128–137.

Alford, J. (2002a). Why do public-sector clients coproduce? *Administration and Society.* (34,1), 32–56.

Alford, J. (2002b). Defining the client in the public sector: a social change perspective. *Public Administration Review.* (62,3), 337–346.

Alford, J. (2009). *Engaging public sector clients: from service-delivery to co-production.* Basingstoke: Palgrave Macmillan.

Alford, J. (2014). The multiple facets of co-production: building on the work of Elinor Ostrom. *Public Management Review.* (16,3), 299–316.

Alford, J. (2016). Co-production, interdependence and publicness: extending public service dominant logic. *Public Management Review.* (18,5),673–691.

Alford, J. and Yates, S. (2016). Co-production of public services in Australia: the roles of government organisations and co-producers. *Australian Journal of Public Administration.* (75,2), 159–175.

Ansell, C. and Gash, A. (2007). Collaborative governance in theory and practice. *Journal of Public Administration Research and Theory.* (18), 543–571.

Arnstein, S. A. (1969). A ladder of citizen participation? *Journal of the American Institute of Planners.* (35,2), 216–224.

Barnes, M., Newman, J., Knops, A. and Sullivan, H. (2003). Constituting 'the public' in public participation. *Public Administration.* (81,2), 379–399.

Bochel, C., Bochel, H., Somerville, P. and Worley, C. (2007). Marginalised or enabled voices? 'User participation' in policy and practice. *Social Policy and Society.* (7,2), 201–210.

Bolzan, N. and Gale, F. (2002). The citizenship of excluded groups: challenging the consumerist agenda. *Social Policy and Administration.* (36,4), 363–375.

Bovaird, T. (2005). Public governance: balancing stakeholder power in a network society. *International Review of Administrative Sciences.* (71,2), 217–228.

Bovaird, T. (2007). Beyond engagement and participation—user and community co-production of public services. *Public Administration Review.* (67), 846–860.

Bovaird, T. (2009). Strategic management in public sector organisations. In Bovaird, T. and Loeffler, E. (eds.), *Public management and governance* (2nd ed.) London: Routledge.

Bovaird, T. and Loeffler, E. (2009). The changing policy context of public policy. In Bovaird, T. and Loffler, E. (eds.), *Public management and governance.* London: Routledge.

Bovaird, T. and Loeffler, E. (2012). From engagement to co-production: how users and communities contribute to public services. In Pestoff, V., Brandsen, T.

and Verschuere, B. (eds.), *New public governance, the third sector and co-production*. New York: Routledge.

Bovaird, T., Stoker, G., Jones, T. and Loeffler, E. (2016). Activating collective co-production of public services: influencing citizens to participate in complex governance mechanisms in the UK. *International Review of Administrative Sciences*. (82,1), 47–68.

Box, R. C. (1999). Running government like a business: implications for public administration theory and practice. *American Review of Public Administration*. (29,1), 19–43.

Boyer, E. J., Van Slyke, D. M. and Rogers, J. D. (2016). An empirical examination of public involvement in public-private partnerships: qualifying the benefits of public involvement in PPPs. *Journal of Public Administration Research and Theory*. (26,1), 45–61.

Boyle, D., Clark, S. and Burns, S. (2006). *Hidden work: co-production by people outside paid employment*. York: Joseph Rowntree Foundation.

Brandsen, T. and Honingh, M. (2016). Distinguishing different types of co-production: a conceptual analysis based on the classical definitions. *Public Administration Review*. (76,3), 427–435.

Brandsen, T. and Pestoff, V. (2006). Co-production, the third sector and the delivery of public services. *Public Management Review*. (8,4), 493–501.

Brudney, J. L. (1987). Coproduction and privatization: exploring the relationship and its implications. *Nonprofit and Voluntary Sector Quarterly*. (16), 11–21.

Brudney, J. L. and England, R. E. (1983). Toward a definition of the co-production concept. *Public Administration Review*. (January–February), 59–65.

Bryer, T. A. and Cooper, T. L. (2012). H. George Frederickson and the dialogue on citizenship in public administration. *Public Administration Review*. (72,SI), S108–S116.

Callaghan, G. D. and Wistow, G. (2006). Publics, patients, citizens, consumers? Power and decision making in primary healthcare. *Public Administration*. (84,3), 583–601.

Christensen, T. and Laegreid, P. (2002). New public management: puzzles of democracy and influence of citizens. *The Journal of Political Philosophy*. (10,3), 267–295.

Christensen, T. and Laegreid, P. (2011). Democracy and administrative policy: contrasting elements of new public management (NPM) and post-new public management. *European Policy Science Review*. (3,1), 125–146.

Clark, B. Y., Brudney, J. L. and Jang, S. G. (2013). Coproduction of government services and the new information technology: investigating the distributional biases. *Public Administration Review*. (73,5), 687–701.

Clarke, J. (2005). New labour's citizens: activated, empowered, responsibilised, abandoned? *Critical Social Policy*. (25,4), 447–463.

Clarke, J. (2007). Unsettled connections: citizens, consumers and the reform of public services. *Journal of Consumer Culture*. (7,2), 159–178.

Clarke, J. and Newman, J. (1997). *The managerial state*. London: Sage.

Crompton, A. (2018). Inside co-production: stakeholder meaning and situated practice. *Social Policy Administration*. 1–14.

Crowley, P., Green, J., Freake, D. and Drinkwater, C. (2002). Primary care trusts involving the community: is community development the way forward. *Journal of Management and Medicine*. (16,4), 311–322.

Denhardt, J. V. and Denhardt, R. B. (2015). *New public service: serving, not steering* (4th ed.). New York: Routledge.

Dougherty, G. W. and Easton, J. (2011). Appointed public volunteer boards: exploring the basics of citizen participation through boards and commissions. *American Review of Public Administration*. (41,5), 519–541.

Dunston, R., Lee, A., Boud, D., Brodie, P. and Chiarella, M. (2009). Co-production and health system reform—from re-imagining to re-making. *The Australian Journal of Public Administration*. (68,1), 39–52.

Evers, A., Lewis, J. and Riedel, B. (2005). Developing child-care provision in England and Germany: problems of governance. *Journal of European Social Policy*. (15,3), 195–209.

Ewert, B. and Evers, A. (2012). Coproduction—contested meanings and challenges for user organisations. In Pestoff, V., Brandsen, T. and Verschuere, B. (eds.), *New public governance, the third sector and co-production*. New York: Routledge.

Farrell, C. M. (2000). Citizen participation in governance. *Public Money and Management*, (January–March), 31–36.

Farrell, C. M. (2010). Citizen and consumer involvement in UK public services. *International Journal of Consumer Studies*. (34), 503–507.

Ferris, J. M. (1988). The use of volunteers in public service production: some demand and supply considerations. *Social Science Quarterly*. (6,9), 3–23.

Fischer, F. (2006). Participatory governance as deliberative empowerment: the cultural politics of discursive space. *The American Review of Public Administration*. (36,1), 19–40.

Fotaki, M. (2011). Towards developing new partnerships in public services: users as consumers, citizens and/or co-producers in health and social care in England and Sweden. *Public Administration*. (89,3), 933–955.

Fotaki, M. (2015). Co-production under the financial crisis and austerity: a means of democratizing public services or a race to the bottom? *Journal of Management Enquiry*. (24,4), 433–438.

Fountain, J. E. (2001). Paradoxes of public sector customer service. *Governance*. (14,1), 55–73.

Frederickson, H. G. (1996). Comparing the reinventing government movement with the new public administration. *Public Administration Review*. (56,3), 263–270.

Fung, A. (2006). Varieties of participation in complex governance. *Public Administration Review*. (Special Issue), 66–73.

Gabriel, Y. and Lang, T. (2006). *The unmanageable consumer*. London: Sage.

Gaster, L. and Rutqvist, H. (2000). Changing the 'front line' to meet citiz3en needs. *Local Government Studies*. (26,2), 53–70.

Gilliatt, S., Fenwick, J. and Alford, J. (2000). Public services and the consumer: empowerment or control? *Social Policy and Administration*. (34,3), 333–349.

Goodsell, C. T. (2006). A new vision for public administration. *Public Administration Review*. (66,4), 623–635.

Greener, I. (2007). Choice or voice? Introduction to the themed section. *Social Policy and Society*. (7,2), 197–200.

Guo, H. and Neshkova, M. I. (2012). Citizen input in the budget process: when does it matter most? *American Review of Public Administration*. (43,3), 331–346.

Haikio, L. (2010). The diversity of citizenship and democracy in local management reform. *Public Management Review*. (12,3), 363–384.

Havassy, H. M. and Yanay, U. (1990). Bridging between local needs and central-ised services: co-optation or co-production. *Community Development Journal.* (23,3), 213–234.

Hirschman, A. O. (1970). *Exit, voice and loyalty: responses to decline in firms, organizations and states.* Cambridge: Harvard University Press.

Hood, C. (1991). A public management for all seasons? *Public Administration.* (69), 3–19.

Hood, C., Dunsire, A. and Thomson, L. (1988). Rolling back the state: Thatcher-ism, Fraserism and bureaucracy. *Governance.* (1,3), 243–270.

Hood, C., Peters, G. and Wollmann, H. (1996). Sixteen ways to consumerise public services: pick 'n mix or painful trade-offs'? *Public Money and Manage-ment.* (October–December), 43–50.

Jakobsen, M. and Andersen, S. C. (2013). Coproduction and equity in public service delivery. *Public Administration Review.* (73,5), 704–713.

Jaspers, S. and Steen, T. (2018). Realizing public values: enhancement or obstruc-tion? Exploring value tensions and coping strategies in the co-production of social care. *Public Management Review.* (21,4), 606–627.

Jones, G. and Needham, C. (2008). Debate: consumerism in public services—for and against. *Public Money and Management.* (28,2), 70–76.

Joshi, A. and Moore, M. (2004). Institutionalised co-production: unorthodox public service delivery in challenging environments. *The Journal of Develop-ment Studies.* (40,4), 31–49.

Jun, K. N. and Bryer, T. (2017). Facilitating public participation in local gov-ernments in hard times. *American Review of Public Administration.* (47,7), 840–856.

Jung, T. (2010). Citizens, co-producers, customers, clients, captives? A criti-cal review of consumerism and public services. *Public Management Review.* (12,3), 439–446.

King, C. S., Feltey, K. and Susel, B. O. (1998). The question of participation: toward authentic public participation in public administration. *Public Admin-istration Review.* (58,4), 129–215.

Kweit, M. G. and Kweit, R. W. (2004). Citizen participation and citizen evalua-tion in disaster recovery. *American Review of Public Administration.* (34,4), 354–373.

Langan, M. (2000). Social services: managing the third way. In Clarke, J., Gewirtz, S. and McLaughlin, E. (eds.), *New managerialism: new welfare?* Lon-don: Sage.

Levine, C. and Fisher, G. (1984). Citizenship and service delivery: the promise of co-production. *Public Administration Review.* (44), 178–189.

Locke, M., Begum, N. and Robson, P. (2003). Service users and charity gover-nance. In Cornforth, C. (ed.), *The governance of public and non-profit organi-zations: what do boards do?* London: Routledge.

Lowndes, V., Pratchett, L. and Stoker, G. (2001). Trends in public participation: part I—local government perspectives. *Public Administration.* (79,1), 205–222.

Lowndes, V., Pratchett, L. and Stoker, G. (2006). Local political participation: the impact of rules-in-use. *Public Administration.* (84,3), 539–561.

Marschall, M. J. (2004). Citizen participation and the neighbourhood context: a new look at the coproduction of local public good. *Political Research Quar-terly.* (57,2), 231–244.

Martin, S. and Boaz, A. (2000). Public participation and citizen-centred local government: lessons from the best value and better government for older people pilot programmes. *Public Money and Management.* (April–June), 47–53.

Mayer, I., Edelenbos, J. and Monniikhof, R. (2005). Interactive policy development: undermining or sustaining democracy? *Public Administration.* (83,1), 179–199.

Meijer, A. J. (2011). Networked coproduction of public services in virtual communities: from a government-centric to a community approach to public service support. *Public Administration Review.* (July–August), 598–607.

Meijer, A. J. (2014). New media and the coproduction of safety: an empirical analysis of Dutch practices. *American Review of Public Administration.* (44,1), 17–34.

Meijer, A. J. (2016). Coproduction as a structural transformation of the public sector. *International Journal of Public Sector Management.* (29,6), 596–611.

Moynihan, D. P. (2010). From performance management to democratic performance governance. In O'Leary, R., Van Slyke, D. M. and Kim, S. (eds.), *The future of public administration around the world.* Washington, DC: Georgetown University Press.

Nabatchi, T., Sancino, A. and Sicilia, M. (2017). Varieties of participation in public services: the who, when and what of co-production. *Public Administration Review.* (77,5), 766–776.

Needham, C. E. (2007). Realising the potential of co-production: negotiating improvements in public services. *Social Policy and Society.* (7,2), 221–231.

Osborne, D. and Gaebler, T. (1992). *Reinventing government.* Reading, MA: Addison-Wesley.

Osborne, S. P. (1994). The language of empowerment. *International Journal of Public Sector Management.* (7,3), 56–62.

Osborne, S. P., Radnor, Z. and Nasi, G. (2013). A new theory for public service management? Toward a (Public) service dominant approach. *American Review of Public Administration.* (43,2), 135–158.

Osborne, S. P., Radnor, Z. and Strokosch, K. (2016). Co-production and the co-creation of value in public service: a suitable case for treatment? *Public Management Review.* (18,5), 639–653.

Ostrom, E. (1972). Metropolitan reform: propositions derived from two traditions. *Social Science Quarterly.* (53), 474–493.

Ostrom, E. (1978). The public service production process: a framework for analysing police services. *Policy Studies Journal.* (7), 381–389.

Ostrom, E. (1989). Microconstitutional change in multiconstitutional political systems. *Rationality and Society.* (1,1), 11–50.

Ostrom, E. (1990). *Governing the commons: the evolution of institutions for collective action.* Cambridge: Cambridge University Press.

Ostrom, E. (1996). Crossing the great divide: co-production, synergy and development. *World Development.* (24,6), 1073–1087.

Ostrom, E. (1999). Coping with tragedies of the commons. Annual *Review of Political Science.* (2), 493–535.

Ostrom, E. (2000). Collective action and the evolution of social norms. *Journal of Economic Perspectives.* (14,3), 137–158.

Pammer, W. J. (1992). Administrative norms and the coproduction of municipal services. *Social Science Quarterly.* (73,4), 920–929.

Parkinson, J. (2004). Why deliberate? The encounter between deliberation and new public managers. *Public Administration*. (82,2), 377–395.

Parks, R. B., Baker, P. C., Kiser, L., Oakerson, R., Ostrom, E., Ostrom, V., Percy, S. L., Vandivort, M. B., Whitaker, G. P. and Wilson, R. (1981). Consumers as co-producers of public services: some economic and institutional considerations. *Policy Studies Journal*. (9,7), 1001–1011.

Percy, S. (1983). Citizen participation in the co-production of urban services. *Urban Affairs Quarterly*. (19,4), 431–446.

Perri 6. (2003). Giving consumers of British public services more choice: what can be learned from recent history. *Journal of Social Policy*. (32,2), 239–270.

Pestoff, V. (2006). Citizens and co-production of welfare services. *Public Management Review*. (8,4), 503–519.

Pestoff, V. (2009). Towards a paradigm of democratic participation: citizen participation and co-production of personal social services in Sweden. *Annals of Public and Cooperative Economics*. (80,2), 197–224.

Pestoff, V. (2012a). Co-production and third sector services in Europe: some critical conceptual issues. In Pestoff, V., Brandsen, T. and Verschuere, B. (eds.), *New public governance, the third sector and co-production*. New York: Routledge.

Pestoff, V. (2012b). New public governance, co-production and third sector social services in Europe: crowding in and crowding out. In Pestoff, V., Brandsen, T. and Verschuere, B. (eds.), *New public governance, the third sector and co-production*. New York: Routledge.

Pestoff, V. (2014). Collective action and the sustainability of co-production. *Public Management Review*. (16,3), 383–401.

Pestoff, V. and Brandsen, T. (2010). Public sector governance and the third sector: opportunities for co-production and innovation? In Osborne, S. P. (ed.), *The new public governance?* Oxon: Routledge.

Pickard, S. (1998). Citizenship and consumerism in health care: a critique of citizens' juries. *Social Policy and Administration*. (32,3), 226–244.

Pollitt, C. and Bouckaert, G. (2004). *Public management reform: a comparative analysis*. Oxford: Oxford University Press.

Porter, D. O. (2012). Co-production and network structures in public education. In Brandsen, T. and Verschuere, B. (eds.), *New public governance, the third sector and co-production*. New York: Routledge.

Potter, J. (1988). Consumerism and the public sector: how well does the coat fit? *Public Administration*. (66), 149–164.

Powell, M., Greener, I., Szmigin, I., Doheny, S. and Mills, N. (2010). Broadening the focus of public service consumerism. *Public Management Review*. (12,3), 323–340.

Roberts, N. (2004). Public deliberation in an age of direct citizen participation. *American Review of Public Administration*. (34,4), 315–353.

Rosentraub, M. (1981). Consumers as producers of social services. *Southern Review of Public Administration*. (4), 502–539.

Rosentraub, M. and Warren, R. (1987). Citizen participation in the production of urban services. *Public Productivity Review*. (10,3), 75–89.

Ross, K. (1995). Speaking in tongues: involving users in day care services. *British Journal of Social Work*. (25), 791–804.

Rummery, K. (2006). Partnerships and collaborative governance in welfare: the citizenship challenge. *Social Policy and Society*. (5,2), 293–303.

Sharp, E. B. (1980). Toward a new understanding of urban services and citizen participation: the coproduction concept. *The American Review of Public Administration*. (14,2), 105–118.

Sicilia, M., Guarini, E., Sancino, A., Adreani, M. and Ruffini, R. (2016). Public service management and co-production in multi-level governance settings. *International Review of Administrative Sciences*. (82,1), 8–27.

Simmons, R. and Birchall, J. (2005). A joined-up approach to user participation in public services: strengthening the 'participation chain'. *Social Policy and Administration*. (39,3), 260–283.

Sundeen, R. A. (1988). Explaining participation in coproduction: a study of volunteers. *Social Science Quarterly*. (69,3), 547–568.

Terry, L. D. (1993). Why we should abandon the misconceived quest to reconcile public entrepreneurship with democracy. *Public Administration Review*. (53,4), 393–395.

Thomsen, M. K. (2017). Citizen co-production: the influence of self-efficacy perception and knowledge of how to co-produce. *American Review of Public Administration*. (47,3), 340–353.

Timney, M. M. (1998). Overcoming administrative barriers to citizen participation: citizens as partners, not adversaries. In King, C. S. and Strivers, C. (eds.), *Government is us: public administration in an anti-government era*. Thousand Oaks: Sage.

Tritter, J. Q. and McCallum, A. (2006). The snakes and ladders of user involvement: moving beyond Arnstein. *Health Policy*. (76), 156–168.

van Eijk, C. J. A. and Steen, T. P. S. (2014). Why people co-produce: analyzing citizens' perceptions on co-planning engagement in health care services. *Public Management Review*. (16,3), 358–382.

Ventriss, C. (1998). Radical democratic thought and contemporary American public administration: a substantive perspective. *American Review of Public Administration*. (28,3), 227–245.

Verschuere, B., Brandsen, T. and Pestoff, V. (2012). Co-production: the state of the art in research and the future agenda. *Voluntas*. (23,4), 1083–1101.

Voorberg, W. H., Bekkers, V. J. J. M. and Tummers, L. G. (2015). A systematic review of co-creation and co-production: embarking on the social innovation journey. *Public Management Review*. (17,9), 1333–1357.

Wagenaar, H. (2007). Governance, complexity, and democratic participation: how citizens and public officials harness the complexities of neighbourhood decline. *The American Review of Public Administration*. (37,1), 17–50.

Whitaker, G. P. (1980). Coproduction: citizen participation in service delivery. *Public Administration Review*. (May–June), 240–246.

Williams, B. N., Kang, S. C. and Johnson, J. (2016). (Co)-contamination as the dark side of co-production: public value failures in co-production processes. *Public Management Review*. (18,5), 692–717.

Wilson, G. (1994). Co-production and self-care: new approaches to managing community care services for older people. *Social Policy and Administration*. (28,3), 236–249.

Wilson, R. K. (1981). Citizen conjecture as a mode of participation: conjectures and models. *Journal of Urban Affairs*. (3,4), 27–49.

# 3 Co-production and the Service Management Theory

## Abstract

This chapter introduces co-production from the service management perspective, which it argues offers a better starting point from which to theorise about co-production. In contrast to the public administration literature, it discusses co-production as an integral element of service delivery due to the inseparable nature of production and consumption. A critical point in the discussion is the differentiation made between the product-dominant logic, which has traditionally been applied to public services and their management, and the service-dominant logic, which centres on the relational exchange between service users and service providers. It further argues that, due to its integral role within the service relationship, the management of co-production should be a priority for service organisations, and teachings from relationship marketing may have an important contribution to make in this respect.

## Introduction

The 'consumerist' movement in public service delivery has drawn upon some elements of service management theory, particularly around public choice theory which, in its simplest form, positions the market as the optimal structure to produce measurable public service outputs and the relevance of private management experience to their delivery (Hood, 1991; Pollitt and Bouckaert, 2004). However, as others have argued, this approach is a partial one that has sought to extract 'the consumer' from the overall service delivery process and fails to understand the logic of this process—and its implications for public service delivery and management (Jung, 2010; Powell et al., 2010). There has also been some debate over the extent to which the public sector can impersonate the private (Allison, 1979), with some commentators highlighting the difference in the nature of the tasks undertaken in each sector (Hood, 1991; Kickert, 1997). Conditions such as citizenship, equity and collective choice, for example, are present in the public sector and absent from the private

(Ferlie et al., 1996) and the societal, political and legal environment makes the public sector distinctive (Kickert, 1997).

Theorising about co-production has traditionally drawn on management theory derived primarily from the manufacturing sector and rooted in product-dominant logic, which suggests that production and consumption are separated as discrete processes (Vargo et al., 2008)—in other words, public services are conceptualised as goods that are produced by public service staff and consumed (relatively) passively by service users. Thus, co-production can only occur at the behest of, and controlled by, service professionals, as discussed in the previous chapter. Until recently the debate around public service production has largely ignored the dedicated theory and literature on service management—despite the fact that this may well have unique insights to offer to the understanding of public service management (Osborne, 2010; Osborne and Strokosch, 2013).

This chapter will introduce co-production from the service management perspective. It will argue that, in comparison to the public administration literature presented in Chapter 2, this body of work offers a better starting point from which to theorise about co-production by understanding services as processes within which the role of the service user is integral and critical.

## Understanding Services: Inseparability, Intangibility and Co-production

The service management theory is a relatively young and evolving field with significant conceptual developments being made over the last fifteen years and the theory is continuing to develop, particularly in relation to the idea of value creation/co-creation. It is important to start by understanding what is meant by service and its distinction from manufactured goods. However, in attempting to encapsulate the essence of the term and distinguish it from goods, definitions of services have been numerous and varied (Sampson and Froehle, 2006). It is not the aim of this work to explore these definitions as this has been conducted comprehensively by Nankervis (2005) who argues that the various definitions of services ultimately seek to emphasise the dynamic interactions between the provider and customer. He suggests three implications from a review of the definitions of service: first, services are distinct from goods in their nature and systems of delivery; second, services rely on the perceptions and expectations of customers; and, third, the output of services is more difficult to quantify compared to goods.

The process nature is a key characteristic of services because it underlines their construction as a series of activities to which various resources contribute (Gronroos, 2007). Gronroos argues that because customers participate in the process, the process becomes part of the solution. As processes, services are therefore inherently relational. The process includes the way the customer is dealt with by the service provider, emphasising the responsiveness of the organization, the flexibility of front-line staff, the degree of personal interaction, the accessibility of personnel and information, the courtesy and competency of staff and the interactions with other customers (Johnston and Clark, 2008).

Service management theory stems specifically from tripartite notions of inseparability, intangibility and co-production (Gronroos, 2007).[1] Services are *intangible*. They are not concrete goods that that can be physically moved, consumed and/or owned at a time of the consumer's choosing (such as a washing machine or car). Rather they are intangible processes, where the subjective experience of the service delivery process by the consumer is a key determinant of the quality (Nankervis, 2005; Gronroos, 2007)—the service experience in a doctor's surgery, for example, is at least as important in the 'performance' of the service, through the receptionist and medical professionals, as is the quality of the professional advice and the effectiveness of the medication provided. However, there is some divergence from the view that all services are intangible. Sampson and Froehle (2006, p. 335) argue, for example: 'Service processes are capable of being perceived, and service outcomes are often as tangible, or more tangible, than manufacturing outputs'. They suggest that all production processes have both tangible (that can be perceived by the senses) and intangible components, concluding that intangibility does not uniquely characterise services. Some services, such as dental treatment, for example, provide both tangible (e.g. facilitating goods such as needles and supporting facilities such as the building within which the service is conducted) and intangible elements (e.g. the subjective experience of the service encounter). Thus tangible elements can support the intangible process of the service (Lusch et al., 2010). Likewise, in the case of manufactured goods, tangible goods may be supported by intangible services (e.g. after purchasing an electrical appliance, the manufacturer may offer a telephone service to receive advice on operating the goods). The important point here is that services always have an intangible element. In the case of dental treatment, for instance, although there are examples of the supply of goods (e.g. receipt of a crown or filling), the service is experienced during the patient's interactions with reception staff, their experience in the dentist's chair while undergoing treatment, their experience afterwards when making a future appointment and also regarding the success of the treatment; all these factors are important determinants of how the final experience is viewed by the service user (and the dental practice in evaluating its services).

Another core component of service management theory is the *inseparable* nature of production and consumption. The process nature of services means that the customer plays a key role in both consumption and production (Nankervis, 2005; Gronroos, 2007; Normann, 1991). This departs from the product-dominant perspective that has been the basis of thinking about public service design and delivery over the last four decades at least, which suggests that, like manufactured goods, public services are designed and delivered by an organisation and its employees and consumed separately by relatively passive consumers. Production and consumption are inseparable because, as processes, services are produced and consumed simultaneously in time and location—rather than with production and consumption being temporally and spatially separated as in the case of manufactured goods (Johnston and Clark, 2008). Thus, whilst manufactured goods are produced in one place (for example, a factory), sold somewhere else (a shop) and then consumed at a third site (perhaps in someone's home), the production and business logic for services is entirely different—production and consumption occur at the same time and in the same place (Vargo et al., 2008). Residential care services provided to elderly or disabled people are good examples of such simultaneous inseparability of production and consumption in the public service setting.

Nankervis (2005) suggests that there are degrees of inseparability in all services. The service encounter is a process that consists of activities or a series of activities within which there is some kind of interaction between the service organisation and the customer (Gronroos, 2007). From the product-dominant logic, the customer has traditionally taken a role of dependency, playing a largely passive role as an observer and reliant on service organisation employees' knowledge and skills to produce and deliver services on his/her behalf. Similarly, the service organisation is dependent on the customer whose primary role is to consume the service. However, the traditional demarcation between consumption and production has become less rigid (Nankervis, 2005). Through inseparability, the service user is more than a passive consumer because he/she plays an active role as participant in the service, and, likewise, the service organisation is more than just service provider, as it has to manage the customer's role in the production process. It is here where the service management literature may have more to offer around how to manage such relationships. This will be discussed later in the chapter.

Finally, from the service management perspective, services are invariably *co-produced* by the service staff and the consumer. Lovelock and Young (1979) were among the first to consider co-production from a service management perspective, forwarding the idea that customers are an important contribution to a firm's productivity. They argued that consumer behaviour is critical for productivity gains in services for three reasons: services typically involve the consumer in the production process, services tend to be labour-intensive and services tend to be time-bound and therefore managers place a strong emphasis on capacity utilisation. Since then, there has been considerable literature on the theory of co-production, although there is currently a dearth of empirical work.

The service management literature situates co-production as an essential and intrinsic process of interaction between any service organisation and the consumer at the point of production of a service (Gronroos, 2007)—what Normann has termed 'the moment of truth' in service provision:

> Most services are the result of social acts which take place in direct contact between the customer and representatives of the service company. To take a metaphor from bullfighting, we could say that the perceived quality is realized at the moment of truth, when the service provider and the service customer confront one another in the arena. At that moment they are very much on their own. What happens then can no longer be directly influenced by the company. It is the skill, the motivation and the tools employed by the firm's representative and the expectations and behaviour of the client which together will create the service delivery process.
>
> (Normann, 1991, pp. 16–17)

The 'moment of truth' is a critical point in the process of service production where the quality or value of the service experienced by the individual service user can be influenced by the service provider (Normann, 1991; Gronroos, 2007; Glushko and Tabas, 2009). At this point, the experience of a service process is shaped as much by the subjective expectations of the consumer and their active role in the service delivery process as by service staff themselves. Service organisations can therefore only 'promise' or offer a certain process or experience—the actuality is dependent upon Normann's (1991) 'moment of truth'. A classic example of this would be in education where the co-produced experience is based on the student-teacher relationship. Teachers make value propositions during class time, exchanging their knowledge of a subject area with students who may interact by completing set work, asking questions and by participating in class discussions. The experience is co-produced through this interaction, but the student's role outside the classroom is critical to building on that learning interaction through, for example, further study. In such services, co-production and inseparability are high, owing to the fact that consumption and production take place at the same point in time, and with direct face-to-face contact between the service user and the service provider (in a classroom, respectively). By contrast, inseparability is rather lower in the example of an individual completing a self-assessment tax form—because production and consumption of such services occur through the medium of an electronic interface that does not have the inter-personal immediacy of face-to-face contact between the service provider and the service user. Yet even such services do still exhibit co-production from a service management perspective—even if the co-production of completing a tax return is less interactive (inputting data about yourself on an online system), compared to the more active case of student-teacher interaction in the classroom.

## Building the Concept of Co-production From the Service Management Perspective

Co-production from the service management perspective has been described as integral to the process nature of the service and therefore unavoidable. However, the concept has been extended in the literature with associations to customer participation. The idea that co-production sits on a continuum is suggested in a strand of the service management literature, which, like the public administration literature, refers to co-production as a form of participation, focusing specifically on consumer mechanisms (Fitzsimmons, 1985; Mills and Morris, 1986; Kelley et al., 1990; Bitner et al., 1997; Bendapudi and Leone, 2003). The suggestion is that customers can become more active in producing and delivering the service than what is facilitated through the inseparable nature of the service encounter. Various mechanisms are available through which individuals can co-produce beyond 'the moment of truth', such as choice, information provision, complaints' procedures, service evaluation forms and self-service activities (Bitner et al., 1997; Gronroos, 2007). Such an approach to co-production has already been discussed in the realm of public service production under the auspices of New Public Management.

Arguments have been forwarded to suggest that services can be classified according to the degree of customer involvement during the service encounter. Nankervis (2005, p. 18), for example, refers to a continuum of active or passive contact from very high to very low. Others have also suggested that customer participation can be plotted onto a continuum. Fitzsimmons (1985) refers to a 'spectrum of service delivery' that places the individual service user according to the degree of involvement they have in service production. He argues that 'productivity can be enhanced by capitalizing on the active participation of the consumer in the service process' (p. 61). Bettencourt et al. (2002) suggest that although co-production exists in all services, it can be more pronounced in certain services, which they describe as knowledge intensive. In such services, the clients are described as knowledgeable and competent and organisations are said to be dependent upon their collaboration for the effective production of the service. Indeed, Betterncourt et al. (2002) suggest that organisations should seek out high-performing clients whose contributions, along with the organisation, will ultimately enhance the operational effectiveness of the service. They promote the idea of the 'partial employee', as do others (Mills et al., 1983; Mills and Morris, 1986; Bowers et al., 1990; Bitner et al., 1997). The creation of partial employees is said to swell the boundaries of the organisation to include temporary members who fulfil tasks that were traditionally undertaken by paid employees (Mills et al., 1983; Bitner et al., 1997). There is, however, a counter argument to the one for partial employees, which reflects the uncertainty that customers bring to the production process and suggests their input should be limited (Bitner et al., 1997).

## Product-Dominant Logic vs Service-Dominant Logic

Over the last decade, and predominantly through the work of Vargo and colleagues (2008), clear distinctions have been drawn between the product-dominant logic and service-dominant logic, which as suggested earlier is important for differentiating between manufactured goods and services. It is this body of literature that has become of interest in the context of public service management, with Osborne et al. (2013) arguing that this theory should inform the conceptual understanding and analysis of public service management. Table 3.1 summarises the key differences between the two opposing approaches.

Both logics focus on the notion of value creation, which in the service management literature refers mainly to the value created for service organisations; value in the public sector context, by contrast, is likely to take a broader focus including community and societal dimensions, as well as individual service users (this is an area in need of further exploration, which unfortunately is not within the remit of this book).

*Table 3.1* Value creation from a product-dominant logic vs a service-dominant logic

|  | *Product-Dominant Logic* | *Service-Dominant Logic* |
| --- | --- | --- |
| Value driver | Value in exchange | Value in use/context |
| Creator of value | Organisation (with input from others in the supply chain) | Various stakeholders— organisation, network partners and service users |
| Process of value creation | Value embedded in goods or services | Organisation proposes value through market offerings, service users continue process through use |
| Purpose of value | Increase wealth of organisation | Increase adaptability, survivability and system well-being through service |
| Resources used | Primarily operand resources, e.g. raw materials, machinery | Primarily operant resources, e.g. skills and knowledge |
| Role of organisation | Produce and distribute value | Propose and co-create value |
| Role of goods | Units of output, embedded with value | Vehicle for operant resources |
| Role of customers | To use or destroy value | Co-create value through the integration of organisation's resources and other public and private resources. |

Adapted from Vargo et al. (2008, p. 148)

The product-dominant logic focuses on goods or products (including both tangible and intangible elements), the value of which is realised through the process of exchange (Spohrer et al., 2008). Put differently, the service provider produces the product in isolation from the service user and embeds value during the manufacturing process; the role of the service user is to consume the service. The service organisation therefore uses tangible assets as factors of production such as raw materials and machinery and these are considered to be the primary source of competitive advantage. The product-dominant logic suggests that the organisation, as sole provider, makes goods as a resource available to the service user and therefore acts as creator of value; through their consumption of the services, the consumer is, by comparison, the destroyer of value. As discussed earlier in Chapter 2, the New Public Management has been criticised for embracing a product-dominant logic by suggesting that the production and consumption of public services are discrete processes to which service users may only contribute to at the behest of public service staff (Dunston et al., 2009; Osborne et al., 2013; Alford, 2016; Osborne et al., 2016).

The central role of the customer further suggests that the service-dominant logic is based on relational exchanges between the service provider and customer. Indeed, Vargo and Lusch (2004) recognise that, although their role is often invisible and intangible, customers contribute to service production as 'active participants in relational exchanges and coproduction', rather than being acted upon (2004, p. 7). Thus, service quality or value are no longer created by the service provider but are perceived and determined by the consumer through 'value-in-use'; the service provider can only make value propositions because value is co-created through the combined efforts of all players. This reflects the relational nature of services, which results from the core principle of inseparability and also suggests there is no value for the consumer until he/she makes use of the service. Ramirez (1999) also differentiates value creation from a goods perspective and the alternative services perspective which suggests value co-production. In relation to services, Ramirez argues 'Value is not simply "added", but is mutually "created" and "re-created" among actors with different values' (Ramirez, 1999, p. 50), a stark contrast from how co-production has been traditionally perceived in the public services (as an extension to public service production, or an 'add-on'). The inference here is that value is co-created by various organisations and individuals within any service system. The service-dominant logic, then, understands services as the application of knowledge and skills for the benefit of another (Spohrer et al., 2008). It avoids the various issues that arise from pegging service users as either consumers or citizens by redirecting focus to *all* stakeholders of the service (Osborne et al., 2013). According to Gummesson and Polese (2009), all stakeholders (organisations and individuals) are operant resources who act rather than react. Each is recognised as having invisible and intangible resources in the form of key skills and knowledge, which are the main source of competitive advantage. The implication is that individual service users are positioned as key contributors to value-creation processes as co-producers of the service.

> This means more than simply being consumer orientated; it means collaborating with and learning from customers and being adaptive to their individual and dynamic needs. A service centred dominant logic implies that value is defined by and cocreated with the consumer rather than embedded in output.
>
> (Vargo and Lusch, 2004, p. 6)

Importantly, the service-dominant logic has endorsed the conception of co-creation (Vargo and Lusch, 2004, 2008), a term coined by Prahalad and Ramaswamy (2000) who discuss the changing role of customers within the service relationship. Although co-creation and co-production have been used interchangeably in much of the literature (Voorberg et al., 2015), Eriksson (2019) distinguishes between the two concepts noting that 'Co-production assumes a process where the public service organisation is dominant and where the logic is linear and based upon product-dominant conceptions of production' while co-creation 'assumes an interactive and dynamic relationship where value is created at the nexus of interaction' (p. 225). In the service management literature, co-creation also represents a shift in thinking away from the product-dominant logic view where value was exchanged when the service was provided to the customer to the service-dominant logic that suggests that value is determined by the customer during service consumption, usage and process (Kristensson et al., 2008; Ordanini and Pasini, 2008; Vargo and Lusch, 2008). Value is recognised as a contested concept (Gronroos and Voima, 2013).

Vargo and Lusch (2008) take the argument further, emphasising the relational dimension of services. They suggest that rather than viewing the customer as a co-producer (as is determined by the nature of services), he/she should be seen as co-creator of value. Value is not created by the service organisation, but rather 'co-created' by customers when they integrate resources (Prahalad and Ramaswamy, 2000, 2004; Vargo and Lusch, 2008; Lusch and Webster, 2011) to co-develop personalised service experiences through an active and equal dialogue with service providers through the service encounter. The role of the service provider is therefore to create value propositions or service offerings, which the service users, as co-creators of value, consume to determine the ultimate value of the service (Vargo and Lusch, 2008). This means that no value is created until the service is used during the interactive process that constitutes service delivery, which the service-dominant logic refers to as 'value in use'. Vargo and Lusch (2008) further argue that because the experience and perception of the customer are critical to their determination of value, the service delivery process can be managed to increase the potential for value creation.

Through co-creation, the service organisation proactively seeks to discover, understand and satisfy 'latent needs', rather than simply reacting to expressed needs (Kristensson et al., 2008). The mechanisms through which customers co-create in service design include brainstorming, interviews, mock service delivery and team meetings (Alam, 2006). The traditional approach was to first scrutinise customer need, and then attempt to satisfy that need. The idea of co-creation is to shift the role of the service provider to 'mere facilitator and partner of consumer ingenuity and agency' (Zwick et al., 2008, p. 173). The task for service managers is establishing and maintaining co-operation with co-creators (both service users and operational staff working on the front line), which Prahalad and Ramaswamy (2000) argue can be achieved by shaping their expectations through two-way communication and education.

### The Innovating Potential of Customers

Vargo and Lusch (2008), contend that the relational element of service is not a normative option—as has been suggested by the public administration literature—but rather, inherent to the premise of the co-creation of value. Co-creation and the service-dominant logic emphasise a close and productive relationship between service providers and customers; a relationship that is mutually beneficial to each (Zwick et al., 2008). This is based on an assumption that customers are skilled workers—which is at odds with the traditional conceptualisation of customers under New Public Management and its implicit assumption that service users are 'lay people' who 'seldom seem to be the driving or shaping force' for public service reforms (Ross, 1995; Timney, 1998; Pollitt and Bouckaert, 2004, p. 31, Millward, 2005)—who should be enabled to freely articulate their needs and share their expertise to shape services. The service management theory suggests that customers are potential innovators who can supplement the creative efforts of the service provider. Thus, the focus becomes the process of the service and the combining of actors' resources, stepping away from any emphasis on output or the intangible product (Vargo and Lusch, 2008). From a public service perspective, recent work by Voorberg et al. (2015, p. 1334) argues that 'co-creation not only influences customer satisfaction and loyalty, but also helps firms achieve competitive advantage'.

The idea of customers as innovators has also been discussed by von Hippel (1998) who argues that service users can be empowered to develop innovative solutions to specific problems. In a later work, von Hippel (2005) refers to the 'democratizing' of innovation, which places the user in the role of service developer. The role of the 'lead user' has been of particular interest to von Hippel, who defines him as one who expects to profit from making innovations and who experience needs in advance of the majority of the remaining market for the product (von Hippel, 1986). In an early paper that discusses innovation, von Hippel (1986) suggests that many services and products are developed and refined by those using them. This is particularly true of instances where an individual faces a specific problem with a product or service and requires him/her to make a modification to it to better suit his/her needs: 'Users can and commonly do create customised end effects for themselves by combining standard products and services to create a customised system' (von Hippel, 1998, p. 641). Any modifications can then be fed back to the provider. It is here that 'sticky information' becomes of interest. 'Sticky' information is a term coined by von Hippel (1994, 1998) and refers to information that is costly to acquire and transfer. Such information emerges from the local level—typically among service users or 'lead users'—and can, according to von Hippel (1998), be important for innovation and the customisation of products according to need: 'when users can innovate for themselves to create precisely what they want, rather than being restricted to a set of options on offer that have been created by others, their satisfaction is significantly higher' (von Hippel, 2007, p. 310). In other words, public service users may therefore hold sticky information required to make innovations to services. Public service organisations can therefore use inherently relational service encounters to benefit from the 'sticky information' held by services users for the purposes of service improvement or innovation (Gronroos and Voima, 2013; Osborne et al., 2016).

Public service users may be understood as suppliers of labour, information and knowledge (Alford, 2009) or owners of 'sticky information' required to make innovations to services. In their discussion of innovation in public services Osborne and Brown (2011) suggest that innovation can only be promoted and sustained through an open system approach rather than within closed organisational boundaries. Innovation can therefore be a product of public service users and networks of organisations rather than individual service providers working alone. Furthermore, such open system approaches to innovation have been described to increase wider social value (Henkel and von Hippel, 2005), therefore potentially benefiting beyond the service users who are co-producing the innovations. However, channelling the expertise of customers from the service management perspective is not without challenges and depends upon continuous dialogue between equals, allowing the customer an opportunity to shape his/her experience. This is dependent upon the co-operation of the customer (Prahalad and Ramaswamy, 2000). According to Prahalad and Ramaswamy (2004), customers who are connected, informed, empowered, active and dissatisfied with the available choices will seek interaction with service organisations with the aim of co-creating value.

*Criticism of the Service-Dominant Logic*

More recently, the service-dominant logic has been criticised particularly for its definitional problems around value co-creation (Gronroos and Voima, 2013; Gronroos, 2018). Gronroos and Voima (2013) argue that the treatment of co-creation under the service-dominant logic has created a metaphorical concept that becomes all-encompassing and therefore difficult to analyse. In other words, the idea that value is always co-created and that the related positioning of both the service provider and the service user as co-creators of value makes any analysis of the relative importance of each actor and their role in the process challenging. Gronroos and Voima (2013) forward a different perspective regarding co-creation, arguing that service users are not only co-creators of value but also the sole creators of their own value and that the focus should be their role in the creation of value-in-use. They describe value as a contested concept which is socially constructed, accumulating over time through past, current and future experiences. The implication is that value is never homogenous but dependent upon who is delivering the service and importantly, who is consuming it and their broader service experience (Gronroos and Voima, 2013).

A central point here is that value is not created by the service provider (as is implicit under the traditional product-dominant logic view of public services, through value-in-exchange where the public service organisation designs and produces the services *for* public service users) but is perceived and determined by the service user through their *use* of the service (which the service-dominant logic already alludes to) and also within the *context* of their own lives (Gronroos and Voima, 2013). The service relationship (and the various encounters it includes, which may be face-to-face or digital) and its management is therefore a crucial opportunity for the service provider to contribute to and influence the process of value creation (Gronroos, 2007; Gronroos and Voima, 2013). Co-production is therefore less about empowering service users to be involved, as it has been in the public service setting and more about how people transform a service offering made by service providers with their resources, skills and experiences and ultimately create value. In this conceptualisation, an additional layer of analysis is included: service users play a key role as creators of value in the context of their own lives (value-in-context) (Gronroos and Voima, 2013) and co-creators through their role in the production, consumption, evaluation and contextualisation of public services (value-in-use) (see, for example, Alves, 2013; Osborne and Strokosch, 2013; Skalen et al., 2018). This means that the value of public services can be contextualised and experienced at the micro level in the context of the service users' own lives (value-in-context), which, by consequence, reinforces the core role played by individuals in creating value for themselves. It is with this reasoning that Gronroos and Voima (2013) argue that service users as individuals are always the *sole creators of value*, while public service organisations (through their staff, processes and procedures) are only ever value *co-creators* when they interact with those using the services.

Gronroos (2018) criticises the service-dominant logic for taking an organisation-driven view of service delivery that emphasises value creation for the organisation or service system, rather than service users, and for starting from the premise that the organisation creates value and steers the process of co-production with which service users are invited to participate through appended processes. He argues that 'a true service approach' has its roots in Aristotle's value theory which advocates that 'the service users, in addition to determining whether the use of resources is valuable to them or not, are the ones who also create value out of the use of such resources' (Gronroos, 2018, p. 3). By consequence then, a service organisation does not create value, but rather develops service propositions and facilitates service user interactions with organisational processes and resources to allow them to create their own value. Gronroos (2018) therefore forwards a modified 'Service Logic' that compensates for the challenges presented under service-dominant logic. It is this theory that has formed the backbone of the evolving Public Service Logic (Osborne et al., 2015). With its roots in the work of Gronroos (e.g. Gronroos and Voima, 2013; Gronroos, 2018) the Public Sector Logic departs from the product-dominant or 'manufacturing' logic that has traditionally been applied to public services (Osborne et al., 2015) and focuses on value, the creation of which is the public sector's primary goal both in terms of individual value to the service user and wider collective value to the public (Alford, 2016). It argues that value is created within a multi-dimensional system that includes various organisations from the public, third and for-profit sectors, but importantly also service users, the wider community and society (see, for example, Skalen et al., 2018). In line with the wider service management literature then, the Public Service Logic conceptualises services as processes (Vargo et al., 2008) and focuses on the interaction between service users and either front-line service staff or organisational processes and procedures, which may include digital platforms. Importantly though, it also suggests that the processes of value creation are complex and interconnecting. As a consequence of this, it moves beyond the transactional approach that is endorsed within the New Public Management narrative to a relational approach that connects various actors (e.g. community organisations, government, for-profit organisations) through different processes of involvement, but which also firmly centres on the service user and their role in these processes of value creation.

## Managing the Service Relationship

In the public sector, marketing has traditionally been grounded in classical economics and, specifically, exchange theory, which was underpinned by an entirely transactional view of marketing (Kotler and Levy, 1969). Osborne et al. (2015) recommend that steps are taken beyond the transactional approach towards a relational, service-focused one, which would be better suited to the reality of public service management. More recently, there has been a shift towards viewing relationships as fundamental resources in public sector marketing, and, as a result, relationship marketing has been promoted as a potential tool to manage and enhance individual relationships between public service organisations and service users (e.g. Laing, 2003; Wright and Taylor, 2007; McLaughlin et al., 2009; McGuire, 2012; Osborne et al., 2013).

Wright and Taylor (2007) argue that, despite the shortcomings of transferring private sector marketing concepts into the public sector, relationship marketing has a potentially significant contribution to make given its focus on relationship building between providers and both their customers and suppliers. They suggest two roles for relationship marketing in the healthcare setting. First, create a shift away from transactional approaches to services by focusing on the service user and the relationship with them; provide services for them rather than to them. Second, they suggest that relationship marketing focuses on the relationship between healthcare employees and their customers to embed customer focus and responsiveness. More recently, McGuire (2012) defined relationship marketing as a partnership approach that redirects attention from short-term transactions, competition and contracts to longer-term relationships built on trust. She makes a methodological contribution, arguing that relationship marketing has something to offer in the context of public services. However, she further discusses the challenges of transferring relationship marketing into the complex and diverse public service context, particularly given its nature as a broad range of approaches. McGuire suggests that relationship marketing reflects a process view of relationships, which are underpinned by collaboration. She adds: 'A fundamental insight from [relationship marketing] is that managing interactions is the key to relational exchanges' (p. 546).

Osborne et al. (2013) argue that relationship marketing may have a significant input to public service management because it will refine the relational nature of performance at the micro, meso and macro levels. The micro level refers specifically to the co-production of public services, the meso level to the relationships between organisations working across organisational boundaries and the macro level refers to the active role of public service organisations in public policy formulation and implementation (Morgan and Hunt, 1994). It is the micro and meso levels that are of particular interest within this book (inter-organisational relationships will be discussed further in Chapter 5). Focusing attention specifically on the micro level and the service encounters, the service management theory has an important contribution to make on how relationship marketing might be used to facilitate the co-production that is integral to the service relationship.

The early service management literature on co-production focused primarily on the business case for customer co-production, highlighting the benefits to the service organisation and particularly increased productivity (Lovelock and Young, 1979) similar to the economic reasoning and rationale suggested by the New Public Management narrative. Co-production was perceived to reduce labour costs and thereby lowering the cost of the service, benefiting organisations' competitiveness and depressing prices. However, the preceding discussion has suggested that as an inherent dimension of service production, co-production can be managed to ensure value-in-use is created for the service user during the 'moment of truth'. Indeed, according to the basic premise of co-production, productivity and quality are interrelated in the service process; as the customer participates in the service process, he/she influences the service outcome and ultimately his/her own satisfaction with the service. Significant import is therefore attached to managing co-production during the service relationship and the service management has forwarded relationship marketing as a key mechanism through which to manage service relationships effectively.

According to Gronroos (2009), marketing is essentially about customer management and Ramirez (1999) suggests that customers should be managed as factors of production, or assets. Indeed, the value gained from the service might depend on how well the customer and service organisation staff relate to one another, which may include how well the customer explains his/her expectations and whether the employee understands his/her expectations (e.g. a patient has to explain the type of symptoms he/she is experiencing to a GP to enable the doctor to then make a diagnosis or, at least, perform the necessary tests to inform the diagnosis). The relationship exists primarily between the service user and front-line staff within the service organisation. Indeed, service organisations depend on employees for their knowledge, skills and motivation to produce an effective service, but the interaction within the service encounter is key:

> a company can influence service quality, consumer satisfaction, and repeat purchase behaviour by focusing on the small dance carried out by the customer and contact employee.
>
> (Bowers et al., 1990, p. 56)

Managing the front-line employee-customer interface is therefore essential to the success of the service, and relationship marketing has been suggested as an appropriate management technique, which Gronroos (2000, p. 98) defines as:

> the process of identifying and establishing, maintaining, enhancing and, when necessary, terminating relationships with customers and

other stakeholders, at a profit, so that the objectives of all parties are met, where this is done by a mutual giving and fulfilment of promises.

As early as 1979, Lovelock and Young recommended a focus on the relationship between customers and front-line employees to promote co-production. They outlined specific steps for managers: develop positive and trustful relationships with customers in order to promote a willing-ness to accept change, take steps to develop an understanding of custom-ers' habits, undertake careful testing of any new procedures, attempt to understand why customers behave the way they do, be prepared to teach customers how to use service innovations, promote the benefits of ser-vice innovation to encourage customers to change their behaviour and monitor and evaluate the performance of new procedures to ensure they are continuing to work effectively over time. More recently, Gummes-son (1998) argued that relationship marketing offers a welcome para-digm shift from traditional marketing management. He emphasises the importance of inter-dependent, collaborative and long-term relationships of mutual respect and trust, where the customer is viewed as a part-ner (Gummesson, 1998; Wright and Taylor, 2007; Kinard and Capella, 2006). Gronroos (2000) also suggests relationship marketing can be used to terminate relationships in a positive way.

In essence, relationship marketing recognises the crucial role of the customer in contributing to his/her own satisfaction with the service (Veloutsou et al., 2004). Relational strategies are typically communicated through advertising, customer care and customer loyalty programmes (O'Malley and Prothero, 2004). The aim is to establish, develop and sustain relationships with customers, which is achieved through nor-mative methods such as trust and commitment rather than contractual arrangements. Thus, there is a shift away from manipulation and the transactional approach towards communication, knowledge sharing and genuine customer involvement (Gronroos, 2007). With a focus on rela-tionships, networks and interactions, relationship marketing does not only consider the customer-provider relationship, but also relationships among suppliers and with competitors (Gummesson, 1998).

## Summary: Co-production From the Service Management Perspective

Two broad dimensions of co-production have been uncovered in the dis-cussion presented in this chapter. First, co-production has been defined as a central construct in the service management literature. It is not a buzzword or rhetoric but an inalienable feature of the service production process and can be managed and fostered to the benefit of service produc-tion for service users, service organisations and wider society. The service

management theory emphasises the interaction between the service producer and the service user and the interdependency between these two, due
to the inseparability of production and consumption. Co-production in
this narrative occurs at the point of service delivery (Normann's 'moment
of truth'). It is not an add-on and does not result from the service organisation providing additional and optional opportunities for the service
user to co-produce—it is an unavoidable element of the service production process. Thus, co-production here does not result from a dedicated
public policy initiative (such as the personalisation reform agenda) or
as a direct consequence of public officials offering means through which
individual service users can voice their opinions. The user's contribution
during service production is not only unavoidable but also crucial to his/
her own satisfaction with the service and the effectiveness of the service
(value-in-use). This satisfaction is thus based upon the perceived experience of a service by its user, including its co-production.

The second dimension of co-production has focused on customer
participation as a means of extending co-production. Although it suggests that customers can become more active during service production
through various consumer mechanisms, unlike the essential form of co-
production, customer participation is facilitated and controlled by the
service provider. This has similarities with the public administration
debate presented in Chapter 2, referring to customer participation as a
means of co-production whereby the customer becomes a more active
contributor to the service.

Co-production has also been developed under the service-dominant
logic and with reference to the co-creation of value. Here, a deeper role
for the service user is implied and his/her participation is embedded
into the whole process of service production (during usage, process and
contextualisation, rather than being confined to the 'moment of truth')
where the aim is to create value for the individual. This involves an active
and equal dialogue in order to create personalised service experiences
and, importantly, emphasises the innovative potential of service users
who possess the 'sticky' information or knowledge (von Hippel, 1994,
2005) required for effective service improvement, transformation and
innovation. However, the discussion has also examined the criticism of
the service-dominant logic through the work of Gronroos who suggests
an alternative 'Service Logic', which has been described as fundamental
to the developing Public Service Logic.

Although the service management theory clearly has important insight
to offer around the understanding of co-production, it also has its limitations. It has no real understanding of the political and policy context
of public services, nor of service production where 'who the user is' of
a service is contested (as in the case of the criminal justice system, for
example) or where the desired outcomes of a service are multiple and/or
contested—as can be the case in a range of childcare services (Osborne,

2010). What it offers is a conception of the process nature of services and the implications this has for how public services might be better managed to improve public services, but its application must be positioned in a public service context that takes account of the motivation and impact of co-production on the individual, organisational and societal levels. This chapter has further suggested that if co-production exists as an inherent dimension of service production—as is suggested by the service-dominant logic—then the management of the interface between service users and front-line staff is of significant importance. Relationship marketing has been discussed as providing an important contribution to that debate.

## Note

1 Nankervis (2005) also includes variability and perishability as defining characteristics of services. Services are variable in the sense that they can be diverse and customised; they are not fixed in the same way as manufactured goods and can be tailored to the specific needs of the customer. Services are also perishable experiences in that they cannot be replicated, stored or reused due to their diverse and customised nature. They are also perishable in the sense that they are time-limited and may therefore only be available for consumption at a certain point in time (Sampson and Froehle, 2006).

## References

Alam, I. (2006). Removing the fuzziness from the fuzzy front-end of service innovations through consumer interactions. *Industrial Marketing Management.* (35), 468–480.

Alford, J. (2009). *Engaging public sector clients: from service-delivery to co-production.* Basingstoke: Palgrave Macmillan.

Alford, J. (2016). Co-production, interdependence and publicness: extending public service dominant logic. *Public Management Review.* (18,5), 673–691.

Allison, G. (1979). Public and private management: are they fundamentally alike in all unimportant respects? In Shafritz, J. and Hyde, A. (eds.), *Classics of public administration.* Wadsworth: Belmont.

Alves, H. (2013). Co-creation and innovation in public services. *The Service Industries Journal.* (33,7–8), 671–682.

Bendapudi, N. and Leone, R. P. (2003). Psychological implications of customer participation in co-production. *Journal of Marketing.* (67), 14–28.

Bettencourt, L. A., Ostrom, A. L., Brown, S. W. and Rowntree, R. I. (2002). Client co-production in knowledge-intensive business services. *California Management Review.* (44,4), 100–128.

Bitner, M. J., Faranda, W. T., Hubbert, A. R. and Zeithaml, V. A. (1997). Customer contributions and roles in service delivery. *International Journal of Service Industry Management.* (8,3), 193–205.

Bowers, M. R., Martin, C. L. and Luker, A. (1990). Trading places: employees as customers, customers as employees. *The Journal of Services Marketing.* (4,2), 55–69.

Dunston, R., Lee, A., Boud, D., Brodie, P. and Chiarella, M. (2009). Co-production and health system reform—from re-imagining to re-making. *The Australian Journal of Public Administration*. (68,1), 39–52.

Eriksson, E. M. (2019). Representative co-production: broadening the scope of the public service logic. *Public Management Review*. (21,2), 1–314.

Ferlie, E., Ashburner, L., Fitzgerald, L. and Pettigrew, A. (1996). *The new public management in action*. Oxford: Oxford University Press.

Fitzsimmons, J. A. (1985). Consumer participation and productivity in service operations. *Interfaces*. (15,3), 60–67.

Glushko, R. J. and Tabas, L. (2009). Designing service systems by bridging the 'front stage' and 'back stage'. *Information System E-business Management*. (7), 407–427.

Gronroos, C. (2000). Creating a relationship dialogue: communication, interaction and value. *The Marketing Review*. (1,1), 5–14.

Gronroos, C. (2007). *Service management and marketing: customer management in service competition* (3rd ed.). Chichester: John Wiley & Sons.

Gronroos, C. (2009). Marketing as promise management: regaining customer management for marketing. *Journal of Business and Industrial Marketing*. (24,5), 351–359.

Gronroos, C. (2018). Reforming public services: does service logic have anything to offer? *Public Management Review*. (21,5), 775–788.

Gronroos, C. and Voima, P. (2013). Critical service logic: making sense of value creation and co-creation. *Journal of the Academy of Marketing Science*. (41,2), 133–150.

Gummesson, E. (1998). Implementation requires a relationship marketing paradigm. *Journal of the Academy of Marketing Science*. (26,2), 242–249.

Gummesson, E. and Polese, F. (2009). B2B is not an island! *Journal of Business and Industrial Marketing*. (24,5), 337–350.

Henkel, J. and von Hippel, E. (2005). Welfare implications of user innovation. *Journal of Technology Transfer*. (30,1), 273–287.

Hood, C. (1991). A public management for all seasons? *Public Administration*. (69), 3–19.

Johnston, R. and Clark, G. (2008). *Service operations management: improving service delivery*. Harlow: Prentice Hall.

Jung, T. (2010). Citizens, co-producers, customers, clients, captives? A critical review of consumerism and public services. *Public Management Review*. (12,3), 439–446.

Kelley, S. W., Donnelly, J. H. and Skinner, S. J. (1990). Customer participation in service production and delivery. *Journal of Retailing*. (66,3), 315–335.

Kickert, W. J. M. (1997). Public governance in the Netherlands: an alternative to Anglo-American 'managerialism'. *Public Administration*. (75), 731–752.

Kinard, B. R. and Capella, M. L. (2006). Relationship marketing: the influence of consumer involvement on perceived service benefits. *Journal of Services Marketing*. (20,6), 359–368.

Kotler, P. and Levy, S. J. (1969). Broadening the concept of marketing. *The Journal of Marketing*. (1), 10–15.

Kristenssen, P., Matthing, J. and Johansson, N. (2008). Key strategies for the successful involvement of customers in the co-creation of new technology-based services. *International Journal of Service Industry Management*. (19,4), 474–491.

Laing, A. (2003). Marketing in the public sector: towards a typology of public services. *Marketing Theory*. (3,4), 427–445.

Lovelock, C. H. and Young, R. F. (1979). Look to consumers to increase productivity. *Harvard Business Review*. (57, May–June), 168–178.

Lusch, R. F., Vargo, S. L. and Tanniru, M. (2010). Service, value networks and learning. *Journal of the Academy of Marketing Science*. (38), 19–31.

Lusch, R. F. and Webster, F. E. (2011). A stakeholder-unifying, cocreation philosophy for marketing. *Journal of Macromarketing*. (31,2), 129–134.

McGuire, L. (2012). Slippery concepts in context: relationship marketing and public services. *Public Management Review*. (14,4), 541–555.

McLaughlin, K., Osborne, S. and Chew, C. (2009). Relationship marketing, relational capital and the future of marketing in public service organizations. *Public Money and Management*. (29,10), 35–42.

Mills, P. K., Chase, R. B. and Margulies, N. (1983). Motivating the client/employee system as a service production strategy. *Academy of Management Review*, (8,2), 201–310.

Mills, P. K. and Morris, J. H. (1986). Clients as 'partial' employees of service organizations: role development in client participation. *Academy of Management Review*. (11,4), 726–735.

Millward, L. (2005). Just because we are amateurs doesn't mean we aren't professional: the importance of expert activists in tenant participation. *Public Administration*. (83,3), 735–751.

Morgan, R. M. and Hunt, S. D. (1994). The commitment-trust theory of relationship marketing. *The Journal of Marketing*. (1), 20–38.

Nankervis, A. (2005). *Managing services*. Cambridge: Cambridge University Press.

Normann, R. (1991). *Service management: strategy and leadership in service business* (2nd ed.). West Sussex: John Wiley & Sons.

O'Malley, L. and Prothero, A. (2004). Beyond the frills of relationship marketing. *Journal of Business Research*. (57,11), 1–8.

Ordanini, A. and Pasini, P. (2008).Service co-production and value co-creation: the case for a service-orientated architecture (SOA). *European Management Journal*. (26), 289–297.

Osborne, S. P. (2010). Delivering public services: time for a new theory? *Public Management Review*. (12,1), 1–10.

Osborne, S. P. and Brown, L. (2011). Innovation, public policy and public services delivery in the UK: the word that would be king? *Public Administration*. (89,4), 1335–1350.

Osborne, S. P., Radnor, Z., Kinder, T. and Vidal, I. (2015). The SERVICE framework: a public-service-dominant approach to sustainable public services. *British Journal of Management*. (26,3), 424–438.

Osborne, S. P., Radnor, Z. and Nasi, G. (2013). A new theory for public service management? Toward a (Public) service dominant approach. *American Review of Public Administration*. (43,2), 135–158.

Osborne, S. P., Radnor, Z. and Strokosch, K. (2016). Co-production and the co-creation of value in public service: a suitable case for treatment? *Public Management Review*. (18,5), 639–653.

Osborne, S. P. and Strokosch, K. (2013). It takes two to tango? Understanding the co-production of public services by integrating the service management and public administration perspectives. *British Journal of Management*. (24), S31–S47.

Pollitt, C. and Bouckaert, G. (2004). *Public management reform: a comparative analysis.* Oxford: Oxford University Press.

Powell, M., Greener, I., Szmigin, I., Doheny, S. and Mills, N. (2010). Broadening the focus of public service consumerism. *Public Management Review.* (12,3), 323–340.

Prahalad, C. K. and Ramaswamy, V. (2000). Co-opting customer competence. *Harvard Business Review.* (January–February), 79–87.

Prahalad, C. K. and Ramaswamy, V. (2004). Co-creation experiences: the next practice in value creation. *Journal of Interactive Marketing.* (18,3), 5–14.

Ramirez, R. (1999). Value co-production: intellectual origins and implications for practice and research. *Strategic Management Journal.* (20), 49–65.

Ross, K. (1995). Speaking in tongues: involving users in day care services. *British Journal of Social Work.* (25), 791–804.

Sampson, S. E. and Froehle, C. M. (2006). Foundations and implications of a proposed unified services theory. *Production and Operations Management.* (15,2), 329–343.

Skalen, P., Karlsson, J., Engen, M. and Magnuson, P. R. (2018). Understanding public service innovation as resource integration and creation of value propositions. *Australian Journal of Public Administration.* (77,4), 700–714.

Spohrer, J., Vargo, S. L., Caswell, N. and Maglio, P. P. (2008). *The service system is the basic abstraction of service science.* 41st Hawaii International Conference on Service Sciences.

Timney, M. M. (1998). Overcoming administrative barriers to citizen participation: citizens as partners, not adversaries. In King, C. S. and Strivers, C. (eds.), *Government is us: public administration in an anti-government era.* Thousand Oaks: Sage.

Vargo, S. L. and Lusch, R. F. (2004). Evolving to a new dominant logic for marketing. *Journal of Marketing.* (68), 1–17.

Vargo, S. L. and Lusch, R. F. (2008). Service-dominant logic: continuing the evolution. *Journey of the Academy of Marketing Science.* (36), 1–10.

Vargo, S. L., Maglio, P. P. and Archpru Akaka, M. (2008). On value and value co-creation: a service systems and service logic perspective. *European Journal of Management.* (26), 145–152.

Veloutsou, C., Saren, M. and Tzokas, N. (2004). Relationship marketing: what if. . .? *European Journal of Marketing.* (36,4), 433–449.

von Hippel, E. (1986). Lead users: a source of novel product concepts. *Management Science.* (32,7), 791–805.

von Hippel, E. (1994). Sticky information and the locus of problem solving: implications for innovation. *Management Science.* (40,4), 429–439.

von Hippel, E. (1998). Economics of product development by users: the impact of 'sticky' local information. *Management Science.* (44,5), 629–644.

von Hippel, E. (2005). *Democratizing innovation.* Cambridge: MIT Press.

von Hippel, E. (2007). Horizontal innovational networks—by and for users. *Industrial and Corporate Change.* (16,2), 293–315.

Voorberg, W. H., Bekkers, V. J. J. M. and Tummers, L. G. (2015). A systematic review of co-creation and co-production: embarking on the social innovation journey. *Public Management Review.* (17,9), 1333–1357.

Wright, G. H. and Taylor, A. (2007). Strategic partnerships and relationship marketing in healthcare. *Public Management Review.* (7,2), 203–224.

Zwick, D., Bonsu, S. K. and Darmody, A. (2008). Putting consumers to work: co-creation and new marketing govern-mentality. *Journal of Consumer Culture.* (8,2), 163–196.

# 4   Co-production
## An Integrated Perspective

## Abstract

This chapter presents an integrated model of co-production. It merges the literature from the public administration and service management perspectives and argues that such an integration of the theory supports the reformulation of the concept of co-production, which is subsequently differentiated into three distinct modes—co-construction, participative co-production and co-design. The chapter discusses each of these modes in detail, referring to their key dimensions and rationale, before examining the limitations of the model.

## Introduction

This chapter will draw on the previous analysis of co-production presented in Chapters 2 and 3, from the public administration and service management literature, respectively, to develop an integrated perspective of co-production. It will present three modes of co-production, namely co-construction, co-production and co-design, suggesting that while service users' involvement is an integral dimension of the service production process, it can also be extended beyond the service interaction through participative mechanisms during both service delivery and design.

## An Integrated Perspective on Co-production

The discussion has demonstrated that the conceptualisation of co-production from the public administration theory is significantly dissimilar conceptually from that portrayed in the service management literature. It is argued here that the understanding of co-production is improved significantly by its differentiation, creating 'opportunities not only to develop better management theory, but also to enhance citizen and service user participation, based on a more contingent understanding of public sector deliberative processes than is available via product logic' (Alford, 2016, p. 688).

The dependence upon product-dominant management theory originating from the manufacturing sector has impaired current public management theory and practice because it does not provide an accurate reflection of how services are produced or the role of individual service users or other organisations in that process. The service management literature, by contrast, arguably offers a better starting point for theorising about the co-production of public services, offering insight into the process nature of services and the related implications for service production and the role played by service users.

The argument presented here is based on the service management theory and suggests that public services are understood and managed as *services*, which can be defined as 'help[ing] someone's relevant processes, such that his or her goal achievement is enabled in a way that is valuable to him or her' (Gronroos, 2018, p. 4) and which departs from the product-dominant logic that is associated with manufactured goods and has been applied to public services over the last four decades (Osborne et al., 2013, 2015). In line with the classical public administration perspective, public services necessitate a concentration on interactional and relational dimensions, rather than a transactional approach (e.g. Pestoff, 2014; Meijer, 2016). Importantly, for public service management, though, the emphasis becomes not only the output as it has been within the New Public Management narrative, but also the service user experience during those interactions (Alford, 2016). It is here that the service management literature has been argued to have another significant contribution to the debate, specifically with regards to the management of service relationships.

Verschuere et al. (2012), in parallel with much of the public administration literature, suggest that the starting point for co-production is the public service organisations and their articulation of the goals: 'From the organisational perspective, it is important that clients fully understand the value that the organisation is seeking, hence the organisation must clarify the value it is seeking to achieve: "what are we trying to do here?" This question is about outcome and effect, rather than input, process or output' (Verschuere et al., 2012, p. 1089). Learning from the service management literature turns this conceptualisation on its head by starting with the service user and his/her goals (Gronroos, 2018). The implication here is that the goals of the organisation should replicate and balance those of the individual service user and society at large and suggests that the public service organisation should seek to understand the goals of the service user and communities through an outside-in approach to service design and delivery. Indeed, Gronroos (2018) argues that organisational processes, resources and competences should be aligned with the needs of the service user, rather than vice versa; the role of public service staff here is therefore to facilitate positive interactions with service users through, for example, relationship marketing.

Although the service management literature has offered a significant development around the role of the service user in the delivery of services, the public administration/management literature offers valuable insight around how co-production can be extended through various participative mechanisms. Taken together, the two literatures add further to the debate, suggesting that co-production can be enhanced both through the use of various mechanisms and by developing deeper relationships with service users to co-create value through the co-design of services.

Drawing on Osborne and Strokosch (2013) and Osborne et al. (2016), Table 4.1 integrates these narratives to produce three modes of service user involvement. Integrating them in this way provides a more comprehensive view of the role of the service user in public services, showing that their involvement exists both as an implicit dimension of the service interaction and that it can be both extended and embedded through various mechanisms of co-production. The starting premise of the model is public service users are never passive, but that they can play a more or less active role in the production of public services. The three modes are termed as *co-construction* (based in service management theory), *participative co-production* (rooted in public administration theory) and *co-design* (that combines elements of the two previous modes).

*Co-construction.* This dimension was formally referred to as 'consumer co-production' (Osborne and Strokosch, 2013), but, in line with theoretical progress in both the service management and public administration literature (which has been discussed in the preceding analysis)

*Table 4.1* Individual modes of co-production

| Co-construction (service delivery/ interactions) | Participative co-production (service delivery and design) | Co-design (service delivery and design) |
| --- | --- | --- |
| The inseparability of production and consumption focuses on the service interaction and implies an integral role for the service user during service delivery. The role of the public service organisation is to facilitate an effective relationship during service interactions in order to maximise his/ her satisfaction with the service ('value-in-use'). | Participative mechanisms used to co-produce services in order to achieve broader societal aims (e.g. integration). Includes both consumer and citizen participation mechanisms. | Service innovations under the goal of service improvement and to enhance the achievement of public policy objectives. The role of the service user through co-construction is extended to whole service process (including operational planning) to develop personalised experiences. |

Adapted from Osborne and Strokosch (2013)

and developments in practice, the concept of co-production is most strongly associated with the product-dominant logic and is therefore used to describe instances where citizens/service users might be 'added into' the process of service design/delivery rather than being integral to it (Gronroos and Voima, 2013; Gronroos, 2018). Distinguishing the service interaction as a dimension of value creation that is distinct from the traditional appended view of co-production adds conceptual clarity and enables greater analytical rigour, which has been a strong criticism of the literature on co-production from both the public management and service management literature (e.g. Gronroos and Voima, 2013; Nabatchi et al., 2017). For the purposes of this analysis, the term 'co-construction' therefore presents an embedded view of co-production (Osborne et al., 2016) that focuses particularly on the service interaction and the role of individual service users during their interactions (or service encounters) with the staff and processes of an organisation.

The act of service consumption is critical to service production, as it is this action that results in the service users' contribution to production at the operational level—their expectations and experiences are central to effective service delivery. This reflects a shift from the dominant value-in-exchange view typically associated with manufactured goods (and public services), and towards value-in-use, where the value is perceived and determined by the service user through their *use* of the service and within the *context* of their own lives (Vargo and Lusch, 2008; Gronroos and Voima, 2013; Skalen et al., 2018). In this first mode, therefore, the interaction between the service provider and service user is an integral component of public service production. This acknowledges that it is *involuntary and unavoidable* on the part of both the service user and the public service organisation. In other words, organisations do not have to employ any special mechanisms to encourage, facilitate or sustain co-production, nor does the service user have to make a conscious choice to co-produce. From this perspective, co-production is not an issue of choice and design, but rather of the management of the relationships between the organisation and the service user; co-construction is a core element of the effective management of public services on a day-to-day, operational basis. Starting with the service encounters suggests that service user involvement is no longer framed as a normative ideal or limited to appended processes of involvement. Service user involvement, through co-construction, is an integral dimension of the service relationship and interactions between the service user and public service staff, the organisation's processes or digital interfaces.

From this perspective, co-production is reframed, suggesting that the service delivery professional alone does not provide the service experience or outcome, but rather it is negotiated between the professional and service user through an interactive relationship. While the service output is essential, the process is the decisive aspect of the service (Gronroos,

2018) and the management of the service is therefore a critical way in which public service organisations might influence the value created. User empowerment has of course been a desire of public service reform for several decades (Osborne, 1994) but co-construction reformulates this aspiration in a way that understands it as a natural part of the service production process and that offers concrete approaches to its achievement. Co-construction is not an issue of choice and design but of the management of the relationships between the public service organisation and the service user, and it is one that is essential to the quality of a service and the satisfaction of service users with the service (Vargo et al., 2008). Relationship management therefore becomes a core element of the effective management of public services on a day-to-day basis. This goes beyond 'simple' consumerism and towards a more sophisticated understanding of a public service as *a service delivery system* (Vargo et al., 2008). It further emphasises the critical role played by the front-line employees delivering services; their role is essential to shaping value-in-use (Gronroos and Voima, 2013) with the quality of the interaction affecting both service user satisfaction and the service outcome (Osborne et al., 2013).

This conceptualisation has further implications for the public service organisation's role in service production. It suggests that an organisation can only 'promise' a certain process or experience—the actuality is dependent upon the 'moment of truth' (Normann, 1991) which is the point at which the organisation's front-line staff (or service processes which can be online) and service user interact through the service relationship or experience. The 'moment of truth' is critical to the process of co-construction where value can be co-created or co-destroyed by front-line staff and public service users. Public service organisations make 'service offerings' based upon a promise of value that should address collective value, deemed important by society, such as an equal and fair or well-educated society (Alford, 2016; Skalen et al., 2018).

An example of co-construction in the public service setting is the service provided by a social worker to a child in the care system. Co-construction suggests that the relationship should not be paternalistic where the professional provides the service and the client is the recipient, but instead rooted within interaction. This core relational element is located during the service interactions—the moment of truth—between the two parties. In order for the child to receive any satisfaction with the services, he needs to share information and communicate with the social worker, who in turn needs to manage an effective relationship with that individual to ensure the best possible outcome. A patient also co-constructs his healthcare with professionals. For example, a doctor can only make an accurate diagnosis if a patient has provided accurate information regarding his symptoms. Failure to provide complete or accurate information could negatively impact the quality of the care. Similarly, education is reliant on the attendance and participation of learners. Their participation may, however, be more or less active (i.e. learners may simply choose to listen to the teacher and take notes or they may also ask questions and provide feedback during the class), but their application to learning is critical to the effectiveness of the service which will eventually be measured by their resulting achievements.

Of course, there are examples of public services that are less relational in nature and some which are delivered without any interaction between service users and public service staff, which could take place through face-to-face encounters or over the telephone. One such case is where individuals complete tax forms online or apply for a new passport. In such instances the relational element is not present, but an interaction (between the service user and the service organisation's online systems and processes) still takes place. This arguably has significant implications for the design and operation of the organisational processes that facilitate the online interaction; if they are not accessible and usable, service users will be unable to interact with them effectively to generate the information required by the organisation or to meet their own needs (e.g. obtain a new passport). This is an area that requires further investigation and analysis, particularly around the potential for organisational processes that support services to create or destroy value for service users.

## Participative Co-production

In the second mode, co-production is extended beyond the consumption logic of a single service alone and into the overall service production process, including planning, delivery and evaluation. This conceptualisation draws substantively on the public administration narrative on co-production, where co-production has been widely defined. The approach here follows that of Nabatchi et al. (2017) who define the classical public administration view of co-production as an umbrella concept, which encapsulates the involvement of both individuals and groups within public service planning and delivery (Parks et al., 1981; Brandsen and Honingh, 2016).

Participative co-production does not necessarily change the nature of operational service delivery, as Bovaird (2007) has noted, but rather in its design and planning at the strategic level. In contrast to co-construction, which seeks to acknowledge the indisputable presence of a service user in the operational production of a service, participative co-production is 'added-on' to the service design process in order to improve the design (and hence effectiveness) of public services. A key element of such co-production is *user participation* (Beresford, 2001; Simmons and Birchall, 2005). Public service users can adopt a more active role in service production than co-producing solely through consumption. This can be achieved, for example, through either citizen participation or consumer mechanisms, which are utilised at the behest of the public service organisation.

Organisations may introduce consumer mechanisms such as choice, complaints procedures and service evaluation forms (Gronroos, 2007). By establishing such consumer mechanisms, they can promote independent advocacy, which can shift responsibility and control away from the service provider and towards the individuals consuming services (Jack, 1995). This includes, for example, a parent and child's choice over which school is attended. This may not be free choice, but rather a suggestion of preference, with the final allocation being decided by authorities and according to postcode and availability. In terms of complaints, all public sector organisations (e.g. National Health Service hospitals, housing associations and prisons) have formal procedures and if a service user is not satisfied with the outcome of following such procedures, they can take their complaint to the Scottish Public Services' Ombudsman who will seek to remedy the issue and share any learning to improve services.

The mechanisms associated with citizen participation suggest a potentially deeper role for public service users through participative co-production, which may extend into service planning. For example, when planning a new service, a public service organisation may consult current or potential service users to gauge their needs and therefore help develop a framework for the service. However, consultation is not synonymous with co-production; their association arguably depends upon the depth of consultation and its outcomes. Pestoff (2014), for instance, argues that co-production cannot be equated with consultation as the former involves a systematic dialogue between service users and organisations, which ultimately gives the service user greater influence and ownership over public services. Co-production in this form therefore tends to be on an ad hoc basis, being added on and its format depends upon the goal of the public service. For example, an organisation may utilise the skills and knowledge of service users during the production of a public service to another group. One example of this might be a volunteer visitor in a hospital who can undertake various activities including supporting the nursing staff on the ward by talking to patients and assisting at meal times. Participative co-production might also include partnership approaches where public service users or their representatives (e.g. guardians or carers) contribute to service planning. For example, parent councils operate in British schools and provide parents with the opportunity to work in partnership with schools by contributing to decision-making.

## Co-design

It is possible to combine elements from the two previous modes and both narratives to achieve co-design, a core dimension of which is in the field of service reform and innovation. Co-design, according to Bovaird and Loeffler (2012, p. 9) integrates 'the experience of users and their communities' into the planning and development stages of public services to design improved services for those who are using them. It extends beyond the service interaction, which is the basis of co-construction, offering a deeper role for service users that is embedded into the whole service production process and enabling the transformation of services by drawing on the resources and skills or 'sticky' knowledge of *experienced* service users (von Hippel, 1994, 2005; Gronroos and Voima, 2013; Osborne et al., 2016). The process of co-design facilitates the proactive discovery, understanding and satisfaction of 'latent' needs by a public service organisation, rather than simply reacting to (existing) needs or professionally determined needs (Ordanini and Pasini, 2008; Vargo and Lusch, 2008). In this sense, the service organisation draws on resources and experience or 'sticky' knowledge of service users in order to transform the service or to develop customised experiences, as opposed to focusing on the service encounter during delivery which is the location of co-construction (von Hippel, 1994, 2005; Gronroos and Voima, 2013; Osborne et al., 2016). The potential for value creation therefore extends beyond the service interaction or 'moment of truth' to all points of interaction between the service user and provider. The operationalisation of co-design therefore takes a more embedded form than co-production; although similar to participative co-production, its application and impact is still controlled by the public service organisation.

Co-design can also embrace forms of service design, taking a holistic approach where service users' lived experiences are used to develop and innovate services in partnership with public service organisations (Radnor et al., 2014). This involves a user-centred design approach to understand how service users experience a service which extends beyond the service interaction—basis of co-construction—and offers a deeper opportunity for customers to shape the service experience. Its conceptualisation draws on the service management literature, which argues that service users' contributions to service design are critical to the design process by building their needs and experiences into the development process (Steen et al., 2011).

Examples of co-design include various service design approaches which are increasingly employed in the public sector service, such as blueprinting (Radnor et al., 2014), persona techniques (Jeong et al., 2016) and collaborative design approaches (Dietrich et al., 2017). Another example of co-design in the public service setting is in the case of self-directed support, which has recently had much interest in social and healthcare services in Scotland. Self-directed support suggests that an extended dialogue takes place between the two parties working in partnership, and the service user may be given a greater degree of control over how needs are met (Hunter and Ritchie, 2007). The role of the professional is one of advocacy, where he/she assists the service user, who is considered an expert in his/her own needs, to navigate through the system. In some instances, the service user may take responsibility for designing his/her own care packages and are therefore in control of his/her own budget—with the assistance of the professional.

This mode seeks to move from expressed to latent need to uncover future needs, and as such is a key element of service innovation (Alam, 2006) and can contribute significantly to our understanding of the nature and process of public service innovation. The public policy narrative has a long history of proposing 'co-production' as the solution to the need for 'social innovation' in public service delivery as part of the reform process of these services, though without ever really exploring what this might mean in theory and practice. Thus Mulgan (2006, p. 159) has argued that the 'absence of sustained and systematic analysis is holding back the practice of social innovation', whilst Osborne and Brown (2011) have similarly maintained the need for greater conceptual clarity on the nature and process of such innovation if we are to drive forward the process of innovation. The framework presented here makes clear the role that this mode of co-production can play in innovation in public services. The suggestion here is that the process of co-construction exists as an intrinsic dimension of service production, but that this relational element of production can be extended by public service organisations recognising that, first, co-construction exists and can be managed and, second, by taking pragmatic decisions over when it is most fruitful to extend co-construction through co-design or when to apply participatory forms of co-production (Osborne et al., 2013). A one-size-fits-all approach is not the recommendation here, but rather an approach that starts with individual service encounters and the service relationship which can be built on and extended by the public service organisation by introducing or embedding participatory processes that seek to utilise the 'sticky' knowledge and experiences of the service user for the purpose of service improvement and innovation.

## Limitations of the Integrated Model

These conceptualisations are not without limitations, especially in the relationship between service professionals and service users. While service users bring important expertise to co-production, so too do service professionals. Co-production is not about the replacement of the role of professionals by public service users, but about bringing these different forms of expertise together. Public service organisations are typically highly professionalised and may be resistant to accept the actual premise of participative co-production or its challenges to their own professionalism (Osborne, 1994; Bovaird and Loeffler, 2009). To take a simple example, one would not want to replace the role of the surgeon by the patient in the co-production of oncology services—the professional expertise of the surgeon is vital here. However, the research has also indicated the significance to clinical outcomes of the co-production of the overall treatment plan between health professionals and patients (Katz et al., 2005). The crucial point here is that the appended forms of co-production should be applied sensitively and appropriately, depending on the service, and this is why it is an area of great import for academics and practitioners alike. Furthermore, specifically with reference to participative co-production and co-design, transferring influence and ownership to service users is, for Pestoff (2014), a substantial risk for public service organisations, who may be wary of allowing individual service users to 'do their own thing' which could potentially result in disparity of service provision.

Another challenge for co-production is that there are inevitably cases where the public service user is an unwilling or coerced user. The prison service is a classic example here. In this context, the professionals of the prison service have a custodial function that is hard to co-produce. Even here, though, it could be argued that the daily service interactions between prison staff and inmates have co-construction at their heart. Furthermore, electronic tagging of a convicted criminal within the community is a form of co-produced custody (Corcoran, 2011); this is an area where further conceptual development is required (Osborne et al., 2013).

All three modes are reliant on the presence of *trust* in the service relationship—because the process of co-production is essentially relational, but it can be risky, uncertain, time-consuming and costly for public service organisations, service users and other organisations, particularly when it is extended to its more participatory forms. Service professionals and planners must trust that they will receive some return from co-production, whilst service users must trust that their contributions will be recognised, valued and acted upon. Developing such trust has of course been a substantive challenge for public service organisations for many decades (van de Walle and Bouckaert, 2003). Tools to assist in the process of this development do exist in the service management literature, such as relationship marketing (Sheth and Parvatiyar, 2002) and some have explored their application to public services (McLaughlin et al., 2009). Without such application, the risks of co-production may counter its benefits in the implementation process. It is important to recognise that simply establishing mechanisms through which to involve service users in service planning and production does not guarantee the participative co-production or co-design. Indeed, the earlier discussion has suggested that these appended forms are subject to a public service organisation taking an active and genuine approach to their application, but there are many examples of passive or even tokenistic approaches to responding to these mechanisms (Sinclair, 2004), which ultimately serve to limit the innovative potential of public service organisations and likely cause an aversion to participate among public service users (Williams et al., 2016).

Finally, co-production is particularly fraught where public services, as is often the case, can have multiple and perhaps conflicting users. In the case of custodial prison services, for example, it is a moot point who the actual service user is—the convicted criminal themselves, or the court, victims of crime or society at large. This dilemma is highlighted particularly by Bovaird (2005). If, as the service management literature suggests, the fundamental aim of co-production is to create value, the question that arises in the public sector context in relation to who that value is created for is particularly complex; do public services aim to create value for the wider public, individual service users, public service organisations and their employees or all of the above? There are likely to be significant tensions between the various types of value that public services seek to create and these require greater exploration and debate.

## Summary: An Integrated Model of Individual Modes of Co-production

This chapter has combined two bodies of literature on co-production to develop an integrated model of co-production. The analysis has focused on the individual service user and locates three modes of co-production: co-construction, participative co-production and co-design.

The discussion has argued that the public service user plays an integral element of service production during the interaction or 'moment of truth' that is specific to the process nature of services through co-construction. The analysis of the service management literature has permitted a reformulation of co-production that starts from co-construction and the importance of managing the service relationship as a process. However, this is not to say that the public administration literature has not also made a significant contribution to the debate on co-production. On the contrary, the literature offers an important contribution to the theory, particularly around its participative and reciprocal characteristics and the motivations and barriers to its practice. It has been argued through the presentation of the integrated model—and in line with the public administration theory on co-production—that there is potential for the role of public service users to be extended beyond the service interaction through different participative mechanisms. However, the discussion has suggested that the conceptualisation and practice of co-production in the public sector over the past four decades has taken an appended form that is controlled by those in power. Significantly, the conceptualisation of co-production has also been influenced heavily by the New Public Management narrative and has recently received increasing criticism, not least for the application of a product-dominant logic version of co-production, which overlooks the process and inherently relational nature of co-production (Dunston et al., 2009; Osborne et al., 2013). Finally, this chapter has suggested that co-production can build and extend co-construction that is integral to service encounters through co-design, which places the service user and his/her experience and 'sticky' knowledge at the centre of the service design process. This appended form of co-production is reliant on the public service organisation and its staff framing service users as operant resources who possess knowledge and skills that can be drawn on to achieve service innovation and reform.

## References

Alam, I. (2006). Removing the fuzziness from the fuzzy front-end of service innovations through consumer interactions. *Industrial Marketing Management.* (35), 468–480.

Alford, J. (2016). Co-production, interdependence and publicness: extending public service dominant logic. *Public Management Review.* (18,5), 673–691.

Beresford, P. (2001). Service users, social policy and the future of welfare. *Critical Social Policy.* (21,4), 494–512.

Bovaird, T. (2005). Public governance: balancing stakeholder power in a network society. *International Review of Administrative Sciences.* (71,2), 217–228.

Bovaird, T. (2007). Beyond engagement and participation—user and community co-production of public services. *Public Administration Review.* (67), 846–860.

Bovaird, T. and Loeffler, E. (2009). The changing policy context of public policy. In Bovaird, T. and Loffler, E. (eds.), *Public management and governance*. London: Routledge.

Bovaird, T. and Loeffler, E. (2012). From engagement to co-production: how users and communities contribute to public services. In Pestoff, V., Brandsen, T. and Verschuere, B. (eds.), *New public governance, the third sector and co-production*. New York: Routledge.

Brandsen, T. and Honingh, M. (2016). Distinguishing different types of co-production: a conceptual analysis based on the classical definitions. *Public Administration Review.* (76,3), 427–435.

Corcoran, M. (2011). Dilemmas of institutionalization in the penal voluntary sector. *Critical Social Policy.* (31), 30–52.

Dietrich, T., Trischler, J., Schuster, L., Rundle-Thiele, S. (2017). Co-designing services with vulnerable consumers. *Journal of Service Theory and Practice.* (27,3), 663–688.

Dunston, R., Lee, A., Boud, D., Brodie, P. and Chiarella, M. (2009). Co-production and health system reform—from re-imagining to re-making. *The Australian Journal of Public Administration.* (68,1), 39–52.

Gronroos, C. (2007). *Service management and marketing: customer management in service competition* (3rd ed.). Chichester: John Wiley & Sons.

Gronroos, C. (2018). Reforming public services: does service logic have anything to offer? *Public Management Review.* (21,5), 775–788.

Gronroos, C. and Voima, P. (2013). Critical service logic: making sense of value creation and co-creation. *Journal of the Academy of Marketing Science.* (41,2), 133–150.

Hunter, S. and Ritchie, P. (2007). With, not to: models of co-production in social welfare. Hunter, S. and Ritchie, P. (eds.), *Co-production and personalisation in social care*. London: Jessica Kingsley.

Jack, R. (1995). Empowerment in community care. In Jack, R. (ed.), *Empowerment in community care*. London: Chapman and Hall.

Jeong, I., Seo, J., Lim, J., Jang, J. and Kim, J. (2016). Improvement of the business model of the disaster management system based on the service design methodology. *International Journal of Safety and Security Engineering.* (6,1), 19–29.

Katz, S., Lantz, P., Janz, N., Fagerlin, A., Schwartz, K., Liu, L., Deapen, D., Salem, B., Lakhani, I. and Morrow, M. (2005). Patient involvement in surgery treatment decisions for breast cancer. *Journal of Clinical Oncology.* (23), 5526–5533.

McLaughlin, K., Osborne, S. and Chew, C. (2009). Relationship marketing, relational capital and the future of marketing in public service organizations. *Public Money and Management.* (29,10), 35–42.

Meijer, A. J. (2016). Coproduction as a structural transformation of the public sector. *International Journal of Public Sector Management.* (29,6), 596–611.

Mulgan, G. (2006). The process of social innovation. *Innovations: Technology, Governance, Globalization.* (1,2), 145–162.

Nabatchi, T., Sancino, A. and Sicilia, M. (2017). Varieties of participation in public services: the who, when and what of co-production. *Public Administration Review.* (77,5), 766–776.

Normann, R. (1991). *Service management: strategy and leadership in service business* (2nd ed.). West Sussex: John Wiley & Sons.

Ordanini, A. and Pasini, P. (2008). Service co-production and value co-creation: the case for a service-orientated architecture (SOA). *European Management Journal.* (26), 289–297.

Osborne, S. P. (1994). The language of empowerment. *International Journal of Public Sector Management.* (7,3), 56–62.

Osborne, S. P. and Brown, L. (2011). Innovation, public policy and public services delivery in the UK: the word that would be king? *Public Administration.* (89,4), 1335–1350.

Osborne, S. P., Radnor, Z., Kinder, T. and Vidal, I. (2015). The SERVICE framework: a public-service-dominant approach to sustainable public services. *British Journal of Management.* (26,3), 424–438.

Osborne, S. P., Radnor, Z. and Nasi, G. (2013). A new theory for public service management? Toward a (Public) service dominant approach. *American Review of Public Administration.* (43,2), 135–158.

Osborne, S. P., Radnor, Z. and Strokosch, K. (2016). Co-production and the co-creation of value in public service: a suitable case for treatment? *Public Management Review.* (18,5), 639–653.

Osborne, S. P. and Strokosch, K. (2013). It takes two to tango? Understanding the co-production of public services by integrating the service management and public administration perspectives. *British Journal of Management.* (24), S31–S47.

Parks, R. B., Baker, P. C., Kiser, L., Oakerson, R., Ostrom, E., Ostrom, V., Percy, S. L., Vandivort, M. B., Whitaker, G. P. and Wilson, R. (1981). Consumers as co-producers of public services: some economic and institutional considerations. *Policy Studies Journal.* (9,7), 1001–1011.

Pestoff, V. (2014). Collective action and the sustainability of co-production. *Public Management Review.* (16,3), 383–401.

Radnor, Z., Osborne, S. P., Kinder, T. and Mutton, J. (2014). Operationalising co-production in public services delivery: the contribution of service blueprinting. *Public Management Review.* (16,3), 402–423.

Sheth, J. N. and Parvatiyar, A. (2002). Evolving relationship marketing into a discipline. *Journal of Relationship Marketing.* (1,1), 3–16.

Simmons, R. and Birchall, J. (2005). A joined-up approach to user participation in public services: strengthening the 'participation chain'. *Social Policy and Administration*. (39,3), 260–283.

Sinclair, R. (2004). Participation in practice: making it meaningful, effective and sustainable. *Children & Society*. (18,2), 106–118.

Skalen, P., Karlsson, J., Engen, M. and Magnuson, P. R. (2018). Understanding public service innovation as resource integration and creation of value propositions. *Australian Journal of Public Administration*. (77,4), 700–714.

Steen, M., Manschot, M. and De Koning, N. (2011). Benefits of co-design in service design projects. *International Journal of Design*. (5,2), 53–60.

van de Walle, S. and Bouckaert, G. (2003). Public service performance and trust in government: the problem of causality. *International Journal of Public Administration*. (26), 891–913.

Vargo, S. L. and Lusch, R. F. (2008). Service-dominant logic: continuing the evolution. *Journey of the Academy of Marketing Science*. (36), 1–10.

Vargo, S. L., Maglio, P. P. and Archpru Akaka, M. (2008). On value and value co-creation: a service systems and service logic perspective. *European Journal of Management*. (26), 145–152.

Verschuere, B., Brandsen, T. and Pestoff, V. (2012). Co-production: the state of the art in research and the future agenda. *Voluntas*. (23,4), 1083–1101.

von Hippel, E. (1994). Sticky information and the locus of problem solving: implications for innovation. *Management Science*. (40,4), 429–439.

von Hippel, E. (2005). *Democratizing innovation*. Cambridge: MIT Press.

Williams, B. N., Kang, S. C. and Johnson, J. (2016). (Co)-contamination as the dark side of co-production: public value failures in co-production processes. *Public Management Review*. (18,5), 692–717.

# 5    Co-production Through
Inter-organisational Relationships

## Abstract

This chapter discusses the existence of co-production at an organisational level and examines the shift from intra-organisational to inter-organisational relationships that has developed within the New Public Governance narrative of public service reform. It focuses on the relationships between organisations across sectors and emphasises, in particular, the role played by third sector organisations within such relationships. Within this discussion, third sector organisations are described as mediators with the potential capacity to articulate the needs of those they represent. The chapter argues that third sector organisations can take two roles in co-production: they can contribute to service delivery (co-management) or to both the delivery and planning of services (co-governance). Once again, the service management literature is drawn on to understand how such inter-organisational relationships might be better managed by focusing on the trust that exists between those employees working across organisational boundaries.

## Introduction

Although inter-organisational relationships are not new, with literature dating back to the 1960s (e.g. Aiken and Hage, 1968; Pfeffer and Nowak, 1976) there has been an increased focus on joint working over the past twenty years, which has led to developments in the conceptualisation and practice of public service management. A strong government push for inter-organisational relationships through partnership, collaboration, networks and joint working is particularly notable across Europe. This chapter will introduce co-production at the organisational level, examining the relationships that exist across organisational boundaries during the production of public services. Although the literature has focused predominantly on the role of third sector organisations in the co-production of public services (Vidal, 2006; Pestoff and Brandsen, 2009), it is feasible that any organisation could co-produce. Indeed, Bode (2006a) notes that social welfare provision is increasingly co-produced through a process or inter-organisational working across the sectors. For the purposes of this work, however, the focus will be on the role played by third sector organisations in co-production due to the sector's particular importance in the case of asylum seekers, which will be discussed in Chapter 6.

The chapter will start by considering the shift from intra-organisational to inter-organisational relationships that has developed within the New Public Governance narrative. The discussion will consider both the enablers and challenges of such relationships. It will then focus on the distinctive characteristics of the third sector, before differentiating co-production on the organisational level with the introduction of the concepts of co-management and co-governance. The chapter will conclude by integrating these organisational dimensions of co-production with the individual modes presented in Chapter 4.

## Moving From Intra-organisational to Inter-organisational Relationships

The New Public Governance was a term coined by Osborne (2006) to reflect the impact upon public management of network governance and collaboration that originated in European governance literature dating back to the 1990s (Kooiman, 1993; Rhodes, 1997). More recently, scholars have argued that public service management has been overly concerned with the capacity of administrative processes and intra-organisational management to increase efficiency, while largely overlooking broader societal needs (Osborne et al., 2013). A focus on inter-organisation relationships has therefore been framed as an alternative to the New Public Management, which Osborne et al. (2013) argue has adopted an overly managerial and market-focus framework which is deeply flawed in its failure to reflect the inter-organisational and interactive nature of public service production. This discussion has continued under the Public Service Logic, which emphasises the complexity and interrelated processes of co-production which should operate in alignment to create value (Alford, 2016).

The New Public Governance builds on organisational sociology and network theory (Osborne, 2006) and suggests that public management is becoming increasingly fragmented and pluralistic, with public services being produced by networks from the for-profit, public and third sectors (Osborne et al., 2015). A relational approach to public service management is therefore necessary at the organisational as well as the individual level. The evolution of the New Public Governance narrative has also been driven by calls for more democracy and engagement as well as a need to reduce the costs of public services. It has recast public service delivery in an open systems framework (Osborne, 2006) and this has important implications for public service management. No longer is it a case of exploring administrative processes through top-down relationships, or dyadic exchanges between public service organisations and the recipients of public services; or the intra-organisational management of public services, which focuses on the internal relations within an organisation. The fragmentation of public service delivery in the post-modern state has placed emphasis upon inter-, rather than intra-, organisational relationships for public service delivery (Osborne, 2010; Osborne et al., 2015). The literature argues that public service delivery is moving towards network production whereby the production process is conducted across various organisations (Brandsen and van Hout, 2006; Bode, 2006a). Working across organisational boundaries is now, therefore, a fundamental role of public service managers (Huxham, 2000).

Network governance theories, although concerned primarily with policy formulation, provide useful grounding for understanding the inter-organisational relationships that exist during public service implementation. This is underpinned by a rich theoretical tradition with the concept of network dating back to the 1970s (Klijn and Koppenjan, 2000). Network governance emphasises partnership approaches and networks, as well as the process of interaction between organisations, in comparison with top-down (hierarchies) approaches, which tend to be results-orientated and concerned with predicting policy outcomes (Schofield, 2001; Bode, 2006a). Rhodes (1997, p. 15, emphasis in original) expands on network governance and refers to '*self-organizing, interorganisational networks* characterised by interdependence, resource exchange, rules of the game and significant autonomy from the state'. Furthermore and importantly for this work, Kooiman (2005) differentiates three modes of governance: hierarchical governance, self-governance and co-governance. Hierarchical refers to top-down governance, where a central actor takes control and directs others. Self-governance is the opposite, referring to bottom-up approaches where a collectivity controls and represents itself (see Prentice, 2006 for a discussion of the role of third sector organisations in planning and delivering childcare services in Canada without government support). Finally, co-governance suggests co-operation between a collectivity through a process of mutual shaping and representation, suggesting that the actors play an equal role in governance. It is the concept of co-governance and implications of mutual relationships among service providers during service production that are of interest here.

Networks are lauded for augmenting representative democracy by increasing participation at the output side of the political system, offering new structures and spaces of influence for those who have a deep interest in a particular issue and by recruiting and empowering those who can challenge traditional power structures (Sorensen and Torfing, 2005, 2009, 2018; Dryzek, 2007). They have also been welcomed for their plurality of actors who are well equipped to develop solutions to complex societal problems (Hajer and Wagenaar, 2003; Koppenjan and Klijn, 2004; Greenaway et al., 2007; Pestoff and Brandsen, 2010; Kennett, 2010; Moore and Hartley, 2010). These actors are typically representatives of certain groups/communities and their involvement is viewed as supplementing traditional representative democracy (Sorensen and Torfing, 2009). Within these relationships, public managers have also been described as playing a significant role as intermediaries between civil society and politicians, linking the two through interactive decision-making (Jeffares and Skelcher, 2011). Public Managers have also been described as key actors who facilitate and participate in horizontal relationships of co-production with service users during service design and delivery (Pestoff, 2006; Sicilia et al., 2016).

### Challenges of Inter-organisational Relationships

The literature outlines three challenges for inter-organisational relationships. First, Kickert and Koppenjan (1997) argue that there are considerable challenges with inter-organisational working, such as the financial, monetary and time costs of the participation of multiple actors and also the need to make compromises. In a similar vein, Rhodes (2000, pp. 74–75) argues that managing networks is 'time consuming, objectives can be blurred, and outcomes can be indeterminate'. Indeed, individual organisations have diverse and diverging interests, motivations and therefore, potentially conflicting objectives (Kickert and Koppenjan, 1997; Evers et al., 2005). Co-ordination is therefore a core challenge for networks (Klijn, 2008).

Second, the inclusiveness of networks has been questioned by some. Critics argue that network membership is exclusive to those with the necessary organisational infrastructure, expertise, knowledge and skills, and who may manipulate the system for their own gains (Ansell and Gash, 2007; Van Tatenhove et al., 2010; Lewis and Marsh, 2012). In order to facilitate negotiation, the membership of governance networks has been criticised for invariably serving a like-minded professional elite at the expense of 'lay people', consumers or citizens (Hendricks, 2008). By consequence, inter-organisational relationships may therefore have a negative impact on participative co-production. Indeed, empirical studies have generally suggested that in practice networks do not offer greater deliberation or direct participation with citizens/communities (Sorensen and Torfing, 2003; Greenaway et al., 2007; Peters, 2010).

Finally, Osborne et al. (2015) argue that the theories from networks and governance are inadequate in explaining the actuality of public service production. They argue that understanding inter-organisational relationships should extend beyond network governance and that public services should be conceptualised as being produced within complex public service systems, rather than by one organisation in isolation or even a network within the system. This leads Osborne et al. (2015, p. 2) to argue 'The task is thus not simply the governance of networks of public service organisations but the operationalisation of these interactive and complex service systems'. This suggests that inter-organisational relationships at the meso level also need to be considered in relation to individual interactions between public service users and public service staff during service planning and delivery.

## Enabling Inter-organisational Relationships Through Interaction and Trust

Inter-organisational relationships are reliant on the existence of credibility, reputation, reciprocity and trust among members (Vidal, 2006; Newman, 2007). Indeed, the process of working in networks involves bringing together expertise, knowledge and resources from across sectors as a way of tackling complex problems and improving services (Brandsen and van Hout, 2006). This involves interaction between multiple actors who are mutually dependent and reliant on one another's resources (e.g. financial, political or informational) (Rhodes, 1997). Interdependence means that co-operation is essential, although it does not preclude conflict. Each actor takes its own perspective, creating tension between dependency and the diversity of goals and interests. The success and failure are thus based upon the extent to which co-operation is achieved on a day-to-day basis (Klijn and Koppenjan, 2000; Klijn, 2008). For Sicilia et al. (2016), building and sustaining trust over time was fundamental to ensuring the collaboration of third sector organisations. Inter-organisational relationships have therefore brought a changed role of public service managers as one that is dependent upon building and sustaining relationships of trust across organisational boundaries:

> As managers no longer maintain control of the services their organisation offers, they increasingly have to operate through incentives and persuasion rather than hierarchy. This is where co-management starts to undermine the managerialist ethic: managers will lose power as their organisations diversify and stretch out. To be more precise, they will have to exercise a different kind of power, with an emphasis on charisma and inspiration rather than rule-making. Also, it will become more important to watch the quality of the organisation's gatekeepers and boundary spanner.
>
> (Brandsen and van Hout, 2006, p. 547)

It is around the management of these inter-organisational relationships that theory from the service management literature can once again provide valuable insight. This literature developed in the late 1980s and through the 1990s (e.g. Ring and Van de Ven, 1992, 1994; Gulati, 1995; Tsai and

Ghosal, 1998; Zaheer et al., 1998) and argues that trust is essentially an individual-level phenomenon that must be translated to the organisational level (Zaheer et al., 1998; Ring and Van de Ven, 1994; Gulati, 1995; Kale et al., 2000). The role of individuals is therefore crucial to building and sustaining inter-organisational trust. Zaheer et al. (1998) argue that establishing trust at the inter-organisational level, through individuals, eases negotiation and reduces conflict within the relationship. Indeed, trust is defined in the service management literature as facilitating learning through close interactions and the exchange of information and know-how, thereby improving the interaction (Kale et al., 2000). This leads Ring and Van de Ven (1994) to argue that personal relationships are core to shaping and changing the structure of inter-organisational relationships through co-operation.

Ring and Van de Ven (1994) suggest that inter-organisational relationships emerge out of three basic interactions that evolve over time through the formal and informal processes of negotiation, commitment and execution: first, personal relationships enhance formal role relationships; second, psychological contracts replace formal legal contracts and, finally, formal agreements such as rules and policy increasingly mirror informal agreements and understandings. However, Nooteboom et al. (1997) warn that conflict can result between the personal and formal role relationships. They suggest that co-operation within inter-personal relationships may cause loyalty to deviate from organisational interests and, furthermore, that staff turnover may result in a breakdown in relations between organisations due to a loss of personal trust. This ties in with ideas from relationship marketing which suggest that business-to-business relationships presented in the service management literature 'are created by the behaviours of a small number of individuals who form and hold the relationships by their words and actions' (Johnston and Clark, 2008, pp. 93–94). As players move on and change, so will the nature of the relationship. The tension that exists between the personal and organisational levels leads Ring and Van de Ven (1994) to argue that trust should not be the sole mechanism of governance:

> Organisations can be like oceans, and in dealing with uncertainties brought upon by their roles, prudence may require that the parties employ 'life jackets' recognised by their organisations (e.g. formalised contracts, exogenous safeguards) in lieu of exclusive reliance on trust.
>
> (Ring and Van de Ven, 1994, p. 96)

## The Third Sector: Mediator and Co-producer

The collaborative role of the third sector in public service design and delivery has been regarded to result in a whole host of benefits such as increased efficiency, shared learning, the spreading of risks and costs (Huxham, 2000) and the increased capacity to contend with broad societal challenges (Bovaird and Loeffler, 2009; Klijn, 2008). There has also been ideological reasoning behind inter-organisational working; such approaches are considered to offer stakeholders an opportunity to participate in decision-making processes or empower them to take a more central role in processes (Huxham, 2000).

The third sector is characterised by its diversity, which is partly the result of the multiple functions undertaken by the organisations, and which leads Kendall and Knapp (1995) to describe the sector as 'a loose and baggy monster'. In the UK, the functions of the third sector continue to fall under various social activities, including advocacy, self-help, support groups for the vulnerable, community activity (e.g. youth groups) and public service provision. To complicate matters, third sector organisations are often multi-functional, taking on more than one of these roles (Kelly, 2007). McLaughlin (2004) splits the sector in two. One is a non-institutionalised sector dependent on voluntary income and working predominantly on the periphery of public service delivery. The other comprises the modernised sector, made up of 'preferred' third sector organisations dependent on government funding and committed to producing public services. For the purposes of this work, the interest is predominantly on this second sub-sector and particularly the role of third sector organisations during service delivery and planning.

In their seminal work, Berger and Neuhaus (1978) describe third sector organisations as *mediating structures*. The argument starts with the presumption that people are the best experts in their own lives, but that mediating structures are necessary to enable the expression of these needs against the mega-institutions of society. Mediating structures are thus defined as 'those institutions standing between the individual and his private life and the large institutions of public life' (Berger and Neuhaus, 1978, p. 2); this includes organisations such as churches and neighbourhood, family and voluntary associations. Their value is their capacity to expand the boundaries of the welfare state without expanding the boundaries of overly bureaucratic government structures that tend to offer little personal meaning to individuals.

According to Berger and Neuhaus, mediating structures play a dual role. They are both in a position to attach political order to the values and realities held by an individual, while, at the same time, they are said to legitimise political order by transferring meaning and value to government structures. Indeed, Schmid (2003) suggests that third sector organisations delivering services act as a buffer between the government and service users, serving to minimise friction between the two. The responsive nature of third sector organisations has also been described as one of the qualities that makes them best placed to understand and articulate local need (Haugh and Kitson, 2007).

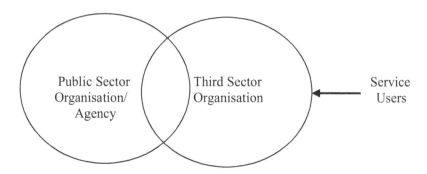

*Figure 5.1* Organisational co-production
Source: Adapted from Brudney and England (1983, p. 61)

Figure 5.1 illustrates that co-production at the organisational level occurs when a public sector organisation/government agency works with a third sector organisation to produce services. Organisations rather than individual service users are the principal actors here. Nevertheless, service users are depicted as feeding into the third sector organisation.

As mediating structures (Berger and Neuhaus, 1978), third sector organisations can facilitate the inclusion of marginal groups, who do not have the necessary resources, capacity or power to articulate their own need (Kearns, 1995; Haugh and Kitson, 2007). Nevertheless, engaging with marginalised groups such as asylum seekers is still challenging because they typically lack the necessary skills, resources and opportunities to seek outside assistance. Success in reaching these groups may therefore depend to a large extent upon the resource capabilities of the organisation (Marshall, 1996). In addition, the extent to which those 'preferred' organisations that are involved in public services are close to citizens, particularly in light of McLaughlin's (2004) depiction of a two-tier sector, is unclear. Furthermore, and significantly for this research, there is an ongoing debate about whether the involvement of third sector organisations genuinely enhances co-production, through the strength of collective action, or actually diminishes it, by placing the third sector organisation between the individual service users and their services—that is, it meets the needs of the third sector organisation rather than the service user (Brenton, 1985; Pestoff et al., 2006).

## Differentiating Inter-organisational Relationships: Co-management and Co-governance

Within the dedicated literature on co-production, the nature of inter-organisational relationships has been discussed in greater detail. The work of Brandsen and Pestoff (2006) is particularly significant in this regard. They differentiate the inter-organisational relationship, suggesting that two relationships exist—co-management and co-governance—which will each now be discussed in detail.

*Co-management* operates at the meso-level (Pestoff, 2012a) and describes instances where third sector organisations contribute to public service *delivery* (Brandsen and Pestoff, 2006; Pestoff et al., 2006):

> co-production can refer both to direct citizen participation in the delivery of publicly financed service, at the site of service delivery, as well as to group provision of such services. Co-production at the site of service provision is nevertheless different from meso level phenomenon of co-management, whether the third sector participates alongside other public and private actors in managing the growing complexity of delivery of diverse publicly financed services, without any direct citizen or user participation.
>
> (Pestoff, 2012a, pp. 16–17)

Brandsen and van Hout (2006) recognise that co-management is not a new phenomenon and that a long history of co-operation across organisational boundaries exists. Indeed, the third sector has been described as playing a crucial role filling gaps in service provision, dealing in particular with marginalised groups (Deakin, 1995; Edelman, 2004) with the advent of the New Public Management in the late 1970s/early 1980s. Such relationships are typically governed by market structures, with third sector organisations bidding for and working under government contracts to deliver services (Tsukamoto and Nishimura, 2006; Bode, 2006a). The contractual relationship makes clear a division of labour, with responsibility for service delivery falling to the third sector organisations and the government controlling the purse strings. The government's day-to-day interaction with public service users is therefore reduced, with third sector organisations delivering services acting as a buffer (Schmid, 2003), while the government retains control of strategic decision-making.

There are, however, three concerns related to third sector organisations working under government contracts. The first relates to the potential for the third sector organisation's role as mediator, including its distinctive characteristics and original values to be diluted by the government agency funding them (Pifer, 1967; Berger and Neuhaus, 1978; Deakin, 2001; Bode, 2006b). The literature suggests that the competition which results from marketisation may prompt internal organisational change, making third sector organisations increasingly like their for-profit counterparts (Taylor and Lansley, 1992; Goodin, 2003). Indeed, to win contracts and, attributing success to the for-profit sector, some third sector organisations may restructure their internal management procedures and processes to model themselves on their opposite numbers. In order to keep a check on those third sector organisations working in the field of public service provision, government has also introduced accountability mechanisms to justify public spending and ensure organisations are meeting centrally devised targets. DiMaggio and Powell (1983) describe this process of modelling as mimetic isomorphism, which involves an organisation modelling itself on another organisation's perceived successful approaches rather than developing novel approaches with the goal of becoming more legitimate or successful. Such an approach has been criticised as both inappropriate and ineffective, although there is some recognition that the third sector can learn from other sectors, with Myers and Sacks (2001) arguing, for instance, that the interpretation of practices should be context-specific and pragmatic.

Second, the increased bureaucracy that is likely to result from organisational changes made to secure government contracts has been criticised for resulting in the loss of independence and flexibility of third sector organisations, leading to suggestions that their decision-making structures have become increasingly distant from clients (Milligan and Fyfe, 2004). Indeed, balancing the needs of funders, donors, beneficiaries, members and employees is challenging (Moxham and Boaden, 2007) and these multiple external pressures make the development of a rational strategy difficult (Parry et al., 2005). It is therefore questionable whether the involvement of the third sector in the mixed economy of welfare contributes to the democratisation of service delivery or whether increasing the reliance of these organisations on state contracts and grants may instead bolster state control over welfare provision (Milligan and Fyfe, 2004, p. 76). One of the core characteristics of the sector, which may be diminished by the contractual relationship, is the autonomous nature of third sector organisations, which is typically associated with their perceived closeness and responsiveness to citizens (Schmid, 2003; Bode, 2006b).

Finally, the traditional adversarial role of third sector organisations may be jeopardised if acting in opposition to government is seen to influence the likelihood of winning contracts. However, Brandsen and van Hout (2006) argue that co-management does not necessarily result in a loss of third sector autonomy because organisations can contribute to policy changes from the ground-up by resolving any challenges encountered during implementation through their capacity to shape services according to local needs.

Since 1997, increasing attention has been paid to the role of third sector organisations in policy formation and, specifically, the shaping and commissioning of public services (Kelly, 2007). This relationship has been coined 'co-governance' (Vidal, 2006; Brandsen and Pestoff, 2006). The interest here is on the co-governance of public services and the role of third sector organisations in the planning and delivery of services, rather than policy formulation, which has been discussed extensively elsewhere (e.g. Kickert and Koppenjan, 1997; Brandsen and Pestoff, 2006; O'Toole et al., 1997). Co-governance, in this sense, introduces an opportunity for third sector organisations to bring their interests and agendas into the realm of planning by contributing to the governance of public services through, for example, Community Planning Partnerships.

Network approaches to service planning and delivery bring together expertise, knowledge and resources from across sectors as a way of tackling complex problems and improving the effectiveness of service provision (Morison, 2000). This involves a process of complex interaction between multiple actors who are mutually dependent and reliant on one another's resources (e.g. financial, political or informational) (Rhodes, 1997). This interdependence means that co-operation is essential, although it does not preclude conflict (Klijn and Koppenjan, 2000). Daily interactions and co-operation between actors are critical to effective decision-making (Klijn, 2008). Indeed, network governance also recognises the critical role of front-line service staff who may exercise a high degree of discretion and control over the way in which policies are implemented on the ground (Schofield, 2001).

Somerville and Haines (2008) argue that co-governance has the potential to enhance democratic accountability and to result in fairer and more effective decision-making. Network members can also seek specialist skills and information from within the network (Brandsen and van Hout, 2006), reducing the likelihood of duplication. However, Hartley and Benington (2006, p. 105) warn that 'knowledge is often hoarded, concealed or fails to transfer because of professional or organisational loyalties, assumptions and roles'. Furthermore, despite having potentially advantageous connections with marginalised groups and a perceived closeness to citizens (Turner and Martin, 2005), the third sector has been criticised for lacking legitimacy as non-democratic (Hill and Hupe, 2003) with a predisposition to advocate certain voices at the expense of others. However, Taylor and Warburton (2003) argue that third sector organisations do not purport to be representative; the fact that individual organisations represent specific sets of needs might be advantageous as long as diverse organisations input to the process. Furthermore, the extent to which third sector organisations have been involved in planning services is contested, with some arguing that their role has predominantly been limited to service delivery (Taylor and Warburton, 2003; McLaughlin, 2004; Evers et al., 2005). Nevertheless, Brandsen et al. (2005) argue that the distinction between decision-making and delivery is often too sharp because those organisations on the ground delivering services will shape them according to local needs.

Another significant challenge is related to the fact that co-governance operates within a context of hierarchies and market mechanisms (Bode, 2006a; Head, 2008). Rhodes (2000, p. 84) argues for example: 'Marketisation undermines trust, co-operation and reciprocity in networks.

Organisational complexity obscures accountability. The search for co-operation impedes efficient service delivery'. Bode (2006a) takes a similar line of argument, suggesting the market rationale has had a negative effect on network relations, essentially disorganising networks that were based on consensus. Competition for contracts might breed secrecy and distrust among service providers while the networks call for inter-organisational co-operation (Goodin, 2003; Brandsen and van Hout, 2006). The consequence for third sector organisations is that they might be expected to work with other organisations to plan services (co-governance), compete for government funding/contracts (market mechanism) and work under government contracts (co-management) and also work within top-down results-orientated systems (hierarchies). Bode (2006a, p. 563) argues, for example, that the continuation of the market-approach has meant that although co-governance plays a part in the public service arena, it is 'a complement to the steering process, given that everyday business is very much subject to public control and market governance'. The co-existence of these different systems may make it difficult to achieve the co-operation that is required for co-governance. The combination of competition and co-operation can be challenging for service managers with the result being differentiation through competition and integration through networks (Brandsen and van Hout, 2006). While sharing information among those in the chain may be important, competition arguably instils a view of maintaining competitive advantage. The co-existence of hierarchies, markets and networks can also cause confusion for service users, who may not understand the respective roles and responsibilities of the various parties:

> Citizens tend to have little regard for bureaucratic sensitivities and often address their demands to whichever organisation they happen to be in touch with . . . there remains a tension between the differentiation within public service delivery and the unitary, messy nature of demand.
>
> (Brandsen and van Hout, 2006, p. 543)

Furthermore, Craig and Manthorpe (1999, p. 70) argue that the 'most damaging of all' factors in the relationship between government and the third sector, is that most third sector organisations 'continue to understand that they are subservient to and dependent on the local authority, rather than equal partners with it in policy development and service delivery'.

## Co-production by Service Users and Organisations

This chapter has introduced the idea that co-production can also exist at an organisational level, focusing on the inter-organisational relationships that can exist between government and third sector organisations. As mediating structures, third sector organisations are often regarded as close to service users and therefore better positioned to articulate and respond to need, while also acting as a mediator between groups of citizens and government (Berger and Neuhaus, 1978). The discussion has suggested that, as co-producers, third sector organisations can take two roles: they can contribute to service *delivery* (co-management) or to both the *delivery and planning* of services (co-governance).

These dimensions are now brought together in a typology along with the individual modes of co-production in Figure 5.2. This combines the insights about co-production at the individual and organisational levels, showing that service users and third sector organisations can co-produce services with public service organisations in different ways. These are displayed in a matrix in order to distinguish between different types of co-production.

On the vertical axis, the typology illustrates that either individual service users or third sector organisations can co-produce public services with public service organisations. The horizontal axis shows that either party can co-produce during service delivery and/or decision-making about the services. By understanding these relationships in this way, five types of co-production can be differentiated and such an approach integrates the traditionally isolated narratives on co-production within the service management and public administration literatures.

The two upper quadrants of the typology comprise individualised co-production, referring to the relationships between the individual service user and the organisation producing the public service. They both differentiate between involvement in service delivery alone and involvement in service planning as well, and between more or less active forms of co-production. Thus, *co-construction* refers to co-production by service users as part of the service encounter. As discussed previously, there is no differentiation between the production and consumption of a service—both take place at

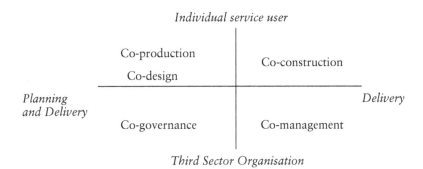

*Figure 5.2* Typology of individual and organisational modes of co-production

the same time and with the service user as co-producer. In this sense, a service user and public service staff have no alternative but to co-produce a service; co-construction is integral to the process nature of services.

*Participative co-production and co-design*, as discussed in Chapter 4, refer to co-production that is explicitly sought by service managers in order to achieve some broader objective, whether in relation to that service (such as innovation) or broader public policy objectives. In this case, it is not the unalienable element of the service production process, but rather it is consciously sought out because it can lead to another goal—such as in relation to social inclusion or citizenship.

The two lower quadrants of the matrix illustrate organisationally based co-production, involving relationships between third sector organisations and public service organisations. In these cases, the public service organisation or government agency may select a third sector organisation as a vehicle for service delivery (*co-management*); here, the aim may be to reduce costs by decentralising the service production process, to capitalise on the third sector's closeness to certain groups and parts of society, or both. Third sector organisations may also contribute to the planning and development of public services (*co-governance*). Their role in co-governance comes earlier than service delivery, and their specialist skills and knowledge are an important contribution to more effective decision-making (Brandsen and van Hout, 2006).

## Summary: Understanding Inter-organisational Relationships

This chapter has introduced inter-organisational relationships that can exist between public and third sector organisations. Because public services are produced in a pluralistic and fragmented way (Osborne et al., 2015) it has argued that organisations from across sectors are working together to plan and deliver services and as such, there is a need to effectively manage these relationships. Chapter 5 has further argued that the third sector, as a mediator, operates in close proximity to certain vulnerable groups and is therefore potentially better positioned to articulate and respond to need and therefore co-produce with other public service organisations and government. The discussion has suggested that third sector organisations can take two roles during inter-organisational relationships: they can contribute to service *delivery* (co-management) or to both the *delivery and planning* of services (co-governance). Theory around governance and networks has been critical to understanding these concepts and their associated challenges, but the service management literature around relational capital and trust has also provided valuable insight into how inter-organisational relationships operate and might be more effectively managed. The chapter concluded by depicting two organisational forms of co-production alongside the individual modes discussed in detail in Chapter 4; the suggestion here is that co-production is not only an individual phenomenon but one that can also be used to explore inter-organisational relationships.

## References

Aiken, M. and Hage, J. (1968). Organizational interdependence and intra-organizational structure. *American Sociological Review*. (33,6), 912–930.

Alford, J. (2016). Co-production, interdependence and publicness: extending public service-dominant logic. *Public Management Review*. (18,5), 673–691.

Ansell, C. and Gash, A. (2007). Collaborative governance in theory and practice. *Journal of Public Administration Research and Theory*. (18), 543–571.

Berger, P. L. and Neuhaus, R. J. (1978). *To empower people: the role of mediating structures in public policy*. Washington, DC: American Enterprise for Public Policy Research.

Bode, I. (2006a). Co-governance within networks and the non-profit-for-profit divide. *Public Management Review*. (8,4), 551–566.

Bode, I. (2006b). Disorganised welfare mixes: voluntary agencies and new governance regimes in Western Europe. *Journal of European Social Policy*. (16,4), 346–359.

Bovaird, T. and Loeffler, E. (2009). The changing policy context of public policy. In Bovaird, T. and Loffler, E. (eds.), *Public management and governance*. London: Routledge.

Brandsen, T. and Pestoff, V. (2006). Co-production, the third sector and the delivery of public services. *Public Management Review*. (8,4), 493–501.

Brandsen, T., van de Donk, W. and Putters, K. (2005). Griffins or chameleons? Hybridity as a permanent and inevitable characteristic of the third sector. *International Journal of Public Administration*. (28), 749–765.

Brandsen, T. and van Hout, E. (2006). Co-management in public service networks: the organizational effects. *Public Management Review*. (8,4), 537–549.

Brenton, M. (1985). *The voluntary sector in British social services*. London: Longman.

Craig, G. and Manthorpe, J. (1999). Unequal partners? Local government reorganization and the voluntary sector. *Social Policy and Administration*. (33,1), 55–72.

Deakin, N. (1995). The pearls of partnership: the voluntary sector and the state, 1945–1992. In Davis Smith, J., Rochester, C. and Hedley, R. (eds.), *An introduction to the voluntary sector*. London: Routledge.

Deakin, N. (2001). Putting narrow-mindedness out of countenance: the UK voluntary sector in the new millennium. In Anheier, A. and Kendall, J. (eds.), *Third sector policy at the crossroads*. London: Routledge.

DiMaggio, P. and Powell, W. W. (1983). The iron cage revisited: collective rationality and institutional isomorphism in organizational fields. *American Sociological Review*. (48,2), 147–160.

Dryzek, J. S. (2007). Networks and democratic ideals: equality, freedom and communication. In Sorensen, E. and Torfing, J. (eds.), *Theories of democratic network governance*. London: Palgrave Macmillan.

Edelman, G. (2004). Improving provision for children with speech, language and communication difficulties: the role of the voluntary sector. *Current Paediatrics*. (14), 223–228.

Evers, A., Lewis, J. and Riedel, B. (2005). Developing child-care provision in England and Germany: problems of governance. *Journal of European Social Policy*. (15,3), 195–209.

Goodin, R. E. (2003). Democratic accountability: the distinctiveness of the third sector. *European Journal of Sociology*. (44,3), 359–396.

Greenaway, J., Salter, B. and Hart, S. (2007). How policy networks can damage democratic health: a case study in the government of governance. *Public Administration*. (85,3), 717–738.

Gulati, R. (1995). Does familiarity breed trust? The implications of repeated ties for contractual choice in alliances. *The Academy of Management Journal*, 38(1), 85–112.

Hajer, M. and Wagenaar, H. (eds.). (2003). *Deliberative policy analysis: understanding governance in the network society*. Cambridge: Cambridge University Press.

Hartley, J. F. and Benington, J. (2006). Copy and paste, or graft and transplant? Knowledge sharing through inter-organizational networks. *Public Money and Management*. (26), 101–108.

Haugh, H. and Kitson, M. (2007). The third way and the third sector: new labour's economic policy and the social economy. *Cambridge Journal of Economics*. (31), 973–994.

Head, B. (2008). Accessing network-based collaborations: effectiveness for whom? *Public Management Review*. (10,6), 733–749.

Hendricks, C. M. (2008). On inclusion and network governance: the democratic disconnect of Dutch energy transitions. *Public Administration*. (86,4), 1009–1031.

Hill, M. and Hupe, P. (2003). The multi-layer problem in implementation research. *Public Management Review*. (5,4), 471–490.

Huxham, C. (2000). The challenge of collaborative governance. *Public Management Review*. (2,3), 337–357.

Jeffares, S. and Skelcher, C. (2011). Democratic subjectivities in network governance: a Q methodology study of English and Dutch public managers. *Public Administration*. (89,4), 1253–1273.

Johnston, R. and Clark, G. (2008). *Service operations management: improving service delivery*. Harlow: Prentice Hall.

Kale, P., Singh, H. and Perlmutter, H. (2000). Learning and protection of proprietary assets in strategic alliances. *Strategic Management Journal*. (21,3), 217–237.

Kearns, A. (1995). Active citizenship and local governance: political and geographical dimensions. *Political Geography*. (14,2), 155–175.

Kelly, J. (2007). Reforming public services in the UK: bringing in the third sector. *Public Administration*. (85,4), 1003–1022.

Kendall, J. and Knapp, M. (1995). A loose and baggy monster: boundaries, definitions and typologies. In Davis Smith, J., Rochester, C. and Hedley, R. (eds.), *An introduction to the voluntary sector*. London: Routledge.

Kennett, P. (2010). Global perspectives on governance. In Osborne, S. P. (ed.), *The new public governance?* Oxon: Routledge.

Kickert, W. J. M. and Koppenjan, J. F. M. (1997). Public management and network management: an overview. In Kickert, W. J. M., Klijn, E. H. and Koppenjan, J. F. M. (eds.), *Managing complex networks*. London: Sage.

Klijn, E. H. (2008). Governance and governance networks in Europe. *Public Management Review*. (10,4), 505–525.

Klijn, E. H. and Koppenjan, J. F. M. (2000). Public management and policy net-works: foundations of a network approach to governance. *Public Management*. (2,2), 135–158.

Kooiman, J. F. M. (1993). *Modern governance*. London: Sage.

Kooiman, J. F. M. (2005). *Governing as governance*. London: Sage.

Koppenjan, J. and Klijn, E. H. (2004). *Managing uncertainties in networks: public private controversies*. London: Routledge.

Lewis, C. and Marsh, D. (2012). Network governance and public participation in policy making: federal community cabinets in Australia. *Australian Journal of Public Administration*. (71,1), 6–19.

Marshall, T. F. (1996). Can we define the voluntary sector? In Billis, D. and Harris, M. (eds.), *Voluntary agencies: changing of organization and management*. London: Palgrave Macmillan.

McLaughlin, K. (2004). Towards a 'modernised' voluntary and community sector? Emerging lessons from government—voluntary and community sector relationships in the UK. *Public Management Review*. (6,4), 555–562.

Milligan, C. and Fyfe, N. R. (2004). Putting the voluntary sector in its place: geographical perspectives on voluntary activity and social welfare in Glasgow. *Journal of Social Policy*. (33,1), 73–93.

Moore, M. and Hartley, J. (2010). Innovations in governance. In Osborne, S. P. (ed.), *The new public governance?* Oxon: Routledge.

Morison, J. (2000). The government-voluntary sector compacts: governance, governmentality and civil society. *Journal of Law and Society*. (27,1), 98–132.

Moxham, C. and Boaden, R. (2007). The impact of performance measurement in the voluntary sector: identification of contextual and processual factors. *International Journal of Operations & Production Management*. (27,8), 826–845.

Myers, J. and Sacks, R. (2001). Harnessing the talents of a 'loose and baggy monster'. *Journal of European Industrial Training*. (25,9), 454–464.

Newman, J. (2007). The 'double dynamics' of activation: institutions, citizens and the remaking of welfare governance. *International Journal of Sociology and Social Policy*. (27,9–10), 364–375.

Nooteboom, B., Berger, H. and Noorderhaven, N. G. (1997). Effects of trust and governance on relational risk. *The Academy of Management Journal*. (40,2), 308–338.

Osborne, S. P. (2006). Editorial: the new public governance? *Public Management Review*. (8,3), 377–387.

Osborne, S. P. (2010). Delivering public services: time for a new theory? *Public Management Review*. (12,1), 1–10.

Osborne, S. P., Radnor, Z., Kinder, T. and Vidal, I. (2015). The SERVICE framework: a public-service-dominant approach to sustainable public services. *British Journal of Management*. (26,3), 424–438.

Osborne, S. P., Radnor, Z. and Nasi, G. (2013). A new theory for public service management? Toward a (Public) service dominant approach. *American Review of Public Administration*. (43,2), 135–158.

O'Toole, L. J., Hanf, K. I. and Hupe, P. L. (1997). Managing implementation processes in networks. In Kickert, W. J. M., Klijn, E-H. and Koppenjan, J. F. M. (eds.), *Managing complex networks: strategies for the public sector*. London: Sage.

Parry, E., Kelliher, C., Mills, T. and Tyson, S. (2005). Comparing HRM in the voluntary and public sectors. *Personnel Review*. (34,5), 588–602.

Pestoff, V. (2006). Citizens and co-production of welfare services. *Public Management Review.* (8,4), 503–519.

Pestoff, V. (2012a). Co-production and third sector services in Europe: some critical conceptual issues. In Pestoff, V., Brandsen, T. and Verschuere, B. (eds.), *New public governance, the third sector and co-production.* New York: Routledge.

Pestoff, V. (2012b). New public governance, co-production and third sector social services in Europe: crowding in and crowding out. In Pestoff, V., Brandsen, T. and Verschuere, B. (eds.), *New public governance, the third sector and co-production.* New York: Routledge.

Pestoff, V. and Brandsen, T. (2009). *The governance of co-production.* Paper Presented at the 13th Annual Conference of the International Research Society for Public Management, Copenhagen.

Pestoff, V. and Brandsen, T. (2010). Public sector governance and the third sector: opportunities for co-production and innovation? In Osborne, S. P. (ed.), *The new public governance?* Oxon: Routledge.

Pestoff, V., Osborne, S. P. and Brandsen, T. (2006). Patterns of co-production in public services. *Public Management Review.* (8,4), 591–595.

Peters, G. (2010). Meta-governance and public management. In Osborne, S. P. (ed.), *The new public governance?* Oxon: Routledge.

Pfeffer, J. and Nowak, P. (1976). Joint ventures and interorganisational interdependence. *Administrative Science Quarterly.* (21,3), 398–418.

Pifer, A. (1967). *Quasi nongovernmental organizations.* New York: Carnegie Corporation.

Prentice, S. (2006). Childcare, co-production and the third sector in Canada. *Public Management Review.* (8,4), 521–536.

Rhodes, R. A. W. (1997). *Understanding governance: policy networks, governance, reflexivity and accountability.* Maidenhead: Open University Press.

Rhodes, R. A. W. (2000). Governance and public administration. In Pierre, J. (ed.), *Debating governance.* Oxford: Oxford University Press.

Ring, P. S. and Van de Ven, A. H. (1992). Structuring cooperative relationships between organization. *Strategic Management Journal.* (13), 483–498.

Ring, P. S. and Van de Ven, A. H. (1994). Developmental processes of cooperative interorganisational relationships. *The Academy of Management Review.* (19,1), 90–118.

Schmid, H. (2003). Rethinking the policy of contracting out social services to non-governmental organizations: lessons and dilemmas. *Public Management Review.* (5,3), 307–323.

Schofield, J. (2001). Time for a revival? Public policy implementation: a review of the literature and an agenda for future research. *International Journal of Management Review.* (3,3), 245–263.

Sicilia, M., Guarini, E., Sancino, A., Adreani, M. and Ruffini, R. (2016). Public service management and co-production in multi-level governance settings. *International Review of Administrative Sciences.* (82,1), 8–27.

Somerville, P. and Haines, N. (2008). Prospects for local co-governance. *Local Government Studies.* (34,1), 61–79.

Sorensen, E. and Torfing, J. (2003). Network politics, political capital, and democracy. *International Journal of Public Administration.* (26,6), 609–634.

Sorensen, E. and Torfing, J. (2005). Network governance and post-liberal democracy. *Administrative Theory and Praxis.* (27,2), 197–237.

Sorensen, E. and Torfing, J. (2009). Making governance networks effective and democratic through metagovernance. *Public Administration.* (87,2), 234–258.

Sorensen, E. and Torfing, J. (2018). The democratizing impact of governance networks: from pluralisation, via democratic anchorage, to interactive political leadership. *Public Administration.* 1–16.

Taylor, M. and Lansley, J. (1992). Ideology and welfare in the UK: the implications for the voluntary sector. *Voluntas.* (3,2), 153–174.

Taylor, M. and Warburton, D. (2003). Legitimacy and the role of UK third sector organizations in the policy press. *Voluntas.* (14,3), 321–338.

Tsai, W. and Ghosal, S. (1998). Social capital and value creation: the role of intrafirm networks. *The Academy of Management Journal.* (41,4), 464–476.

Tsukamoto, I. and Nishimura, M. (2006). The emergence of local non-profit-government partnerships and the role of intermediary organizations in Japan. *Public Management Review.* (8,4), 567–581.

Turner, D. and Martin, S. (2005). Social entrepreneurs and social inclusion: building local capacity or delivering national priorities? *International Journal of Public Administration.* (28), 797–806.

Van Tatenhove, J., Edelenbos, J. and Klok, P. J. (2010). Power and interactive policy-making: a comparative study of power and influence in eight interactive projects in the Netherlands. *Public Administration.* (88,3), 609–626.

Vidal, I. (2006). Reflections on the market, networking and trust. *Public Management Review.* (8,4), 583–589.

Zaheer, A., McEvily, B. and Perrone, V. (1998). Does trust matter? Exploring the effects of interorganisational and interpersonal trust on performance. *Organization Science.* (9,2), 141–159.

# Part 2

# Case Study Research

Asylum Seekers and Social Welfare
Services in Glasgow

# 6  Asylum Seekers in Scotland
## Marginalised Non-Citizens

## Abstract

This chapter introduces the case of asylum seekers living in Glasgow and the legal, social and economic barriers they face as a result of exclusionary immigration policies that have been enacted in the UK. By consequence, the discussion frames asylum seekers as a disempowered and marginalised group who are not bestowed the same benefits and access rights as others in society. It then reflects on the Scottish context where the integration policy has been developed to support asylum seeker inclusion into society, mainly for economic reasons. However, arguments are presented to suggest that while the Scottish policy on integration perhaps enables social inclusion, significant barriers may continue to impede this goal. The discussion then focuses on the citizenship status of asylum seekers but argues for a broader definition of citizenship that extends beyond legal status to include the practice of citizenship rights and obligations. Finally, this chapter introduces the empirical research design, which takes an embedded case study approach.

## Introduction

Asylum is currently a worldwide concern with the movement of millions of people from the Middle East and Africa into Europe. This huge movement of people has been accompanied by various challenges for governments, specifically regarding where to house asylum seekers and how to meet their social and economic needs during the transitionary period during which they await the outcome of their application.

This chapter is split into three parts. The first introduces the case of asylum seekers living in Glasgow, examining the immigration policies that affect them and the public services they are in receipt of. It starts with an introduction of the UK context and the exclusionary impact of immigration policies. This discussion emphasises the marginal position of asylum seekers who face multiple barriers to inclusion due to their legal, social and economic position which has been shaped by policies of deterrence. The focus then turns to the Scottish context and specifically the social welfare services provided to asylum seekers. This part discusses asylum seekers as non-citizens, but also as public service users and presents the distinctive social inclusion policy forwarded in Scotland, both of which potentially impact the nature and extent of co-production in practice. The final part of the chapter introduces the empirical research design, which takes an embedded case study approach.

## The UK Context: The Impact of Exclusionary Policies

Asylum seekers occupy a contentious position, having exercised their legal right under the United Nations Geneva Convention (1951) to apply for asylum but remaining non-citizens while they await the outcome of their case. Although the term 'asylum seeker' is not outlined in the Geneva Convention, refugees are defined as those whose applications to remain in the country have been accepted and are therefore granted the same rights as a UK citizen. Thus, refugees are those who have proved that they have left their indigenous country and are unable to return because they have a well-founded fear of persecution due to their race, religion, nationality, political opinion or membership of a particular social group. Asylum seekers, by contrast, are those following the application process[1] of the host country to attain refugee status. Immigration issues, including asylum are reserved to UK government under Schedule 5 of the Scotland Act 1998.

The UK government has a duty under human rights law to provide adequate support for those seeking asylum. However, successive UK governments have pursued an agenda that aims to limit the number of asylum applicants and the success of those who do apply through heightened border controls and by curtailing economic, social and political 'pull factors' that may encourage asylum applications, particularly around social welfare provision and access to the paid labour market. Indeed, while awaiting the outcome of their application, asylum seekers are regulated and constrained by strict immigration laws which are within and built upon 'policies of deterrence' (Williams, 2006). Since the mid-1980s, successive UK governments have taken increasingly strict measures to deter asylum seekers and/or contain them within their home countries (e.g. visa requirements). The curtailment of asylum seekers' rights and welfare entitlements have been defined within a strong and enduring rhetoric, which reasons that deterrence policies are necessary to avoid the economic and social 'pull' factors that lure asylum seekers to the UK, who subsequently threaten to overwhelm diminishing resources (Bloch and Schuster, 2002; Doerschler, 2006; Tyler, 2010; Mayblin and James, 2019). The assumption that welfare and employment opportunities incentivise those from less well-off countries to apply for asylum has nevertheless been challenged by some. Mayblin (2016) argues that asylum seekers would require both a comprehensive understanding of the rights that different countries would afford them and would make a rational choice on that basis. Furthermore, research has suggested that asylum seekers do not necessarily come to the UK voluntarily (smugglers may choose the destination) and often have limited prior knowledge of the UK and the rights afforded to them (Bloch and Schuster, 2002; Gilbert and Koser, 2006). There are also significant 'push' factors at play, such as war, repression of minorities, poverty and fear from persecution (Castles and Loughma, 2003).

In the early to mid-1990s the rise of migration was of increasing threat to European countries and, as such, the conception of 'Fortress Europe' was embedded through various asylum and immigration policies and procedures that aimed to deter entry and suppress the rights and assistance of those who did gain access (Zetter, 2007). In the UK, consecutive pieces of legislation gradually withdrew mainstream rights and services from asylum seekers. The result has been a widening gap between asylum seekers and the indigenous population. For instance, the 1993 Asylum and Immigration Appeals Act introduced constrained access to social housing and the 1996 Asylum and Immigration Act removed entitlement to social security benefits for those who applied for asylum in-country (this was reversed by the 1999 Act) and those appealing a Home Office decision (Bloch, 2000).

Those seeking asylum claim social welfare benefits through a separate system, with the Immigration and Asylum Act 1999 (amended in 2002 by the Nationality, Immigration and Asylum Act) making clear distinctions between the social rights of asylum seekers and UK citizens and non-citizen residents. Bloch and Schuster (2002) argue that limited access to benefits reinforces the categorisation of asylum seekers as undeserving. While awaiting the result of their application, asylum seekers can claim a living allowance that is 70% of the basic income support available to UK citizens, although they are placed in fully furnished accommodation rent-free and have their utilities paid for. Under section 95 of the Immigration and Asylum Act 1999, individual asylum seekers receive £37.75 per week to pay for essential items such as clothes, food and toiletries. Additional support is provided to pregnant women and young children (£3 extra per week for pregnant women and for those with children aged 1 to 3, and an additional £5 per week for those with a baby under one year). One-off maternity payments of £300 can also be applied for if a baby is due in eight weeks or less or if that child is less than six weeks old. Nevertheless, access to mainstream services can be made difficult by bureaucratic procedures such as complicated registration processes. To apply for benefits, for example, individuals must show that they have made an application for asylum as soon as was reasonably practicable on arrival in the UK and that they are destitute with no other means of support. Such bureaucratic hoops may perpetuate the exclusionary nature of immigration policies.

Moreover, the 1999 Act excluded those subject to immigration control from non-contributory benefits, increased policing by extending powers of search, arrest and detention, and prohibited asylum seekers from entering paid employment while they are awaiting the outcome of their application. The inability to work has led many to argue that asylum seekers cannot be fully integrated into society and instead promotes feelings of frustration among asylum seekers who become dependent and lose their confidence. Indeed, Bloch (2000) recognises that access to employment is crucial to the settlement and integration of refugees as it provides economic independence, builds self-esteem and immerses them into the language. Although they cannot gain paid employment, the motivation to work among the group tends to be high with asylum seekers being generally well-educated and qualified (Sim and Bowes, 2007).

If refused asylum, an individual must return to his/her country as soon as possible, but can claim support under Section 4 of the Immigration and Asylum Act 1999 in circumstances where his/her application for asylum has been refused but he/she is destitute and cannot leave the UK. Such support comes in the form of accommodation and vouchers (totalling £35.39) to cover the cost of food and other basic essential items. If an individual does not accept the offer of accommodation, he/she will not receive the payment card. Refused asylum seekers can also apply for a one-off £250 maternity payment and will have support for the costs of medical prescriptions, dental care and eyesight tests. The Home Office (2018) reported that there were 4,179 people receiving section 4 support at the end of June 2018, which represented an 8% increase from the previous year.

Annual immigration statistics produced by the Home Office report that the number of applications for asylum in the year ending June 2018 was down 1% to 27,044, which represents a return to the figures seen before the 2015 Humanitarian crisis.[2] In that same year, 14,308 applications for asylum were granted. The Home Office (2018) reported that between 2014 and 2016 the outcome of known asylum applications was 52% granted and 48% refused/withdrawn. Asylum applications came from various countries, including Iran, Iraq, Pakistan, Sudan, Albania, Eritrea, Bangladesh, Afghanistan, India and Vietnam with the majority from male applicants (Home Office, 2018). A total of 42,808 people in the UK were in receipt of Section 95 support in June 2018 and the Home Office report that at the end of 2017, Glasgow City had the highest number of asylum seekers in receipt of such support (3,649). The accuracy of this data is, nevertheless, disputed because it fails to include those asylum seekers and refugees who are not supported by government programmes (Wren, 2007). Beyond the official figures, an unknown number of asylum seekers enter the UK illegally and others are thought to have gone 'underground' after receiving a negative decision in their asylum application. Such groups do not benefit from the available support services, but instead stay with friends or family and might work illegally without having gone through the necessary procedures or receiving the required documentation.

The 1999 Act also introduced, for the first time, a nationally coordinated approach to asylum seeker resettlement and support. Key to the legislation was the introduction of 'no choice' dispersal, which attempted to lessen strain on London and the South East of England, which had experienced a high concentration of asylum seekers in the years previous to the legislation. Contracts between the Home Office and housing providers from throughout the UK were entered into, which were formally signed in 2012. However, asylum seeker dispersal began in 2000 and Darling (2014) links the policy to programmes of fiscal austerity and the decline of support for asylum seekers and third sector organisations during that time. Through no-choice dispersal, asylum seekers have typically been placed in areas of high social deprivation and unemployment, which Darling (2014) argues heightens their isolation and marginalisation. Interestingly, Zetter (2007) explores the relationships between the lived reality of asylum seekers and refugees and public policy through the concept of labelling. He argues that the labelling 'dispersed asylum seeker' is more than a bureaucratic classification, but a 'transformative process which is imposed not chosen, which excludes not incorporates' (Zetter, 2007, p. 182). The potential implication, according to Zetter, is both the marginalisation of asylum seekers from social and cultural settings and an increased likelihood of poverty.

The legislation has built a very much stratified system of social rights which limits asylum seekers' access to services and singles them out as a visibly in-need group distinct from mainstream society (Sales, 2002). Barriers to social integration, such as exclusion from paid employment, limited access to social welfare benefits and the no-choice dispersal policy are legally enforced but also have significant social and moral implications. Kirkwood and McNeill (2015) warn, for example, that the inability of asylum seekers to enter paid employment while awaiting the outcome of their case is a significant barrier for their integration and risks the deskilling and demotivation of asylum seekers. The implication of such a disadvantageous social, economic and political backdrop for asylum seekers has been social exclusion. As a group, risk factors such as poverty, poor housing, poor access to health and social welfare services, limited English language support, isolation and limited supportive social networks are all therefore challenges for asylum seekers (Spicer, 2008).

The impact of the policies of deterrence has been compounded by negative media attention and political rhetoric (see, for example, Hickley, 2009). Indeed, in his exploration of how asylum seekers and refugees were discursively constructed in the media between 2010 and 2011, Parker (2015) notes that the UK media has focused on the need to remove asylum seekers, who are understood as 'unwanted invaders', 'criminals', 'dishonest' and 'tragic' so are therefore in need of assistance. Political rhetoric centres on a potentially convincing argument that juxtaposes 'good' migrants who enter the country through the appropriate processes and with the intention of contributing economically and 'bad' migrants who arrive in a host country illegally (Mulvey, 2010). Indeed, Kofman (2005) argues that European immigration policies have largely been biased towards those considered most advantageous to the economy and who will complement the pre-existing national culture and therefore not unsettle social cohesion. The right to migration and eventual citizenship is by consequence increasingly restricted to the highly skilled, while it serves to alienate asylum seekers as 'the Other' who have no right to belong (Zetter, 2007).

## The Scottish Context: Dispersal, Public Services and Social Inclusion

### No-Choice Dispersal and Public Services in Glasgow

As discussed in the previous section, asylum seekers have been dispersed throughout the UK on a no-choice basis. At the end of December 2016, the Home Office reported that there were 3,350 asylum seekers in Scotland. Glasgow City Council was the only local authority in Scotland to enter into an agreement to house asylum seekers and at the time of this study the YMCA (renamed Y People since this research was conducted) and the for-profit organisation Angel also provided asylum seeker accommodation in the city. Since 2012, housing provision for asylum seekers has been supplied by a for-profit organisation named Serco.[3] Although all Scottish Local Authorities have agreed to resettle refugees under the Syrian resettlement scheme, Glasgow remains the sole authority to which asylum seekers are dispersed under the Home Office agreement.

Responsibility for immigration policy lies clearly with the UK government, but the Scottish government is responsible for the devolved policy agenda, and Scottish Local Authorities are tasked with delivering essential support to asylum seekers, including access to healthcare, education for children and social care needs (Wren, 2007). All asylum seekers residing in the UK are entitled to free healthcare under the National Health Service, free prescriptions, dental care and eyesight tests, as well as support in paying for spectacles. It is also mandatory for asylum seeker children aged between five and seventeen to attend school; all state schools are free and asylum seekers can apply for free school meals. This suggests that asylum seekers are public service users, which likely has implications for their participation, particularly in terms of co-construction, which exists as an inherent dimension of the service relationship.

Significantly, there are also differences in Scotland compared to England, in terms of demography, political climate and, importantly, social inclusion policy. In Scotland a concern about the population decline, coupled with an ageing population (Wren, 2007) has shaped a more positive view of asylum seekers who have been viewed as a potential resource who could fill the skills gap (Sim and Bowes, 2007). Research conducted by Lewis (2006) found a greater tolerance to asylum seekers in Scotland than England, with the Scottish media latterly becoming less suspicious of asylum seekers (see, for example, Johnston, 2003; Anon, 2001, 2005). However, Lewis did find some concerns, particularly among younger people and those in social classes C2DE, that asylum seekers were a threat to local jobs and housing.

The initial dispersal of asylum seekers into Glasgow brought with it a steep learning curve for public service providers, particularly around the provision of appropriate public services, but also with regards to integration. The pace of dispersal was faster than expected and gave service providers limited preparation time, causing them to respond reactively with services being delivered on an ad hoc basis to those in desperate need (Wren, 2007). This was attributed partly to the fact that service providers in Glasgow had very limited contact with asylum seekers or refugees prior to 1999. Indeed, Sim and Bowes (2007) recognise that historically Glasgow has had limited experience of multiculturalism compared to some English cities. Furthermore, the areas within Glasgow where asylum seekers have been placed have not necessarily had ethnic minority communities already living there, which has meant that ethnic minority organisations may not have had strong links with these communities; Glasgow's settled minority ethnic population is of Pakistani, Indian or Chinese heritage, the majority of whom do not reside in the communities where asylum seekers have been housed.

On arrival, asylum seekers in receipt of accommodation support were placed in very deprived communities where housing was readily available due to low take up by the indigenous population. Such areas are typically characterised by above average rates of unemployment, limited community facilities, low-income households and multi-storey housing blocks (Sim and Bowes, 2007; Spicer, 2008). Asylum seekers' needs were therefore placed in competition with the longstanding acute needs of the community, reinforcing the likelihood of social exclusion. The longer-term impact of placing asylum seekers in deprived communities may increase the likelihood that, if given refugee status, they are directed into low-paid work and low-skilled work. The exclusionary impact on asylum seekers suggests a lack of commitment to their inclusion into society. However, according to Wren (2007), placing asylum seekers in the community rather than temporary centres suggests the process of integration begins during the application process and therefore has a positive inclusionary impact.

## Asylum Seeker Integration in Scotland

The longstanding process of integration in Scotland begins during the application process rather than after refugee status is awarded, as is the approach in England (Wren, 2007). The Scottish strategy for the integration of refugees and asylum seekers—the 'New Scots Refugee Integration Strategy'—was implemented in two phases. The first ran from 2014 to 2017 and the second phase outlined the Scottish government's strategy for the period between 2018 and 2022. Taken as a whole, these documents articulate and emphasise the support and integration of asylum seekers into Scottish communities immediately upon their arrival in the country. The strategy ascribes to a model of partnership where collaborative networks share experience, good practice and awareness, and take a coordinated approach to identifying and meeting asylum seekers' needs. It also refers to the Community Empowerment (Scotland) Act 2015, which placed Community Planning Partnerships on statutory footing and compelled them to involve the third sector and community bodies at all stages of Community Planning, with a specific focus on equalities. Thus, in theory, the voice of the community as a collective was strengthened during decision-making about public services.

Ager and Strang (2008) propose a framework to summarise what constitutes successful integration, upon which the Scottish strategy for asylum seeker integration has been built. They construct integration as both a process and an achievement, specifying ten domains that are grouped under four key categories. In the first category 'means and markers' are used to indicate both the extent to which a person is integrated and the factors that assist his/her integration. This category includes access to employment, housing, education and health. The second includes social connections in the community, including ethnic or religious identity, social bonds with members of other communities and social links with institutions. This category builds on the concept of social capital (Putnam, 1993) and from this perspective, reflects the social resources available to an individual through their formal and informal social networks including family, friends and work colleagues. According to Spicer (2008), social networks are particularly important for supporting the social inclusion of asylum seekers because they offer 'assistance in accessing health and other social welfare services, interpretation, and financial and emotional support that may help them to develop confidence and self-esteem and reduce feelings of isolation and depression' (Spicer, 2008, p. 493). 'Facilitators' form the third of Ager and Strang's categories and include those factors that are required for enabling integration, such as language, safety, stability and cultural knowledge. Finally, 'foundation' refers to the rights and responsibilities associated with citizenship, which includes the entitlement and obligations to remain in a nation state and engage politically. It is this category and its implications that the authors argue create the most confusion and disagreement and this will be discussed in greater depth in the next section. Ager and Strang (2008) argue that while these domains of integration are not likely to be accessed equally by all members of a society, their normative prescription should be aspired to.

The legal, social and political positioning of asylum seekers has implications for integration, and the discussion so far suggests that asylum seekers have only partial access to the domains of integration outlined by Ager and Strang (2008). In terms of their first categorisation—'means and markers'—asylum seekers have restricted access to housing (on a no-choice basis), education and health, but cannot undertake paid employment unless their application is successful. The extent to which they have social connections and bonds is likely to vary depending upon the communities within which they are placed and specifically whether the community 'facilitates' an appropriate social network to support their integration. Finally, the preceding discussion has highlighted that asylum seekers cannot engage politically due to their transitionary status. Bloch (2000) argues that the direction of government policy has had an adverse effect on asylum seekers' participation in society. She contends that because they do not receive the same benefits and access rights as others in society, asylum seekers are disempowered and marginalised, which makes any attempt to support their participation or inclusion difficult.

> as immigrants, asylum seekers and refugees seek integration (as opposed to assimilation) in their country of adoption, they often join the poor and oppressed in an ongoing struggle for genuine inclusion and participation in order to exercise their civic rights as well as duties.
>
> (Nash et al., 2006, p. 345)

However, the available research says little about the working links between asylum seekers and statutory agencies during service planning and delivery through co-production—a key dimension of this work. Nevertheless, through public service provision, the Scottish government has been commended for promoting the integration of asylum seekers into Scottish communities, through initiatives such as English language classes and translation assistance, which support the rights and obligations of asylum seekers in line with Ager and Strang's fourth category.

## Citizenship, Rights and Asylum

As discussed earlier in this chapter, a key strand of the deterrence policy that has defined and shaped the UK response to asylum has been the dismantling of social rights for asylum seekers, and this, according to Cemlyn and Briskman (2003) detaches asylum seekers from any provisions associated with citizenship. Ager and Strang (2008) argue that to develop an effective policy on integration, it is necessary to clearly articulate what citizenship means within a country by setting out the rights and responsibilities associated with citizenship.

Citizenship is a contested concept, which is in receipt of considerable debate regarding its meaning and the scope of its membership: 'citizenship is continually recreated through complex legal, political, social and pedagogical practices' (Tyler, 2010, p. 71). On the most basic level, a 'citizen' refers to a person who is recognised under custom or law as belonging to a particular nation state. Citizenship is a legal status 'bestowed on those who are [deemed by law as] full members of a community' (King and Waldron, 1988, p. 84). Legal citizenship, including a sense of belonging and equal access to participation in society, is not afforded to all the indigenous population as a given. It is a right that can be withdrawn or refused (e.g. sectioned patients or offenders) and, importantly, does not automatically connect with a sense of belonging. Asylum seekers are between states or stateless and, as such, have no expectation of citizenship rights and are not afforded equal access to the rights and entitlements of the indigenous population. However, citizenship can also be understood in broader terms as a process that defines the 'relationships between society, government and individuals: who belongs to the "public" and what obligations and rights membership in that "public" confers' (McCluskey, 2003, p. 786).

This broader definition resonates with the idea of social citizenship, which was introduced by the seminal work of Marshall (1950) and diverges from the legal definition of citizen. Marshall's concept has been explored and criticised extensively in the literature. Its roots are in the ideas of the welfare state and it focuses on three fundamental components: civil rights required to attain individual freedoms, such as freedom of speech, the right to own property and the right to justice; political rights to participate and exercise political power and the social right to economic welfare and security. Political, social and economic rights have been core dimensions of citizenship, with influential theorists including Aristotle, Machiavelli and Tocqueville emphasising their necessity for full participation in public life. However, a key criticism of Marshall's work was that it promoted a universal concept of citizenship that centred on the white, working class man and as a by-product produced a second-class citizenry who were not privy to equal membership to the rights or duties implied by three dimensions of citizenship (Roche, 1992; Harris, 1999). Within Marshall's conceptualisation, then, asylum seekers are likely to be portrayed as second-class citizens who exercise less rights and responsibilities compared to the indigenous population.

In the 1980s the Marshallian conception of citizenship eroded with a shift in focus towards the ideas of nationality, immigration and security which have featured strongly in the asylum policy discussed in the previous section. As a process, citizenship can essentially then be applied to create and support either inclusionary or exclusionary dimensions (Turner, 2001). In Marshallian terms it offers (not necessarily equal) access to civil, political and social rights, but its formulation in law and its application in the political and societal context highlight its threatening potential to certain groups and individuals. Indeed, the analysis of the literature shows that citizenship has historically been constructed as a means of excluding outsiders, or at least conceptualising those who do enter the country as the 'Other' (Cemlyn and Briskman, 2003; Tyler, 2010). The political narrative on asylum seekers, for example, has been associated with the need to protect the rights of citizens within the western world, or the privilege of citizenship (Choules, 2006). The impact of such responses on human rights and social justice has been significant, with Brysk and Sharif (2004) describing the disparity in rights afforded to citizens compared to outsiders as the 'citizenship gap' and leading Tyler (2010) to describe citizenship as playing 'a central role within this securitised state, enabling specific groups and populations to be legitimately targeted and criminalised as non-citizens or failing citizens' (Tyler, 2010, p. 64).

Much of the narrative on citizenship, including Marshall's conceptualisation of social citizenship and Ager and Strang's fourth category 'foundation', suggests that citizenship rights are entangled with responsibility and obligation on the part of individuals (Harris, 1999; Turner, 2001). In the preceding discussion, asylum seekers were presented as a disenfranchised group who do not share the social, political or economic rights bestowed on the indigenous population. Their exclusion from the labour market and inability to pay associated taxes places asylum seekers in a position of dependency where the social and economic obligations of citizenship are not met. Under the welfare state, Marshall characterised public service users as passive 'client-citizens'. In this conceptualisation, participation was therefore reserved for expressing political voice (e.g. through voting) and the role of professionals was to skilfully design and deliver public services. Significantly for citizenship rights, asylum seekers also have limited political agency, being unable to vote or influence policymaking or rules regarding immigration.

More recently, Choules (2006) has built a broader conceptualisation of citizenship that offers a potentially more inclusive approach than Marshall's social citizenship. She contends that citizenship is constructed upon three fundamental dimensions: membership of a political community, membership of a community of shared character and membership of a welfare state. Importantly though, Choules' definition of citizenship offers a different point of departure for considering the status of asylum seekers and their potential to co-produce public services as service users. It is the exploration of these dimensions that will be the focus of later analysis. The first category has formed the basis of traditional definitions of citizenship, but the second two offer a potentially broader definition and application of the concept, which may have implications for asylum seekers. This suggests that, as a group of shared character, asylum seekers (and perhaps refugees) might access Choules' second dimension of citizenship. In line with this argument, Niiranen (1999) focuses on the collective dimension of citizenship, which he suggests is developed through community participation. Niiranen also supports the third of Choules' dimensions, suggesting that the role ascribed to public service users within the welfare state forms a type of citizenship at the individual level. This, he argues, demonstrates that citizenship can be attached to individual rights, where individuals as consumers of public services can make use of associated consumer rights. Rouban (1999) also argues that the success of public services is reliant on participation: 'It is, in fact, highly likely that there cannot be quality, or in other words, true effectiveness, without user, or citizen, adhesion or actual participation' (Rouban, 1999, p. 1).

More broadly, participation has been framed in much of the literature as a core human and citizenship right, often being described as a central component of citizenship (Powell, 2002; Brannan et al., 2006). It has also been framed as a core element supporting asylum seeker integration within Ager and Strang's (2008) framework, but it has also been recognised as a challenge for marginalised groups in society, such as asylum seekers who do not have the necessary rights to participate on a political level. Brannan et al. (2006, p. 995) argue that participation should be viewed as a core element of citizenship rather than a 'bolt-on optional extra'. Interestingly, Dreydus (1999) argues for an extended conception of citizenship that can be applied where 'the activities of the State apparatus are under the control of the people who are involved in the decision-making process or at least are informed of the decisions, especially when they are affected by them' (Dreydus, 1999, p. 7). Co-production and what it can offer is a key facet of this debate:

> the progressive decline of citizenship and the sense of moi commun (a shared ideal in which the individual is fully part of the whole community, literally 'common self') has prompted scholars and practitioners to look for new public service delivery mechanisms that will reinvigorate the role of citizens in their communities beyond simply voter and customer.
>
> (Nabatchi et al., 2017, p. 767)

A question therefore arises as to whether asylum seekers, as non-citizens in the legal meaning of the concept, can participate in the welfare state as public service users through the various modes of co-production identified in Chapters 4 and 5. Lister's (2003) work is helpful in analysing the potential impact of co-production on asylum seekers. She differentiates between citizenship as a status and a practice: status is about *being* a citizen, while practice is about *acting* as a citizen. Asylum seekers certainly do not have the legal status of citizens, but perhaps co-production provides a route for them to practise a partial form of citizenship through their membership of the welfare state. As a practice, citizenship enfolds both rights/obligations and political participation through meaningful interaction (Lister, 2003, 2007).

## Role of the Third Sector in Asylum Seeker Context

In Scotland there has been a history of collaborative working in the delivery of public services within which the third sector has played a crucial role that has latterly become embedded by the 2015 Community Empowerment (Scotland) Act. Indeed, the Scottish government describe the third sector as playing a core role in the growth of Scotland's economy, the well-being of the Scottish people and also the improvement of public services (www.scotland.gov.uk/Topics/People/15300, accessed 2017). In relation to asylum seekers, the Race Equality Statement situated the third sector in a core role, with various third sector organisations in the field of asylum/refugees being described as 'strategic partners' (Scottish Government, 2008). This ongoing legacy of collaborative working makes Scotland a particularly rich area for exploring the co-production of public services. Furthermore, due to the complexity of their needs, a multi-agency approach to public service planning and delivery is regarded as fundamental to supporting asylum seekers entering Scotland (Scottish Government, 2006).

Historically, the third sector has played a leading role in supporting asylum seekers, responding on an ad hoc basis in reaction to individual crises and establishing support programmes for specific groups (Wren, 2007). While some commentators have suggested that the strong presence of the third sector has had an exclusionary impact for asylum seekers as the sector serves to deplete statutory service provision (Bloch and Schuster, 2002; Sales, 2002) it has generally been considered to play a core role, particularly in the delivery of public services (Griffiths et al., 2006; Scottish Government, 2008). Although Wren (2007) argues that third sector provision is not directly substitutable for statutory service provision that can better meet the diverse needs of asylum seekers.

According to Griffiths et al. (2006), the role of third sector organisations dealing with asylum seekers and refugees has predominantly been one of gap filling and meeting basic needs, rather than active involvement in the development of policies and/or services. The authors further argue that organisations typically play their role on the periphery of the community, which may hinder the integration of asylum seekers and refugees. More recently, Mayblin and James (2019) argue that while the role of the third sector has been under-researched, it provides essential support to the asylum seeker/refugee population that is not satisfied by the state despite reduced government funding. They suggest that, rather than playing a role of strategic collaboration or as contractors, the role of the third sector in relation to asylum seekers is one of gap filling. Zetter (2007) corroborates that view, arguing that the role of third sector organisations has changed: 'These organisations are less the prime mediators of refugee integration, as in the past. Now they exist for the essentially defensive and immediate tasks of advocacy, protecting basic rights, supporting asylum claims, and filling the increasingly large void left by the withdrawal of state support, not for longer-term settlement' (Zetter, 2007, p. 187).

A diverse number of organisations contribute to the provision of public services for asylum seekers—including churches and refugee community groups—many of which have no contractual relationship with the UK government which, as discussed previously, retains reserved responsibility for immigration and asylum (Barclay et al., 2003). Furthermore, the boundaries between statutory and third sector service provision, in particular, have been described as increasingly blurred (Sales, 2002). Wren's (2007) research, for example, found confusion among asylum seekers over which organisations were responsible and accountable. Such confusion is of concern to Wren who questioned the accountability and legitimacy of third sector organisations providing public services.

It was recognised that due to the complexity of their needs, a multi-agency approach was fundamental to adequately supporting asylum seekers in Scotland (Scottish Government, 2006). Through Community Planning Partnerships, the third sector's role was integrated during service design, planning and delivery for which the Community Empowerment (Scotland) Act 2015 provided the statutory basis. However, in practice, it is unclear whether this has resulted in closer involvement of a limited number of actors from government departments and national third sector organisations or whether it has been more inclusive (Osborne and McLaughlin, 2004). Inter-organisational relationships were also formally established through the inauguration of the Scottish Refugee Integration Forum (SRIF) in January 2002 by the then Scottish Executive to support partnership working among Scotland's statutory and third sector organisations to aid the integration of refugees/ asylum seekers into communities. The SRIF Action Plan was published the following year and outlined key actions related to improving access to services, translation and interpretation support and breaking down barriers to employment (for refugees). These actions were to be implemented by the Scottish government, local authorities and various public service providers through a partnership approach. Furthermore, Integration Networks were established throughout the city of Glasgow. They were funded primarily by the Scottish government with partners from across organisational boundaries and sectors sitting together to plan services at an operational level. Regardless of government funding, Wren (2007) found that networks evolved and functioned at the local level and tended to be independent of outside control.

## Empirical Research Design

The case of marginalised asylum seekers presented earlier offers a fertile ground through which to explore co-production. The preceding discussion has raised three important issues that require further investigation. First, to what extent is co-production dependent upon citizenship, or in other words can asylum seekers as non-citizens co-produce public services? Second, if asylum seekers co-produce regardless of their citizenship status, what are the implications for social inclusion and citizenship? And finally, what is the role of the third sector in co-producing public services? To examine these areas of interest, the remainder of this chapter will introduce an illustrative case study that was conducted in Glasgow. It will start with a brief overview of the research design for the empirical study, before presenting the analysis. The discussion will focus particularly upon the Scottish context and the social welfare services received.

An empirical study was conducted to explore the nature and extent of co-production between asylum seekers, public service organisations/ government agencies and third sector organisations. The study comprised of three stages and took a mainly qualitative approach, with policy interviews, a small-scale postal survey and an embedded case study design. The methods will now be discussed in brief.

In-depth interviews were conducted with seven key national and city-wide organisations in Scotland who are responsible for asylum seeker policy, the third sector and public service provision. Respondents were selected through the use of a purposive sampling technique. The respondents are detailed in Table 6.1. The semi-structured format of the interviews allowed for both flexibility and comparability (Robson, 2005; Bryman, 2008).

The second stage was a Glasgow-wide postal survey of public service organisations providing social welfare services to asylum seekers,

*Table 6.1* Policy respondents

| POLICY RESPONDENTS | ROLE |
| --- | --- |
| Scottish Government Policy 1 | Third Sector policy |
| Scottish Government Policy 2 | Asylum seeker policy |
| Scottish Government Policy 3 | Asylum seeker policy |
| UK Government Agency | Immigration policy at the UK level |
| Charity Manager | Policy and operations of the |
| Accommodation Manager Strategic Manager | Charity |
| | Policy and operations of the |
| Community Planning Partnership Manager | Accommodation Provider |
| | Community Planning |

including third sector organisations working on behalf of asylum seekers. The survey aimed to sample the whole population of organisations providing social welfare services to asylum seekers in Glasgow due to the small numbers involved; in total 107 questionnaires were distributed. Developing the sample was a challenge given that no definitive list of such organisations exists; this has been an issue in previous studies and is a reason for the lack of research in this area in the past (see Mayblin and James, 2019). In order to develop as comprehensive a sample as possible, organisations such as the Glasgow Council for the Voluntary Sector and the Scottish Refugee Council were approached, who provided invaluable advice and access to their online directories of service providers. The questionnaires were sent to named individuals where possible and were coded to keep track of responses. This allowed for non-responses to be chased up by telephone in an attempt to boost response rates. In total, forty-three completed questionnaires were returned, providing a response rate of 40%.

The survey was used to map the nature and extent of co-production in social welfare services for asylum seekers. The questions predominantly used nominal levels of measurement, although a number of ordinal attitudinal questions were also asked. There was also space at the end of the questionnaire for respondents to include open-ended comments, which were completed by ten respondents. Due to the small sample size, analysis was limited to descriptive statistics.

An embedded case study design was adopted to take a concentrated focus on the city of Glasgow which homes the highest number of asylum seekers in Scotland (Home Office, 2018). The embedded design accommodated for the complexity of the context and also provided an opportunity for extensive analysis into the case (Yin, 2009). The case study was split into eight sub-units, each of which is described in Table 6.2. A mixture of community-based organisations, large third sector organisations and statutory agencies were selected in an attempt to generate different narratives and a detailed account of the context through various interviews and observations. In addition, two core structures in the provision of social welfare services for asylum seekers were investigated: Framework for Dialogue Groups and Integration Networks.

Through the case study approach, data triangulation was achieved through the collection of multiple sources of evidence, using interviews with various respondents, observations of service delivery and document analysis.

Across the sub-units in-depth interviews were conducted with two strategic managers, thirteen service managers and four front-line staff. Those accessed within each sub unit are a reflection of the type of organisation providing the service. Accessing asylum seekers was an essential element in the research design, as their input provided valuable insight into the extent and nature of co-production. Nine individual, face-to-face

*Table 6.2* Case study sub-units

|  | CASE DESCRIPTION | METHODS |
|---|---|---|
| Church A | Small community organisation providing various services to asylum seekers, e.g. drop-in sessions for women and children and English classes. | • Service manager interview<br>• Observation<br>• Document analysis |
| Church B | Small community organisation providing services to asylum seekers, including computer and English classes. Also provides ad hoc support and signposts to other services. | • Service manager interview<br>• Asylum seeker interview<br>• Observation<br>• Document analysis |
| Accommodation provider | Public sector organisation responsible for housing asylum seekers in Glasgow under a contract with the Government Agency | • Service manager interview<br>• Strategic Manager interview x2<br>• Observation |
| Humanitarian Organisation | National organisation developed services in response to asylum seeker dispersal, such as an International Tracing Service; Orientation Service; Newspaper; volunteer drop-in sessions; and outreach work with schools. | • Service manager interview<br>• Front-line staff interview<br>• Document analysis |
| Development Organisation | City-wide organisation that offered services to asylum seekers, including Adult Literacy and Numeracy classes. A broader aim was to help underrepresented groups (e.g. asylum seekers) find volunteering opportunities. | • Service Manager interview x2<br>• Front-line staff interview (duo)<br>• Asylum seeker interview (duo)<br>• Observation<br>• Document analysis |
| Young Persons' Group | A thematic Social Inclusion Partnership to support young people leaving institutional care around housing, employment and training, health and well-being, and social support. | • Service manager interview<br>• Asylum seeker group interview<br>• Observation<br>• Document analysis |
| Framework for Dialogue Group | One of eight professionally led groups facilitated and administrated by community development workers from the public sector and the Charity. Provided information and also a forum for asylum seekers to influence the planning of services | • Service manager interview x2<br>• Asylum seeker interviews x6<br>• Observation<br>• Document analysis |
| Integration Network | One of ten such networks operating in the city. The group is comprised of members from across the public and Third Sector who are responsible for asylum seeker services. The group meets regularly to plan services. | • Service manager interview x4<br>• Observation<br>• Document analysis |

interviews were conducted with asylum seekers and a group interview was conducted with four young asylum seekers. This method was considered more appropriate given the age of the asylum seekers as it was thought that they would be more relaxed in an interactive group setting (Robson, 2005). Only two individual asylum seeker interviews and the group interview with young people were digitally recorded, at the request of the interviewees who sometimes felt uncomfortable being recorded. Comprehensive notes were taken for the remaining seven interviews and were written up immediately afterwards. The interviews were relatively brief, lasting around twenty minutes each. Screening was employed prior to undertaking the interviews to ensure that respondents were indeed asylum seekers awaiting the results of their application to reside in the UK. In addition, steps were taken to interview asylum seekers from a variety of ethnic backgrounds, from both genders, in order to achieve multiple perspectives. Out of the thirteen asylum seekers who were interviewed, there were seven men and six women. They came from various countries including Pakistan, Sri Lanka, the Democratic Republic of Congo, Iraq, Serbia, Nigeria and Afghanistan. Asylum seekers were accessed through the sub case units and service providers played a crucial role in generating interest around the research and then encouraging people to participate.

Steps were taken to ensure that those asylum seekers who participated were not limited to 'the usual suspects' who are typically English speakers. During four interviews interpreters were present. Various difficulties arise in relation to the need for interpretation. For example, interpretation means that data from the interviews is modified prior to analysis which creates bias. This bias could be reduced by back translating transcripts and supplying these to respondents for confirmation prior to analysis, but this was not possible due to financial constraints and time pressures. Furthermore, the presence of the interpreter complicates the interview, adding two additional relationships between the respondent and interpreter, and the interviewer and interpreter (Farooq and Fear, 2003). Three interpreters were used; one for two interviews and one each for the remaining two interviews. The interpreters were fully briefed on the aims and the purpose of the research prior to commencing the interviews and were asked to take a passive stance, adding and omitting nothing, acting purely as a neutral conduit between the interviewer and respondent and translating what is said verbatim to ensure the quality of the data (Wallin and Ahlström, 2006).

Interviews that did not progress to sub-units within the case study design were valuable and reliable sources of data and were therefore included in the analysis as contextual stakeholder interviews (see Table 6.3).

Seven observations were also conducted within the embedded case study design. Observation provides an important opportunity for cross checking and data triangulation (Tjora, 2006) and is a valuable source of data collection where the understanding of behaviours and interactions

*Table 6.3* Contextual interviews

---

### STAKEHOLDER INTERVIEW RESPONDENTS

---

- Charity Service Manager
- Small Voluntary Organisation Service Manager
- Local Authority Arm's Length Company Service Manager
- Small Charity Service Manager
- Women's Voluntary Organisation Service Manager
- Scottish Refugee Policy Forum Representative

---

is sought in 'real' world contexts because they enable a deep exploration of the situation (Robson, 2005). Indeed, while interviews provided an opportunity to uncover experiences and perceptions, the observations generated a partially independent (of the research respondents') view of the experience (Tjora, 2006). Essentially, they offered an opportunity to collect naturally occurring events in natural settings, permitting a more accurate account of the 'real life' situation. For ethical reasons, the researcher took the role of complete observer (Angrosino, 2005). Although a concern associated with this approach is the extent to which the context would be managed or modified for the benefit of the observer, Watts (2011) argues that although the initial presence of the researcher as observer may distort behaviour, people cannot maintain a 'front' for a long period of time and are typically more concerned with the task at hand rather than the presence of an outsider.

The observations were used to generate rich data around the interactions between public service providers, service users and third sector organisations during service planning and delivery and the theoretical work that was conducted in the initial part of this study identified some core issues that need to be explored further. An unstructured observation sheet was developed in order to log the data during the observations; because various situations, different people and different activities were observed each time, a structured approach was not appropriate.

Finally, document analysis was conducted within each case study sub unit to systematically review and evaluate organisational documents (Bowen, 2009). The purpose of document analysis was not to compare like with like, but rather to explore organisational narratives about co-production, providing valuable insight into the extent to which each type of co-production is present within different organisations and groups. The documentation was investigated using content analysis, which Bryman and Bell (2007, p. 304) define as 'an approach to the analysis of documents and texts that seeks to quantify content in terms of predetermined categories and in a systematic and replicable manner'. The content analysis was conducted by counting the frequency of words associated with co-production. In total, forty-two words were predefined, including involvement, empower, consult, engage and choice; these words were selected both as a result of the theoretical work and after early analysis of the primary research findings, again emphasising the iterative approach to this research design. The frequency of characters or significant actors (Bryman and Bell, 2007) associated with co-production was also counted (e.g. customer, volunteer, charity). The counts were used to establish the extent to which different organisations have embedded co-production within their policies and practices. In addition to the quantitative element of the analysis, the context was further examined through qualitative content analysis. This ensured that the frequencies were not misconstrued by including the context within which individual words have been used in the text. The following contextual issues were considered: subject matter; how co-production is viewed (favourably or not); what goals or intentions are revealed in relation to co-production; which actors are using these mechanisms.

## Summary: Asylum, Support and Rights

This chapter has introduced the case of asylum seekers, examining the barriers they face legally, socially and economically. It argued that as a disempowered and marginalised group, asylum seekers are not bestowed the same benefits and access rights as others in society. Their lives are regulated and constrained by strict immigration laws, which are rooted within and built upon 'policies of deterrence' (Williams, 2006) that seek to discourage applications for asylum by overriding the potential 'pull factors' that might encourage people from other countries to move to the UK without the required legal documentation. As a consequence of this political approach, the legislation defining and regulating immigration has built a very much stratified system of social rights that limits asylum seekers' access to public services and singles them out as a visibly in-need group distinct from mainstream society (Sales, 2002). They are often demonised in the media and by politicians as 'scroungers' and this, along with their legal position as non-citizens, makes asylum seeker integration challenging.

The discussion in this chapter has also considered the unique context in Scotland where the government has taken a more open approach to asylum, compared to the UK government, for reasons of economic sustainability. Significantly, for the work presented in this book, the Scottish government policy supports integration as soon as an application for asylum is made (rather than if refugee status is granted, which is the approach of the UK government). However, the discussion has also suggested that the Scottish approach to integration, based on Ager and Strang's (2008) framework, is met by significant barriers particularly in relation to asylum seekers' limited access to social rights and their inability to participate at a political level.

The marginalised position of asylum seekers and their limited access to social rights have severe consequences for their citizenship status. This chapter therefore discussed various definitions of citizenship and their application to asylum seekers. It argued that while asylum seekers are not legal citizens, a broader conceptualisation which articulates citizenship as a practice may be helpful in understanding their rights and obligations in society and, importantly, their potential to co-produce public services. However, membership to each of Choule's three domains will change according to which country an asylum seeker is entering. Within this discussion, co-production and its participative foundation is described as a potential mechanism through which asylum seekers may practise a partial form of citizenship (Lister, 2003). Reflecting on their marginalised position and the fact that the Scottish government is responsible for the provision of public services to asylum seekers, the chapter then posed the following questions: whether asylum seekers can co-produce the public services in any of the ways described by the framework introduced in Chapter 4 (i.e. through co-construction, co-production or co-design); and, if they can co-produce public services, whether this might have implications for their integration into society and their position as non-citizens. The chapter then concluded with a presentation of the case study methodology through which these issues will be explored.

## Notes

1. Prior to 2007, the application process was typically a lengthy affair that could take a number of years, leaving asylum seekers uncertain over their future in the UK and hindering the process of resettlement (Spicer, 2008). The asylum process was overhauled in 2007 and, since the introduction of the New Asylum Model, the decision-making process has sped up considerably. Since March of that year, the New Asylum Model introduced a single case owner approach to asylum cases, where one individual was responsible for each new asylum case from beginning to end. That caseworker aims to conclude applications within a six-month timescale with the applicant either gaining refugee status within that timeframe or being sent home either voluntarily or through enforced removal.
2. The expansion of the Vulnerable Persons Resettlement Scheme was announced in September 2015, under which it was proposed that 20,000 Syrians in need of protection would be resettled in the UK by 2020. In July 2017 this was expanded to include vulnerable refugees of any nationality that have fled the conflict in Syria and are unable to return to their home country safely. Since the scheme began in 2014, 12,851 people have been resettled in the UK (Home Office, 2018).
3. In early 2019, Serco lost the Home Office contract for housing asylum seekers in Glasgow; from October of that year housing will be provided by the Mears Group.

## References

Ager, A. and Strang, A. (2008). Understanding integration: a conceptual framework. *Journal of Refugee Studies*. (21,2), 166–191.

Angrosino, M. V. (2005). Recontextualising observation: ethnography, pedagogy, and the prospects for a progressive political agenda. In Denzin, N. K.

and Lincoln, Y. S. (eds.), *The Sage handbook of qualitative research* (3rd ed.). Thousand Oaks: Sage.

Anon. (2001). Let Scotland sort out the asylum mess. *The Glasgow Herald*. 14 August.

Anon. (2005). Deal means asylum seeker raid continue. *The Scotsman*. 25 November.

Barclay, A., Bowes, A., Ferguson, I., Sim, D. and Valenti, M. (2003). *Asylum seekers in Scotland*. Edinburgh: Scottish Executive.

Bloch, A. (2000). Refugee settlement in Britain: the impact of policy on participation. *Journal of Ethnic and Migration Studies*. (26,1), 75–88.

Bloch, A. and Schuster, L. (2002). Asylum and welfare: contemporary debate. *Critical Social Policy*. (22), 393–414.

Bowen, G. A. (2009). Document analysis as a qualitative research method. *Qualitative Research Journal*. (9,2), 27–40.

Brannan, T., John, P. and Stoker, G. (2006). Active citizenship and effective public services and programmes: how can we know what really works? *Urban Studies*. (43,5–6), 993–1008.

Bryman, A. (2008). *Social research methods* (3rd ed.). Oxford: Oxford University Press.

Bryman, A. and Bell, E. (2007). *Business research methods*. Oxford: Oxford University Press.

Brysk, A. and Sharif, G. (2004). Introduction: globalization and the citizenship gap. In Brysk, A. and Sharif, G. (eds.), *People out of place: globalization, human rights and the citizenship gap*. New York: Routledge.

Castles, S. and Loughma, S. (2003). *Trends in asylum migration to industrialized countries: 1999–2001*. Discussion Paper 2003/31. United Nations University, World Institute for Development Economics Research.

Cemlyn, S. and Briskman, L. (2003). Asylum, children's rights and social work. *Child and Family Social Work*. (8), 163–178.

Choules, K. (2006). Globally privileged citizenship. *Race, Ethnicity and Education*. (9,3), 275–293.

Darling, J. (2014). Asylum and the post-political: domopolitics, depoliticisation and acts of citizenship. *Antipode*. (46,1), 72–91.

Doerschler, P. (2006). Push-pull factors and immigrant political integration in Germany. *Social Science Quarterly*. (87,5), 1100–1116.

Dreydus, F. (1999). What kind of a citizen for what kind of state? In Rouban, L. (ed.), *Citizens and the new governance: beyond new public management*. Amsterdam: IOS Press.

Farooq, S. and Fear, C. (2003). Working through interpreters. *Advances in Psychiatric Treatment*. (9), 104–109.

Gilbert, A. and Koser, K. (2006). Coming to the UK: what do asylum seekers know about the UK before arrival? *Journal of Ethnic and Migration Studies*. (32,7), 1209–1225.

Griffiths, D., Sigona, N. and Zetter, R. (2006). Integrative paradigms, marginal reality: refugee community organizations and dispersal in Britain. *Journal of Ethnic and Migration Studies*. (32,5), 881–898.

Harris, J. (1999). State social work and social citizenship in Britain: from clientism to consumerism. *British Journal of Social Work*. (29), 915–937.

Hickley, M. (2009). 90% of failed asylum seekers remain in the UK—and the backlog of undecided cases doubles in a year. *Daily Mail*. 23 January.

Home Office. (2018). *Statistical news release: immigration statistics.* London: Home Office.

Johnston, I. (2003). Work ban on asylum seekers condemned. *Scotland on Sunday.* 25 May.

King, D. S. and Waldron, J. (1988). Citizenship, social citizenship and the defence of welfare provision. *British Journal of Political Science.* (18), 415–443.

Kirkwood, S. and McNeill, F. (2015). Integration and reintegration: comparing pathways to citizenship through asylum and criminal justice. *Criminology and Criminal Justice.* (15,5), 511–526.

Kofman, E. (2005). Citizenship, migration and the reassertion of national identity. *Citizenship Studies.* (9,5), 435–467.

Lewis, M. (2006). *Warm welcome? Understanding public attitudes to asylum seekers in Scotland.* London: Institute for Public Policy Research.

Lister, R. (2003). *Citizenship: feminist perspectives* (2nd ed.). Basingstoke: Palgrave Macmillan.

Lister, R. (2007). From object to subject: including marginalised citizens in policy making. *Policy and Politics.* (35,3), 437–455.

Marshall, T. H. (1950). *Citizenship and social class.* Cambridge: Cambridge University Press.

Mayblin, L. (2016). Complexity reduction and policy consensus: asylum seekers, the right to work, and the 'pull factor' thesis is the UK context. *British Journal of Politics and International Relations.* (18,4), 812–828.

Mayblin, L. and James, P. (2019). Asylum and refugee support in the UK: civil society filling the gaps? *Journal of Ethnic and Migration Studies.* (45,3), 375–394.

McCluskey, M. T. (2003). Efficiency and social citizenship: challenging the neoliberal attack on the welfare state. *Indiana Law Journal.* (78), 783–875.

Mulvey, G. (2010). Problematising of immigration and the consequences for refugee integration in the UK. *Journal of Refugees Studies.* (23,4), 437–462.

Nabatchi, T., Sancino, A. and Sicilia, M. (2017). Varieties of participation in public services: the who, when and what of co-production. *Public Administration Review.* (77,5), 766–776.

Nash, M., Wong, J. and Trlin, A. (2006). Civic and social integration: a new field of social work practice with immigrants, refugees and asylum seekers. *International Social Work.* (49,3), 345–363.

Niiranen, V. (1999). Municipal democracy and citizens' participation. In Rouban, L. (ed.), *Citizens and the new governance.* Amsterdam: IOS Press.

Osborne, S. P. and McLaughlin, K. (2004). The cross-cutting review of the voluntary sector: where next for local government-voluntary sector relationships? *Regional Studies.* (38,5), 571–580.

Parker, S. (2015). 'Unwanted invaders': the representation of refugees and asylum seekers in the UK and Australian print media. *eSharp.* (23).

Powell, M. (2002). The hidden history and social citizenship. *Citizenship Studies.* (6,3), 229–244.

Putnam, R. D. (1993). The prosperous community: social capital and public life. *American Prospect.* (13), 35–42.

Robson, C. (2005). *Real world research* (2nd ed.). Malden: Blackwell.

Roche, M. (1992). *Rethinking citizenship: welfare, ideology and change in modern society.* Cambridge: Polity Press.

Rouban, L. (1999). Citizens and the new governance. In Rouban, L. (ed.), *Citizens and the new governance: beyond new public management*. Amsterdam: IOS Press.

Sales, R. (2002). The deserving and undeserving? Refugees, asylum seekers and welfare in Britain. *Critical Social Policy*. (22), 456–478.

Scottish Government. (2006). *Transforming public services: the next phase of reform*. Edinburgh: Scottish Government.

Scottish Government. (2008). *Race equality statement*. Edinburgh: Scottish Government.

Sim, D. and Bowes, A. (2007). Asylum seekers in Scotland: the accommodation of diversity. *Social Policy & Administration*. (41,7), 729–746.

Spicer, N. (2008). Places of exclusion and inclusion: asylum-seeker and refugee experiences of neighbourhoods in the UK. *Journal of Ethnic and Migration Studies*. (34, 3), 491–510.

Turner, B. S. (2001). The erosion of citizenship. *British Journal of Sociology*. (52,2), 189–209.

Tjora, A. H. (2006). Writing small discoveries: an exploration of fresh observers' observations. *Qualitative Research*. (6,4), 429–451.

Tyler, I. (2010). Designed to fail: a biopolitics of British citizenship. *Citizenship Studies*. (14,1), 61–74.

Wallin, A-M. and Ahlström, G. (2006). Cross-cultural interview studies using interpreters: systematic literature review. *Journal of Advanced Nursing*. (55,6), 723–735.

Watts, J. H. (2011). Ethical and practical challenges of participant observation in sensitive health research. *International Journal of Social Research Methodology*. (14,4), 301–312.

Williams, L. (2006). Social networks of refuges in the United Kingdom: tradition, tactics and new community spaces. *Journal of Ethnic and Migration Studies*. (32,5), 865–879.

Wren, K. (2007). Supporting asylum seekers and refugees in Glasgow: the role of multi-agency networks. *Journal of Refugee Studies*. (20,3), 391–413.

Yin, R. K. (2009). *Case study research: design and methods* (4th ed.). Los Angeles: Sage.

Zetter, R. (2007). More labels, fewer refugees: remaking the refugee label in an era of globalization. *Journal of Refugee Studies*. (20,2), 172–192.

# 7 Understanding Co-production

## An Empirical Case Study of Asylum Seekers Living in Glasgow

## Abstract

This chapter discusses the case study findings in order to map the nature and extent of asylum seeker co-production in the context of social welfare services in Scotland. Importantly, the analysis shows that, as public services users, asylum seekers can and do co-produce public services through the three modes of co-production previously differentiated. It is argued that asylum seekers co-produce at different times during the service production process and through different mechanisms, but critically that co-construction during direct interactions or service encounters is an important means through which relationships can be built between the vulnerable group and public service staff. The data presented here also indicates that asylum seekers co-produce though various mechanisms of participative co-production and, to a lesser extent, co-design. It is important to note, however, that various challenges were also presented in relation to each mode of co-production and the management of the service relationship was described as a key factor in handling these challenges.

## Introduction

This chapter reports a discussion of the case study research findings. It focuses particularly on the existence of the modes of co-production that were differentiated in Chapter 4. The discussion starts with the Scottish context, examining the focus on integration and the public services provided to asylum seekers in Glasgow. It then examines the implications of asylum seekers' legal status as non-citizens, defining the group as occupying a powerless position who bear limited influence over policymaking and strategic decisions, but suggests that, as public service users, asylum seekers play an integral role in service delivery and can also influence service planning on the operational level. It will differentiate asylum seeker co-production in this case with examples of the three modes—co-construction, participative co-production and co-design—in practice, before concluding with the challenges associated with each of the modes.

# Asylum in Scotland: Integration, Public Services and Non-Citizens

## *Asylum in Scotland: The Integration Divide*

Although the numbers of asylum seekers coming to Scotland have varied over time, there was a constant influx of asylum seekers into Glasgow at the time of this research: 'Since 2001, maybe 80% of asylum seekers who come to the UK are sent to Glasgow, something like that, 70 to 80 a week' (Refugee Policy Forum). Asylum seekers were considered a transient community, even more so with the introduction of the new asylum model where decisions had to be taken on an asylum seeker's status within six months. Decisions were being made much quicker than they had previously, with asylum seekers sometimes hearing the outcome of their case within a few weeks, which could potentially impact the extent to which they could be integrated into communities. There was also some recognition from respondents that not all asylum seekers reported to the authorities and some who had not received permission to remain in the UK had chosen to go 'underground' rather than returning home to their native country.

Confirming the literature discussed in Chapter 6 (e.g. Cemlyn and Briskman, 2003; Williams, 2006), asylum seekers were generally considered to occupy a powerless legal position. This was closely associated with the impact of immigration legislation and policies that restricted the extent to which asylum seekers control their lives by, for example, providing authorities at the UK level with full discretion over where they are housed and prohibiting asylum seekers from undertaking paid work. Policy respondents were also clear in confirming the limited power the Scottish government had over influencing the rights of the group in a country where 'the balance is tipped very much against the interests of asylum seekers' (Community Planning Partnership).

As discussed in the previous chapter, the policy on social inclusion is divided between Scotland and England (Wren, 2007) and this was confirmed by the empirical analysis. Scotland and particularly Glasgow was considered a welcoming place for asylum seekers. One respondent referred to England as 'more negative' (Accommodation Provider Strategic Manager), making particular reference to the detrimental media coverage on asylum and immigration more generally. Various respondents reinforced this demarcation and explained that, from the Scottish perspective, integration should start as soon as asylum seekers arrive in the country rather than waiting until they are awarded status, as is the case in England:

> if people arrive in Glasgow, the first thing we try and do is help integrate them into the community for however long their stay is. So

that's a different view from us . . . to the Central Government. And that's caused some tensions in the past.

(Accommodation Provider Strategic Manager)

Such a stance coincided with the Scottish government's policy on integration and the impetus of strong economic drivers was a strong factor supporting and advancing the early integration of asylum seekers. Indeed, respondents noted that regardless of the political persuasion of those in power, there had been a commitment to maintaining a Scottish population of above five million and, to achieve that, inward migration was essential. The Scottish government did not believe in deskilling asylum seekers while they awaited a decision on their application and were therefore eager to encourage opportunities for volunteering and education. Asylum seekers entering Scotland also had the option of signing onto English for Speakers of Other Languages classes, for example, because these were considered to have a beneficial impact upon community integration and potential that groups such as asylum seekers could provide to the economy, suggesting that Ager and Strang's 'facilitators' have been implemented at the operational level to support integration: 'Community integration and the economic . . . you know when they move up they'll provide to the economy' (Interview with a Scottish Government Policymaker).

Through the document analysis, integration was clearly a key goal for organisations delivering services to asylum seekers and was articulated at both the strategic and operational levels. For example, one Humanitarian Organisation newspaper referred to integration from arrival as 'essential' and that organisations and communities had to 'work together' to achieve 'integration'. The integration of asylum seekers in the community through service provision and projects was also paramount for some organisations. For example, Church A's application for funding referred to the Mother and Toddlers' Group providing a space where 'children are able to mix and play together', while Church B associated participation with a broader goal, stating that participation in services promoted 'integration'. However, the centralised nature of immigration policies was a substantial barrier for respondents working in the Scottish context, which operated against the drive for early integration. Respondents also spoke of the challenges that emerged from asylum seeker policies being made in Croydon and therefore often failing to reflect Scottish differences, such as the legal system and different stance around integration.

## Provision of Welfare Services to Asylum Seekers

Of the survey respondents, thirty-four described themselves as working for third sector organisations, five for government agencies and four for further education colleges. The organisations surveyed varied in size,

*Table 7.1* Services provided by survey respondents

| Service type | Frequency | Percentage |
|---|---|---|
| Counselling | 8 | 19% |
| Befriending scheme | 9 | 21.4% |
| Training | 13 | 31% |
| Information and advice | 31 | 73.8% |
| Languages | 21 | 50% |
| Drop in | 17 | 40.5% |

from small community organisations to large public organisations; the average number of paid staff was 420 and the average number of unpaid staff was 45.

Table 7.1 illustrates the types of services that were provided by the organisations surveyed. Information and advice (73.8%) was a key aspect of public service provision. Service providers in various settings provided asylum seekers with information about other services available and advice on their asylum claim. Language courses (50%) and drop-in centres (40.5%) were also key services provided by respondents.

In addition to the services mentioned in Table 7.1, a variety of other services was provided by a smaller proportion of respondents, such as computer classes, employability support by offering opportunities for asylum seekers to volunteer and social events to allow asylum seekers to network and integrate. The qualitative responses to this survey question further confirmed the varied nature of service provision, including for example: family reunion, crisis support, access to education, practical help, support to find volunteering opportunities and employability support. Interestingly, only one organisation said that it provided an advocacy service. The interviews confirmed this to some extent, with respondents suggesting that they did less work around advocacy than they had previously, when asylum seekers had first come to Glasgow, with a greater focus on service provision to meet identified asylum seeker needs. However, the analysis revealed examples of softer forms of advocacy, with some organisations working to ensure that asylum seekers received appropriate services from public sector organisations and that structures were in place for integration. Interestingly, the document analysis showed higher counts for 'support', 'advice', 'help' and 'information', but smaller counts for words such as 'advocacy', 'lobby' and 'campaign', although these were mentioned in some third sector documentation. Church B, for example, made reference to a campaign to stop the deportation of a failed asylum seeker and the Integration Networks referred to lobbying around local policy issues as a key goal.

## Asylum Seekers: Powerless Non-Citizens

A central issue to the analysis is the position of asylum seekers as non-citizens. Chapter 6 described asylum seekers as a marginal and disenfranchised group who do not possess the political agency necessary for citizenship (Haikio, 2010) and as such are typically described as the 'Other' with limited rights (Cemlyn and Briskman, 2003; Choules, 2006). The empirical research confirmed that asylum seekers did not exercise political agency equal to that of the indigenous population due to their legal status and did not have equal levels of economic agency because they were not permitted to work for remuneration.

The status of asylum seekers as non-citizens prevented their engagement at the UK policymaking level. Asylum seekers were generally described by respondents as 'powerless', with immigration legislation and policies restricting their capacity to contribute to civic life. Comments from the Government Agency respondent reflected the professional ambivalence to forms of co-production. She argued that it was not always appropriate for asylum seekers to be directly involved in decision-making at a strategic level, either because they were not equipped for this level of involvement or because these strategic issues (often involving an implicit assumption of citizenship and a commitment to broader social goals) were deemed inappropriate for discussion with asylum seekers as service users.

> Not at the strategic level because a lot of things that we discuss is not for disclosure. And it really wouldn't be an appropriate forum for them anyway because to be fair, we're not talking about the operational issues, we're talking about business planning, forecasting for the future.
>
> (Government Agency)

In particular, co-production by individual asylum seekers at the policy level was marred by their status as non-citizens. Respondents noted that it was difficult for asylum seekers to engage around issues of Immigration policy and legislation: 'because of their status, asylum seekers are not formally meant to engage' (Accommodation Provider Strategic Manager). The relationship between the Government Agency and asylum seekers in Scotland appeared to be relatively one-sided with asylum seekers being legally obliged to inform the Government Agency of any material changes to their circumstances: 'If you have a change in circumstance you're legally obliged to let [the Government Agency] know' (Government Agency). The respondent further suggested that the Government Agency did not want to have a close relationship with individual asylum seekers regarding issues of accommodation, but instead used the

Accommodation Provider and its complaint procedure to mediate with asylum seekers:

> the way to do that [report an issue with the accommodation] is not to constantly phone us five times a day and say that . . . and let them know what the avenue of that referral process would be so it's actually logged and dealt with appropriately.
>
> (Government Agency)

## Co-production and Asylum Seeker Public Service Users

### The Locus of Co-production

Although co-production with asylum seekers at the policy level was rebuffed by the Government Agency, this view was not shared by the vast majority of respondents working in the Scottish context. Policy respondents, for example, said that asylum seekers should be and were engaged in debates around the delivery of public services in Scotland despite their non-citizen status: 'they are still service users and there are still public duties around engagement there' (Community Planning Partnership). Importantly, asylum seekers were viewed as *public service users* and respondents generally spoke of the importance of asylum seeker co-production to ensure buy-in and use of the services.

Respondents providing services to asylum seeker service users typically referred to them as *clients* rather than customers or consumers and focused on serving their needs but also reflected on the fact that asylum seekers have limited capacity to make choices particularly when it came to housing. The public administration narrative on co-production has taken a contradictory perspective on the classification of public service users as clients. Earlier literature argued that the term was too strongly associated with the welfare state and hierarchical forms of service production and management where the service user is passive and dependent and hence, inappropriate in the discussion of co-production (Whitaker, 1980; Levine and Fisher, 1984). The empirical analysis further suggested a preference among certain service providers to refer to and treat asylum seekers as *people* as opposed to giving them titles such as consumer or client, or towards more specific terms relating to the type of service being produced, such as learner or patient. The disagreement over what public service users should be called was recognised by Jung (2010), who suggests that a lack of clarity about respective roles could result.

The survey analysis indicated the main motivations of asylum seeker involvement during public service design and delivery. In line with the public administration literature (e.g. Pestoff, 2014) two thirds of survey respondents agreed/strongly agreed that asylum seeker involvement can improve the effectiveness of the service and almost half agreed that asylum seeker involvement was a cost-effective initiative. Along similar lines, one respondent noted in the qualitative response that some service users cannot be overlooked simply because service provision is more costly for them:

> We provide a service to adults and young people contemplating suicide and/or who self harm. We see a number of asylum seekers. The involvement process we use as standard normally takes longer with someone from a different cultural background, with an interpreter present, and someone who has uncertain expectations of the services. This can/does impact on resources, but is NOT a reason to avoid involvement. We have targeted asylum seekers for early intervention/ preventative work.
>
> (Survey Respondent)

Survey respondents were also asked at what stage they involve asylum seekers in service provision. The results displayed in Table 7.2 show that asylum seekers are involved at each stage of service provision, but particularly during service delivery (69%). Almost half of respondents said they involved asylum seekers after services had been delivered (47.6%) and just over one third said asylum seekers were involved in planning services (35.7%). Furthermore, the majority (69.1%) of survey respondents agreed that asylum seeker involvement was important when designing new services, with only 2.4% disagreeing with the statement. However, almost half of respondents (47.6%) disagreed that asylum seekers have plenty of opportunities to influence decisions regarding services. The response to whether asylum seekers' views are sought before making significant changes to the way that services are delivered was split, with 35.7% agreeing with this statement and 40.5% disagreeing, highlighting that service redesign is not necessarily user-led. The case study analysis also highlighted the challenge of involving asylum seekers in service design, particularly when professionals were defined as the experts with the requisite skill and knowledge to design services effectively. One respondent, whose focus was the social and economic integration

*Table 7.2* When are asylum seekers involved?

| Stage of involvement | Frequency | Percentage |
|---|---|---|
| Planning | 15 | 35.7% |
| Delivery | 29 | 69% |
| After delivery | 20 | 47.6% |

N.B. five counts (11.9%) of missing data

of asylum seekers, responding to the qualitative element of the survey explained why they did not involve their 'clients' in designing services.

> Because our service is specialised and is [in] direct response to the gap in knowledge that clients have, the ability and usefulness of designing services is limited. It is up to us to provide the expert knowledge and a professional service and while we take on board feedback on programme and incorporate suggestions on delivery or content accordingly, our main influence on service provision are employers, the economy, the labour market and the needs and sustainability of these elements. . . . Asylum seekers have so few rights and live in such a specific manner with their own case being the most important thing to them; experience shows that their voice is often not the most appropriate for service delivery and more focused on lobby or policy which is not our remit. Other organisations would disagree.
>
> (Survey Respondent)

The survey also asked respondents about the mechanisms they used to involve asylum seekers during service delivery and design. The results are displayed in Table 7.3. Feedback was the most commonly used mechanism, with over half of respondents stating they used it (52.4%). This was closely followed by consultation and choice (both 42.9%). The least used mechanism was board meetings (21.4%). Respondents also suggested other ways in which asylum seekers were involved in service production such as service user focus groups, informal communication on a constant basis through teacher-student relationships and volunteering.

### Differentiating Co-production in the Case of Asylum Seekers

The results from the data also confirmed the idea that service providers are not facilitating a single type of co-production, but rather involve asylum seekers at different times during the service production process and

*Table 7.3* Mechanisms of involvement

| Mechanism of involvement | Frequency | Percentage |
| --- | --- | --- |
| Consultation | 18 | 42.9% |
| Self-directed-support | 11 | 26.2% |
| Community meetings | 14 | 33.3% |
| Choice | 18 | 42.9% |
| Feedback | 22 | 52.4% |
| Board meetings | 9 | 21.4% |
| Complaints | 11 | 26.2% |

N.B. nine counts (21.4%) of missing data

through different mechanisms. The analysis of the qualitative interview data also suggested that there was some disparity in views around the locus of asylum seeker co-production and whether involvement should extend beyond the service relationship to participative co-production and co-design. For example, whilst one respondent suggested that asylum seekers 'should be at the heart of planning' (Scottish Government Policy-maker), another argued that the expectation of co-production during service planning was overly 'ambitious' (Community Planning Partnership).

The case study sub-units exhibited clear examples of asylum seeker co-production across the case study and these were not limited to the classical form of co-production advocated in the public administration literature. Table 7.4 shows that the three modes of co-production explicated earlier were indeed taking place across the case study sub-units and emphasises specifically the dominance of the first mode. The discussion that follows will consider the occurrence of each of the three types in detail.

### Co-construction

Table 7.4 illustrates the presence of asylum seeker involvement during the service interaction as *co-construction*, confirming the fundamental assertions made in the service management literature: where there is a service encounter, co-construction occurs (Normann, 1991; Gronroos, 2007; Glushko and Tabas, 2009). Co-construction is defined as an inherent component of service production due to the nature of services, which are characterised by the inseparability of production and consumption and, as such, is *involuntary and unavoidable* on the part of both the service user and front-line public service staff (Normann, 1991; Nankervis, 2005; Gronroos, 2007; Osborne and Strokosch, 2013). The service user, as an individual therefore never plays a passive role and co-construction emphasises the inherently relational nature of the service production process (Dunston et al., 2009).

*Table 7.4* The existence of individual co-production across the sub-units

|  | Church A | Church B | Accommo-dation Provider | Humani-tarian Organisation | Development Organisation | Young Persons' Group |
|---|---|---|---|---|---|---|
| Co-construction | X | X | X | X | X | X |
| Participative co-production |  | X |  | X | X | X |
| Co-design |  |  |  | X | X |  |

According to the basic premise of the service management theory, productivity and quality are interrelated in the service process; as the customer participates in the service process, he/she influences the service outcome and ultimately his/her own satisfaction with the service (Normann, 1991; Gronroos, 2007; Glushko and Tabas, 2009). Each service encounter observed during the fieldwork involved face-to-face interactions between the service user and front-line provider. The relationships observed reflected Normann's (1991) conception of the 'moment of truth' and the importance of individual interactions and relationships at the point of service delivery (Johnston and Clark, 2008). In its most simple form, co-construction is predicated upon dialogue and interaction between the service provider and service user during the service encounter; it emerges from the inseparable nature of production and consumption (Normann, 1991; Gronroos, 2007). Indeed, respondents attributed importance to the service interaction as a means of building a relationship and trust with the vulnerable group of service users. The Accommodation Provider, for example, utilised the co-construction that exists as an inherent dimension of the service encounter to promote service user satisfaction and service improvement. The nature of the Accommodation Provider's work meant that front-line project workers had direct and early service encounters with asylum seekers arriving in Glasgow. The observation highlighted that support and advice were provided on an individual basis with the project worker stepping beyond his delineated remit—defined by the parameters of the Home Office contract—of checking accommodation to ensure the well-being of individual asylum seekers, establishing their needs and also feeding information on to public service providers with different remits to allow them to respond to service needs.

Asylum seeker respondents also confirmed the existence of co-construction with respondents broadly stating that they had input to services at the point of delivery. They typically associated this to the propensity of service providers to listen to their service needs and act upon them:

> Yes, everybody used to be asked what they would like to do next week and people's opinions used to be asked and they used to ask what people want to do.
>
> (Asylum Seeker)

> I get support and I'm listened to by all the organisations, like schools and GPs. The only organisation that doesn't listen is the Home Office.
>
> (Asylum Seeker)

These service encounters were invariably in services previously designed by service professionals with little direct input from service users. Co-construction in this setting, therefore, shaped the enactment of a pre-defined service, but had little impact on its design or creation. In other words, asylum seeker services were generally developed and designed by professionals, although their creation was typically driven by need. Church B, for example, sought to deliver responsive services which met asylum seeker need and filled gaps in provision:

> when the asylum seekers first came . . . they didn't have the infra-structure for them, so really what happened was they gravitated towards the Church as a place where they were looking for clothing, prams, shoes, sheets . . . and then they saw that they needed help with their English classes . . . so they set up English classes for them.
>
> (Church B Service Manager)

This was also demonstrated in the case of the Young Persons' Group, where the service users contributed to the content and format of the group during the service delivery but to a much lesser extent during operational service planning, which was conducted at the organisational level.

The findings further suggest that any value or service user satisfaction gained from the service was dependent upon how well the customer and front-line staff related to one another (Nankervis, 2005; Gronroos, 2007). During the group interview, the young asylum seekers spoke at length of the importance of developing relationships with social workers. The health of these varied between individuals, with some having positive reflections such as, 'my social worker is good to me', and others saying 'I don't have relationship with my social worker'. The young people described this as a 'personal thing': 'For my friend, they can't stand their social worker. . . . It depends on the individual but mine is ok'. Taking a similar perspective, the Young Persons' Group service manager described the relationships with service users as friendships, although she noted that there was a core element of professionalism as well. Other respondents also provided some insight into the types of relationships that existed between service providers and service users. They described the development of 'friendships', which aided the service provider build a trusting professional relationship with asylum seekers to uncover need and provide related advice or information about available services.

> [Our] involvement with asylum seekers in projects such as the pro-duction of a community play or the publication of an anthology of stories or the formation of an international choir has fostered friend-ships between staff and participants. This often leads to helping peo-ple with advocacy and interaction with official bureaucracy.
>
> (Women's Voluntary Organisation Service Manager)

Likewise, various front-line staff were at pains to point out the impor-tance of developing relationships and building trust with those whom they described as a vulnerable and marginalised group of service users. Developing relationships through the service interaction was critical to meeting need and ensuring that asylum seekers were accessing the public services they required (and to ensure service uptake in order to secure long-term funding for the service). The service manager from Church B, for example, suggested that relationship-building was an important element of the service, saying that dialogue was crucial to the provision of responsive services:

> it's making sure that you communicate with them; it's making sure that you consult them; it's making sure that you regard them as being on equal footing, and in fact that you're serving them. . . . You're actually doing what they want.
>
> (Church B Service Manager)

This confirms the assertions made in the service management literature that relationship marketing is essential to supporting the service relationship and the related success of the service in producing a positive experience for service users and ultimate satisfaction (Lovelock and Young, 1979; Gummesson, 1998; Gronroos, 2009).

In two sub units—Church A and the Accommodation Provider—co-construction was the only form of individual co-production that was evidenced. Although Church A had an asylum seeker 'volunteer' involved in part of their services, the analysis suggested that her role was much more withdrawn compared to those volunteers from the indigenous population. Indeed, she spoke of making use of the service as a means of integrating with others but there was little evidence to suggest that she was contributing as a volunteer. The Accommodation Provider, similarly, provided a core service but also offered support and advice to asylum seekers. Developing relationships and building trust with clients was deemed crucial to meeting need. The Accommodation Provider relied on asylum seekers sharing information and communicating their needs to ensure that they (or other public service organisations) could deliver appropriate services. Building relationships with newly arrived asylum seekers was a key goal of front-line staff, despite this being deemed a long, slow process.

> the project workers were getting told, probably more than they should have been with people who they'd built up trust, like if they had been victimised or raped or tortured'
>
> (Accommodation Provider Service Manager)

Asylum seeker respondents also broadly agreed that trust was 'important' (Asylum Seeker 2). A trusting relationship was typically associated with the qualities espoused by service providers:

> I can trust people if the people in this organisation are good people, like X and Y and people from other groups.
>
> (Asylum Seeker 8)

[The Charity] do listen but it depends on who you speak to. Some help and some don't help. Some are very difficult.

(Asylum Seeker 5)

### Participative Co-production

Various examples of the classic formulation of *participative co-production* that is presented in the public administration literature were also found, where asylum seekers as public service users were involved in service delivery or redesign to inform the improvement of existing services. Here, co-production extended beyond the consumption logic of a single service and into the entire service production process, including planning and evaluation. Importantly, this mode was enabled by professionals within public service organisations, who defined and controlled the nature and extent of participative co-production. Asylum seeker service users could therefore take on a more active role in service production than is afforded by the integral relationship that exists through co-construction. However, the type and extent of the role they play in co-production was determined by the public service organisation and was dependent upon the goal aspired to.

Four sub-units evidenced participative co-production (see Table 7.1), but the mechanisms employed to support co-production can been divided into two categories. The first set is associated with the New Public Management agenda (and to a certain extent by the service management literature) and the marketisation of public services, empowering service users as consumers who can exercise choice, complaints and evaluation during service delivery (e.g. Greener, 2007). The second category related to operational service planning and typically took place during the service encounter and took the form of citizen participation, including consultation, partnership and volunteering where service user involvement during service delivery and/or planning was actively facilitated by a public service organisation (e.g. Pestoff, 2006; Bovaird, 2009). Encouraging asylum seekers to contribute to operational service planning was considered to increase their commitment to the services and led to feelings of ownership, corroborating Pestoff's (2014) argument, and also was ultimately thought to have a positive impact on service quality.

Although public service organisations were wary of describing service users as consumers (as discussed earlier, 'client' was the preferred term), *market mechanisms* were in operation, with asylum seekers given some leeway to make individual choices over the services they received. On a basic level, and with the exception of housing, asylum seekers were largely able to choose and exit social welfare services provided predominantly by the third sector and typically took the form of drop-in sessions and adult education (as opposed to essential mainstream services such as healthcare or education). Public services provided by third sector organisations for asylum seekers were therefore provided on a voluntary basis; asylum seekers had a choice over whether to use services and also the extent of their involvement. Choice was generally restricted (e.g. by postcode, language barriers), but it provided individuals with some opportunity of empowerment through active involvement (Parks et al., 1981). Indeed, social welfare services were advertised through the Framework for Dialogue Groups, and, although a large degree of competition was not witnessed, it reflected upon the need to retain service users to ensure funding and therefore the longevity of the services. The provision of choice and information sharing was necessary, according to those providing services, to ensure service user commitment and confidence in their role in service production. This emphasised the strong New Public Management narrative that continues to influence the social welfare services being produced in Scotland.

The availability of channels to complain about services, and particularly statutory care services, was viewed by some as an important and significant conduit for social integration among a highly marginalised group such as asylum seekers. However, there was some scepticism raised in the public administration theory to suggest that consumer mechanisms do not result in the inclusion of marginalised groups (Bolzan and Gale, 2002). Two predominant methods of complaint were uncovered during the research: direct complaints to organisations responsible for service provision or policymaking; and complaints via a mediating organisation that voiced opinions/concerns to public service organisations on the behalf of asylum seekers. Complaints through mediating organisations seemed to be the preferred option for both public service providers and asylum seeker service users. While service providers highlighted a preference for complaints and feedback to be collated, asylum seekers showed some confusion over which organisations were responsible for which services and were therefore unclear of whom to raise complaints with.

There were also various examples of public service organisations obtaining feedback or seeking to formally evaluate the services they provide. Indeed, the majority of public service organisations interviewed said they were doing some form of evaluation. Polarised examples of evaluation emerged from the study, with more or less formalised approaches being used. Some respondents considered regular feedback and evaluation to establish service user input and also ensure services were needs-led. Public service organisations were generally willing to modify the service in line with the service users' feedback and needs, proactively responding to suggestions or to tick a box with funders.

> But again it's regularly reviewed and evaluated so young people can tell us, 'I don't want this, I want less of this and I want more of this'.
> (Young Persons' Organisation Service Manager)

The adult literacy classes at the Development Organisation were evaluated every six to eight weeks. While the front-line tutor recognised that funders wanted 'value for money', he said that evaluation was also conducted to make improvements to the service: 'We don't do happy sheets that are filed away and never looked at again; we do read them and take things on board'. Other service managers also explained that while evaluation was linked to accountability to government funders, there was also a need to be accountable to the rest of the sector and also to promote service improvement.

> if we want to be challenging and we want to think of how we're doing things, and we want to continually be held accountable to . . . by the refugee community and by people who work in the sector to say, 'yeah, this is good, this is bad, improve, get better.'
> (Humanitarian Organisation Service Manager)

Asylum seekers also co-produced during *operational service planning—* as opposed to policymaking where immigration is reserved to the UK government and was, by consequence, out with the realms of co-production for asylum seekers. The third sector was described as more inclined to facilitate participative co-production during operational service planning, but this was also described as challenging. Indeed, respondents from across the public and third sectors spoke of attempting to involve asylum seekers in network planning sessions or board meetings, but mentioned logistical difficulties (e.g. language barriers) and also sometimes the unwillingness of organisations to have asylum seekers contribute. Church A, for example offered various services to asylum seekers, including a craft session for women and an after-school drop-in session for families. The observation of these sessions highlighted that such services were accessed as and when asylum seekers chose. Asylum seeker service users were also encouraged to decide which activities they would participate in during the craft sessions, but were not involved in the operational or strategic planning services at Church A: 'Not here, we don't specifically have asylum seekers and refugees helping to plan things out here' (Church A Service Manager). This was attributed to the informal structure of the service provider and was confirmed by the observations.

The service manager from the Young Person's Organisation also suggested that participative co-production at the strategic level was not feasible. Having participative co-production at the operational level and feeding views back to the strategic level was deemed more appropriate. Although young people had previously sat on the Board of the Partnership, this was no longer the case, primarily due to funding issues but also as the result of specific challenges related to the strategic nature of these needs. The service manager explained that the information being shared and discussed might be inappropriate for asylum seeker young people, who were not always equipped to contribute at this level. Furthermore, strategic players were not always welcoming or willing to listen to young asylum seekers.

> I think some things for a young person to hear first-hand can be quite distressing . . . some young people's level of understanding, and the speed at which some things can take place as well can be quite frustrating.
>
> There are some organisations that are very young person friendly and have an understanding of the value and importance of young people being there. Equally I think there are people who sit round tables and think 'what are these young people doing in here?'
>
> (Young People's Group Service Manager)

Despite this, the service manager was of the view that the core aim of giving young people a voice was still achieved.

> unaccompanied young people's voices are still being heard through other routes and that's been fed into the Board when they've met, within papers and within other documents, within consultation papers and things like that.

Overall, there was some general agreement among service providers that co-production through mechanisms of citizen participation resulted in more personalised services that better met service users' needs. Indeed, the analysis highlights that participative co-production was taking place to differing extents and through three key mechanisms—information provision, consultation and volunteering—which could be usefully positioned in Arnstein's (1969) ladder of participation and the wider discussion of the classical view of co-production forwarded in the public administration literature, in order to understand their impact.

Framework for Dialogue Groups operating throughout the city were used as 'information provision networks'. The analysis showed that although there was potential for the Framework for Dialogue Group structures to be used as consultative mechanisms, providing easy access to a group of asylum seekers, their use seemed to centre strongly on information provision. Although, this sits at the lower end of Arnstein's (1969) ladder, information is still a core element supporting co-construction and participative co-production. Indeed, much of the information provided was about available services, how to access them and opportunities to participate in the service production process; importantly, it was typically conveyed during existing service interactions with front-line public service staff using already established relations to ensure service users' wider needs were met.

Consultation was a key tool utilised by public service organisations, either directly or more typically through the Framework for Dialogue

Group structures and was considered fundamental to service planning: 'What we're saying is you don't develop services for a client group without having clear ways of consulting with that client group' (Charity Service Manager). The case study data suggested that consultation was implemented as a way of promoting integration. For example, one activity detailed in the work plan of the Integration Networks was the provision of a sports and arts programme to integrate young asylum seekers and refugees. Another was to build on links with local schools to promote integration with the indigenous population.

The document analysis found that the term 'consultation' was mentioned as a means of gathering views from asylum seekers, other organisations and the indigenous population. Examples of consultation were also embedded during operational service planning and delivery. Various respondents discussed the issue of providing asylum seekers with a 'voice', whether it is through an organised meeting such as a Residents' Association or by expressing their views via the Framework for Dialogue structures that exist. For example, the Charity used group-based brainstorming events through sticky note exercises in order to gather views on reviewing its organisational strategy during a Framework for Dialogue meeting which was observed. Such an exercise capitalised both on the inseparability of service production and consumption and on the relaxed atmosphere in which public service organisations had established trust with the asylum seekers. Consultation was also used in various formats by the Young Persons' Group to strengthen the voice of the young people and ensure needs were being met. It was a core element of the group's activities, with various organisations using the group as a means of accessing the young people. The analysis also uncovered some novel approaches to consultation, highlighting that it was not confined to a formal written method, but tailored to the group being consulted: 'We've had a talking wall, you know put stuff up and draw bricks on the wall and we've just put post-its up as well' (Young Persons' Group Service Manager).

Interviews with asylum seekers suggested a difference in the extent to which they were consulted by different organisations, or at least their awareness of such mechanisms being used. Indeed, when asked whether organisations such as social work ask for their input to or feedback on services, the respondents responded negatively: 'No, they don't ask'. However, the observation showed otherwise, with an example of a service manager from a public sector organisation consulting to 'get views, opinions and ideas' about how the young people would like to participate in the services provided by the organisation. In this example, the service manager from the Young Persons' Group acted as a mediator between the public sector organisation and the young asylum seekers. Thus, the feeling of not being consulted by public sector organisations might have stronger associations with a lack of understanding of the roles played by organisations, with mediators perhaps unintentionally camouflaging the engagement work conducted by other organisations. The asylum seekers did, however, seem to be more aware of the consultative work conducted by third sector organisations such as the Charity.

The analysis also uncovered volunteering as a vehicle for integration. Volunteering was described by respondents as contributing to wider policy objectives, such as social inclusion and also contributing to personal outcomes (e.g. empowerment), leading to benefits on the social and individual levels. Documents from across the sub-units referred to 'volunteers' or 'volunteering', suggesting that volunteering was a core element of the various organisations' work, whether that be asylum seekers volunteering or the indigenous population. Third Sector organisations invariably provided volunteering opportunities for asylum seekers or encouraged them to volunteer for other organisations delivering public services. Volunteering was considered to lead to a host of benefits for asylum seekers including improving their English language, fostering cultural exchange and giving them a sense of self-worth through engaging with the community, thereby offering a means of integration in line with Ager and Strang's (2008) framework. Asylum seeker volunteers were seen, in some instances, to improve service provision (Ferris, 1988) given their experience and cultural knowledge. Thus, the associated benefits of volunteering were tied to both social integration and service improvement, but volunteering was not confined to service delivery. It was also offered to asylum seekers as a means of retaining a form of economic activity, given that they are prohibited from working for remuneration. The challenge here was the difficulty in getting funding for childcare for female asylum seekers who wanted to volunteer:

> Asylum seekers, without exception, want to work. Volunteering is the next best alternative for them. People who use our services tell us that it is very depressing for them to sit in the house all the time. It is difficult for them if they have no language skills (English) . . . we managed to get some short-term funding that paid for childcare and travel expenses for asylum seekers. In eighteen months we were able to connect 110 people into volunteering opportunities, which in turn enabled them to connect with their new communities. Unfortunately, the funding ended and no more was available. All of the women (98 in total) who were placed into volunteering had to give it up as there was no alternative childcare.
>
> (Survey Respondent)

## Co-design

*Co-design* is based on an integrated view of the two theories. It is not situated in the realm of high-level policymaking or strategic planning, but rather is concerned with deep involvement in the operational design of public services, whereby the knowledge and experience of the service user is valued. A key facet of co-design then is that it builds on the embedded nature of service user involvement during service delivery—co-construction—and extends this through heightened participation. Co-design thus suggests a deeper role for service users during the entire service production process—rather than simply during service delivery as is the case in co-construction—enabling the transformation of services by drawing on the resources and skills or 'sticky' knowledge of *experienced* service users (von Hippel, 1994, 2005; Gronroos and Voima, 2013; Osborne et al., 2016) in order to discover and meet latent needs (Ordanini and Pasini, 2008; Vargo and Lusch, 2008). Their involvement through co-design enables the creation of personalised service experiences and typically involves their long-term, embedded involvement (Prahalad and Ramaswamy, 2004; Vargo and Lusch, 2008). The operationalisation of co-design can take a more embedded form than participative co-production, although its application and impact is still controlled by public service organisations. Co-design may include various forms of service design, but fundamentally it involves a holistic approach where service users' lived experiences are used to develop and innovate services in partnership with public service organisations (Radnor et al., 2014). It therefore involves a user-centred design approach to understand how service users experience a service that extends beyond the service interaction—basis of co-construction—and offers an opportunity for service users to shape the service experience.

Examples of co-design were less frequent compared to other modes but some were uncovered in the case of asylum seekers. The analysis suggests that it exists on a continuum with two clear examples being found that could be described as existing at different ends of the spectrum.

The first was witnessed in the Development Organisation through the provision of adult literacy services. A core goal underpinning this service was the inclusion and integration of asylum seekers; this goal was espoused both at the operational and policy levels. The observation demonstrated the informal and fluid nature of the service, which, although directed by the tutor, was shaped by the contributions of the service users throughout the process of service planning, delivery and evaluation. The service users also contributed to their individual learning plans, to tailor what they would learn and then again during the course of the class, through interactions with the tutor. Afterwards evaluations were undertaken to make improvements to the service, which shows that more than one form of co-production can be employed at any one point in time. One respondent spoke of learner forums that are used in relation to English for Speakers of Other Languages and how they provided asylum seekers with a 'voice': 'the learner forums allow them to voice what they think about the quality, the quantity and what's needed to help them to progress in their learning. It's giving them a voice' (Scottish Government Policymaker).

Another, perhaps more tangible example of co-design, was the provision of a client-led Orientation Service by the Humanitarian Organisation, which was planned and executed on an individual level. The aim of the service was to 'help asylum seekers with the integration process'. In this case, asylum seeker service users played a more active role than in the previous example, again suggesting that co-design exists on a continuum of service user activeness. The service delivered by the Humanitarian Organisation was based on the idea that asylum seekers were experts in their own lives and therefore in a position to make important contributions to the service. This suggests that asylum seeker service users were regarded as valuable resources through their possession of sticky knowledge about their own needs and experiences and that this could be used as an important contribution to the innovation and customisation of the services being designed and delivered (von Hippel, 1998).

In this service, the needs of the asylum seeker shaped the service, and the interactions between the asylum seeker and caseworker were crucial to tailoring the service to individual needs, highlighting the importance of the service interaction and co-construction as the basis of co-design. There was a focus on fostering asylum seeker independence in a supportive way rather than dictating their needs. The caseworkers were typically volunteers who had been granted refugee status and were therefore considered well placed to provide support as they had experienced the hardships of the asylum process. Working on a one-to-one basis was considered to provide fertile ground for a relationship to develop, which in turn led to greater information sharing by both parties and therefore better equipped the caseworker to facilitate the meeting of asylum seeker needs. Such an approach placed service users in a central role in the service innovation process as co-designers, while the caseworker facilitated them through service interactions in uncovering and satisfying latent need:

> We call it . . . non-directional advocacy, so you can advocate on behalf of somebody . . . it's assisting someone who can't quite make their point, not going . . . into a meeting and saying 'She needs this, she needs that'. It is about that person saying I would like this service.
> (Humanitarian Organisation Service Manager)

### Challenges of Asylum Seeker Co-production

The analysis also uncovered various challenges for each of the modes of co-production. In terms of *co-construction*, considerable emphasis is placed on public service staff recognising the involvement of service users during service interactions or the 'moment of truth'. This has significant implications for how public service production is understood and managed and requires a shift from the product-dominant view that has traditionally characterised public service management (Osborne et al., 2013). This shift further implies that the role of front-line staff is critical, not in creating co-construction—as it is inherent to service production—but rather in creating a positive service experience during interactions (Osborne and Strokosch, 2013; Osborne et al., 2015; Skalen et al., 2018). This is a significant challenge for public service organisations, particularly during a time of increasing financial difficulties and already increasing workloads among public service staff. The emphasis of co-construction as the creation of a positive service experience may therefore exert further pressure on already burdened front-line staff. In the case of asylum seekers, language barriers, a potential aversion or fear of professionals and a preoccupation with their claims for asylum may make it even more difficult for public service staff to build, develop and manage trusting relationships that are likely to support co-construction. A clear example of this was found in the case of Church A, which noted the challenge in engaging effectively with male members of the community where cultural differences caused an indifference to accessing the services intended for integration.

The analysis highlights three distinct challenges for the operationalisation of the classic view of *participative co-production*. First, there was a belief among a few respondents that public services required professional management. Associated to this, there were suggestions that extending the role of the service user was not warranted because of their lack of experience or understanding of the service production process, a suggestion that was also made in the public administration literature (Percy, 1983; Verschuere et al., 2012). For example, in the case of the Young Persons' Group, professional support was considered imperative to the effective delivery of services and, although asylum seekers had previously contributed to the Board, some organisational representatives did not welcome such an approach. This is perhaps indicative of the presence of a service user-provider dichotomy, where the professionals retain power and control over the process of service production (Bolzan and Gale, 2002). This can be contrasted with the work of von Hippel (1998) who argues that service users can possess 'sticky information' which professionals do not hold and therefore have an important contribution to make in terms of service innovation and customisation. Other staff comments also reflected the professional ambivalence to co-production, arguing that it was not always appropriate for asylum seekers to be directly involved in decision-making at a strategic level, either because they were not equipped for this level of involvement or because these strategic issues were deemed inappropriate for discussion with asylum seekers as service users. This was also discussed in the theory, where it was suggested that professionals might resent or resist the inclusion of untrained and inexperienced service users in the public service production process (Pestoff, 2006; Bovaird, 2007). This suggests that a cultural change is necessary, which would shift the perception of public service users from 'lay people' to experts in their own lives and of their own experiences of services (von Hippel, 1994).

Second, the theory suggested that public service organisations and asylum seeker service users may not have the time or inclination to co-produce through participative mechanisms (Osborne et al., 2002; Lowndes et al., 2006; Bovaird, 2007). Logistical challenges were also associated with having a dialogue with asylum seeker service users, particularly given that multiple interpreters can be party during group consultations, which made for long and convoluted discussions. Participative co-production was also challenging for public service organisations because asylum seekers were deemed to have a lack of trust in authorities and had a perceived poor understanding of the democratic system operating in the UK. The most commonly espoused concern was related to the negative impact involvement might have upon a claim for asylum:

> I could say that the Home Office could prevent me from saying something.
>
> (Asylum Seeker)

> Asylum seekers are very wary of doing anything that will jeopardize their claim.
>
> (Accommodation Provider Strategic Manager)

These challenges suggest that the success of co-production rests strongly on the willingness and inclination of service managers and front-line staff (Gaster and Rutqvist, 2000; Boyle et al., 2006) to implement and facilitate co-production. They further suggest—in line with the survey data and previous research—that participative co-production can be overly time-consuming and resource-intensive for public service organisations (Martin and Boaz, 2000).

Language barriers and asylum seekers' focus on their own asylum cases and personal aspirations (e.g. education) were also frequently mentioned barriers to co-producing beyond co-construction. Although various community mechanisms were in place to facilitate wider consultation among the indigenous population about public services, respondents recognised that asylum seekers did not engage with such mechanisms. This finding suggests that, as Bovaird (2007) highlights, the participative and appended nature of co-production, may be more suited to well-off sections of society. Respondents also suggested that there were two potential reasons for this: the mechanisms needed to be tailored to asylum seekers as a particular group, through the provision of interpreters for example; and the focus of asylum seekers was invariably upon their own individual needs rather than those of the wider service or indeed, broader social objectives.

Although the asylum seekers who participated in the study were largely keen to speak up about the services they received—'Nothing would stop me voicing my opinion'—there was some concern that views would not be listened to, highlighting the issue around tokenistic forms of engagement that is facilitated by participative co-production and this forms the third challenge for this mode. Various respondents expressed the need to provide genuine opportunities for asylum seekers to have their voices heard, rather than offering tokenistic forms of involvement. Church B's service manager talked about asylum seekers' 'right to participate' in order for them to have ownership over the services they are using: 'You want them to own it, as being theirs. . . . I mean otherwise you're just imposing things on people and you're not actually giving them the dignity of making their own decisions'. However, the observation of the craft group at Church B provided contrary evidence to the description provided by the service manager. Although there were opportunities for the participants to decide on the format of the group, these were sometimes relatively tokenistic, when the views of service users were discounted by the service manager, who exercised ultimate control over the format of the sessions. Another asylum seeker also noted the fear that their participation would make limited impact: 'when we started, I felt that what we're going to say about it is just going to be thrown in the bin. It's not important for people'. In the traditional linear model of participative co-production, public service staff exert control and power over the nature and impact of participative co-production. Public service users, as a result, have few opportunities to negotiate the meeting of their needs, being recipients of professionally predefined and delivered services. Bolzan and Gale (2002) argue that professionals act as gatekeepers, controlling access to resources, with front-line staff responsible for managing resources and balancing them against need. The disadvantage placed before asylum seekers is made more acute by the marginalised position of this population and their status as non-citizens throws their ability and role in co-production into stark relief.

The application of *co-design*, through the embedded participation of asylum seekers was sparse, suggesting that, as a form of co-production, it was perhaps too difficult to apply in practice or that service providers were unwilling to embed such forms of participation. Indeed, channelling the knowledge and resources of service users can be challenging and depends upon continuous and equal dialogue between the service user and provider (Prahalad and Ramaswamy, 2000). The analysis of the Humanitarian Organisation's service suggested that allowing service users to shape their own services was dependent upon the development of a close but professional relationship of trust. The respondents from the Humanitarian Organisation discussed the importance of promoting trust within the service relationship; this was considered to be of particular importance given the vulnerability of the group. A core aim of the Orientation Service offered by the Humanitarian Organisation, for instance, was to foster a one-to-one relationship based on trust in order to 'help them with the integration process' (Humanitarian Organisation Service Manager). However, building trust was also perceived as a significant challenge for public service organisations particularly given the marginalised nature of asylum seekers.

> At our first meeting they don't tell you everything but as you give them another appointment, another appointment, another appointment they come out and they tell you. So by that time, you know exactly where you're going to refer them, what they are going through. . . . Just give them time to get used to the idea and begin to trust you.
>
> (Humanitarian Organisation Frontline)

Furthermore, the asylum seeker community was described as transient, particularly now with the New Asylum Seeker Model where decisions are taken within six weeks. Thus, there is less time for public service organisations to set-up and develop dialogue with service users. Furthermore, the discussion has suggested that the dominant narratives of public service reform have typically positioned public service users as 'lay people' whose expertise and knowledge of their own needs and experiences are not sufficiently valued (Pollitt and Bouckaert, 2004) and this is likely to have implications for the extent to which co-design is initiated and embedded. Furthermore, the position of asylum seekers as public service users is also compounded by the fact that they have limited social, economic and legal rights, which limits their right to participation beyond co-construction.

## Summary: Asylum Seekers and Social Welfare Services in Scotland

The findings from this chapter have helped to map the nature and extent of asylum seeker co-production. The status of asylum seekers as noncitizens prevents their engagement at the UK policymaking level. Indeed, asylum seekers were generally described as 'powerless', with immigration legislation and policies restricting their capacity to contribute to civic life. The analysis identified, however, clear differences in approaches to asylum seekers in Scotland compared to England. Social inclusion through integration was a key example of this; asylum seekers were encouraged to integrate as soon as they arrive in Glasgow, as opposed to England where they must first receive refugee status. This is in line with the Scottish government's objective to maintain the population and to maintain any skill that exists within the asylum seeker population which may aid the economy in the future. However, the Scottish government was also described as being in a relatively powerless position when it comes to immigration policy and legislation. Thus, it has no say over asylum cases, nor the granting of asylum.

The goal of integration underpinned the majority of the services explored in this Scottish case study. As *public service users* of social welfare services, examples of asylum seeker co-production during public service delivery and design were uncovered. The results from the data confirmed the idea that social welfare service providers are not facilitating a single type of involvement, but rather involve asylum seekers at different times during the service production process and through different mechanisms. It also highlighted the proposition made in the service management theory that the service interaction or 'moment of truth' was a critical site of service user involvement. The fact that co-construction is integral to the process nature of services is critical to the debate. The analysis confirms the existence of co-construction, which results from the inseparability of the production and consumption of services and, hence, the integral role of the service user at the 'moment of truth' (Normann, 1991). Asylum seekers were also found to co-produce through various mechanisms of participative co-production of which feedback, consultation and choice were the most prominent. Essentially then, in line with the theory, participative co-production was found to take place both through mechanisms of consumer and citizen participation. Examples of co-design were also found but were evidenced less frequently.

This chapter has also discussed the challenges of each of the modes of co-production in the case of asylum seekers and highlighted that although co-construction is an intrinsic dimension of the service interaction, its success in terms of meeting need is reliant on its effective management by front-line public service staff. The potential for co-construction to be extended, particularly through co-design, is also reliant on the management of the service relationship and importantly the re-positioning of public service users as experienced and knowledgeable resources that can contribute to service improvement and innovation.

# References

Ager, A. and Strang, A. (2008). Understanding integration: a conceptual framework. *Journal of Refugee Studies*. (21,2), 166–191.
Arnstein, S. A. (1969). A ladder of citizen participation? *Journal of the American Institute of Planners*. (35,2), 216–224.
Bolzan, N. and Gale, F. (2002). The citizenship of excluded groups: challenging the consumerist agenda. *Social Policy and Administration*. (36,4), 363–375.
Bovaird, T. (2007). Beyond engagement and participation—user and community co-production of public services. *Public Administration Review*. (67), 846–860.
Bovaird, T. (2009). Strategic management in public sector organisations. In Bovaird, T. and Loeffler, E. (eds.), *Public management and governance* (2nd ed.) London: Routledge.

Boyle, D., Clark, S. and Burns, S. (2006). *Hidden work: co-production by people outside paid employment*. York: Joseph Rowntree Foundation.

Cemlyn, S. and Briskman, L. (2003). Asylum, children's rights and social work. *Child and Family Social Work*. (8), 163–178.

Choules, K. (2006). Globally privileged citizenship. *Race, Ethnicity and Education*. (9,3), 275–293.

Dunston, R., Lee, A., Boud, D., Brodie, P. and Chiarella, M. (2009). Co-production and health system reform—from re-imagining to re-making. *The Australian Journal of Public Administration*. (68,1), 39–52.

Ferris, J. M. (1988). The use of volunteers in public service production: some demand and supply considerations. *Social Science Quarterly*. (6,9), 3–23.

Gaster, L. and Rutqvist, H. (2000). Changing the 'front line' to meet citizen needs. *Local Government Studies*. (26,2), 53–70.

Glushko, R. J. and Tabas, L. (2009). Designing service systems by bridging the 'front stage' and 'back stage'. *Information System E-business Management*. (7), 407–427.

Greener, I. (2007). Choice or voice? Introduction to the themed section. *Social Policy and Society*. (7,2), 197–200.

Gronroos, C. (2007). *Service management and marketing: customer management in service competition* (3rd ed.). Chichester: John Wiley & Sons.

Gronroos, C. (2009). Marketing as promise management: regaining customer management for marketing. *Journal of Business and Industrial Marketing*. (24,5), 351–359.

Gronroos, C. and Voima, P. (2013). Critical service logic: making sense of value creation and co-creation. *Journal of the Academy of Marketing Science*. (41,2),133–150.

Gummesson, E. (1998). Implementation requires a relationship marketing paradigm. *Journal of the Academy of Marketing Science*. (26,2), 242–249.

Haikio, L. (2010). The diversity of citizenship and democracy in local management reform. *Public Management Review*. (12,3), 363–384.

Johnston, R. and Clark, G. (2008). *Service operations management: improving service delivery*. Harlow: Prentice Hall.

Jung, T. (2010). Citizens, co-producers, customers, clients, captives? A critical review of consumerism and public services. *Public Management Review*. (12,3), 439–446.

Levine, C. and Fisher, G. (1984). Citizenship and service delivery: the promise of co-production. *Public Administration Review*. (44), 178–189.

Lovelock, C. H. and Young, R. F. (1979). Look to consumers to increase productivity. *Harvard Business Review*. (57, May–June), 168–178.

Lowndes, V., Pratchett, L. and Stoker, G. (2006). Local political participation: the impact of rules-in-use. *Public Administration*. (84,3), 539–561.

Martin, S. and Boaz, A. (2000). Public participation and citizen-centred local government: lessons from the best value and better government for older people pilot programmes. *Public Money and Management*. (April–June), 47–53.

Nankervis, A. (2005). *Managing services*. Cambridge: Cambridge University Press.

Normann, R. (1991). *Service management: strategy and leadership in service business* (2nd ed.). West Sussex: John Wiley & Sons.

Ordanini, A. and Pasini, P. (2008). Service co-production and value co-creation: the case for a service-orientated architecture (SOA). *European Management Journal*. (26), 289–297.

Osborne, S. P., Beattie, R. and Williamson, A. (2002). *Community involvement in rural regeneration partnerships in the UK*. Bristol: Policy Press.

Osborne, S. P., Radnor, Z., Kinder, T. and Vidal, I. (2015). The SERVICE framework: a public-service-dominant approach to sustainable public services. *British Journal of Management*. (26,3), 424–438.

Osborne, S. P., Radnor, Z. and Nasi, G. (2013). A new theory for public service management? Toward a (Public) service dominant approach. *American Review of Public Administration*. (43,2), 135–158.

Osborne, S. P., Radnor, Z. and Strokosch, K. (2016). Co-production and the co-creation of value in public service: a suitable case for treatment? *Public Management Review*. (18,5), 639–653.

Osborne, S. P. and Strokosch, K. (2013). It takes two to tango? Understanding the co-production of public services by integrating the service management and public administration perspectives. *British Journal of Management*. (24), S31–S47.

Parks, R. B., Baker, P. C., Kiser, L., Oakerson, R., Ostrom, E., Ostrom, V., Percy, S. L., Vandivort, M. B., Whitaker, G. P. and Wilson, R. (1981). Consumers as co-producers of public services: some economic and institutional considerations. *Policy Studies Journal*. (9,7), 1001–1011.

Percy, S. (1983). Citizen participation in the co-production of urban services. *Urban Affairs Quarterly*. (19,4), 431–446.

Pestoff, V. (2006). Citizens and co-production of welfare services. *Public Management Review*. (8,4), 503–519.

Pestoff, V. (2014). Collective action and the sustainability of co-production. *Public Management Review*. (16,3), 383–401.

Pollitt, C. and Bouckaert, G. (2004). *Public management reform: a comparative analysis*. Oxford: Oxford University Press.

Prahalad, C. K. and Ramaswamy, V. (2000). Co-opting customer competence. *Harvard Business Review*. (January–February), 79–87.

Prahalad, C. K. and Ramaswamy, V. (2004). Co-creation experiences: the next practice in value creation. *Journal of Interactive Marketing*. (18,3), 5–14.

Radnor, Z., Osborne, S. P., Kinder, T. and Mutton, J. (2014). Operationalising co-production in public services delivery: the contribution of service blueprinting. *Public Management Review*. (16,3), 402–423.

Skalen, P., Karlsson, J., Engen, M. and Magnuson, P. R. (2018). Understanding public service innovation as resource integration and creation of value propositions. *Australian Journal of Public Administration*. (77,4), 700–714.

Vargo, S. L. and Lusch, R. F. (2008). Service-dominant logic: continuing the evolution. *Journey of the Academy of Marketing Science*. (36), 1–10.

Verschuere, B., Brandsen, T. and Pestoff, V. (2012). Co-production: the state of the art in research and the future agenda. *Voluntas*. (23,4), 1083–1101.

von Hippel, E. (1994). Sticky information and the locus of problem solving: implications for innovation. *Management Science*. (40,4), 429–439.

von Hippel, E. (1998). Economics of product development by users: the impact of 'sticky' local information. *Management Science*. (44,5), 629–644.

von Hippel, E. (2005). *Democratizing innovation*. Cambridge: MIT Press.

Whitaker, G. P. (1980). Coproduction: citizen participation in service delivery. *Public Administration Review*. (May–June), 240–246.

Williams, L. (2006). Social networks of refuges in the United Kingdom: tradition, tactics and new community spaces. *Journal of Ethnic and Migration Studies*. (32,5), 865–879.

Wren, K. (2007). Supporting asylum seekers and refugees in Glasgow: the role of multi-agency networks. *Journal of Refugee Studies*. (20,3), 391–413.

# 8 Understanding Organisational Modes of Co-production Through the Empirical Case of Asylum Seekers in Glasgow

## Abstract

This chapter explores the nature and extent to which inter-organisational relationships took place through co-management and co-governance in the case of asylum seekers and social welfare services in Glasgow. It presents data to show that organisational forms of co-production are operating in practice, with organisations from across sectors collaborating together through individual partnerships and broader networks. Through relationships of co-management and co-governance, third sector organisations are understood as playing a leading role in the planning and delivery of public services. The discussion also points to the importance of personal relationships that existed between staff working across organisational boundaries and which facilitated both types of inter-organisational working. Although this is not to say that relationships of co-management and co-governance operated without friction; they were facilitated by the support of sufficiently trained and capable service staff, who had time to build relationships and had trust in one another.

## Introduction

The previous chapter revealed the existence of individual modes of co-production, despite the marginalised position afforded to asylum seekers as a result of their non-citizen status and the powerful influence of policies of deterrence that shape their social and economic rights. This chapter will broaden the discussion to consider the inter-organisational relationships that are operating within the case of asylum seeker social welfare service provision in Glasgow. It commences with an examination of the role of the third sector emphasising its role as mediator, collaborator during social welfare service design and delivery and also advocator of the rights of asylum seekers living in Scotland. It then explores the nature and extent to which inter-organisational relationships took place through co-management and co-governance with evidence from the case study research. Chapter 8 then concludes with an examination of the factors enabling inter-organisational relationships and also the challenges that have obstructed its effective operationalisation in the case of social welfare services for asylum seekers.

## The Importance of the Third Sector

### Working With the Third Sector

Asylum seekers' public services have already been described as having a strong foundation within the third sector (Wren, 2007) and the results of the empirical study add further weight to this argument. Respondents commented that although the City of Glasgow was ill prepared for the arrival of asylum seekers in 2000, the support of the third sector was key to the provision of appropriate and effective social welfare services. Over time, the third sector had established into a key service provider, partner for the public sector and advocate lobbying on behalf of asylum seekers.

In the document analysis voluntary organisations, charities, community organisations and third sector were mentioned on thirty-four occasions in total. This reflected the environment within which social welfare services for asylum seekers were designed and delivered. However, that is not to say that statutory agencies and the government were not mentioned. The analysis highlighted the fundamental role played by the Government Agency in policymaking around immigration and the documentation confirmed the role of the Scottish government in promoting integration. Nevertheless, the strong role of the third sector in service provision has caused the boundaries between third sector and statutory sector service provision to become increasingly blurred (Sales, 2002). Indeed, Wren's (2007) research and the empirical findings suggest confusion among asylum seekers over which organisations were responsible and accountable for public services. There was also some suspicion from asylum seekers regarding the role of service providers such as the Accommodation Provider, which was associated with their fear of the Home Office and the potential that any information they shared would impact their application for asylum and therefore their likelihood to remain in the country. This was often described by respondents as resulting in a reluctance among asylum seekers to develop relationships or share information with organisations that would enable the better meeting of their needs.

The third sector offered various services to asylum seekers living in Glasgow, including information, advice, counselling, training, empowerment initiatives and, in some instances, campaigning. A majority (83.3%) of survey respondents said that they worked with third sector organisations when providing services to asylum seekers, including Glasgow Housing Association, the YMCA, Scottish Refugee Council and Community Groups such as Red Road Women's Centre. Of those, 31% said they did so during the development of policies, 78.6% said they did so during service delivery and 47.6% said they involved third sector organisations after service delivery.

Respondents were also asked to describe their relationships with third sector organisations: two thirds said they worked in partnerships (61.9%) but networks followed at 50%. Interestingly, only 9.5% of organisations described their relationship with third sector organisations as contractual. The responses are shown in Table 8.1. The majority of respondents said they worked with third sector organisations through informal communications (76.2%) and formal meetings (73.8%) (see Table 8.2)

The role of the third sector was generally viewed positively by survey respondents. Two thirds of all questionnaire respondents agreed to some extent that third sector organisations represented asylum seekers' needs. A similar percentage of respondents agreed to some extent that involving third sector organisations was a cost-effective approach in service provision. Furthermore, the majority of respondents (78.2%) disagreed to some extent with the following statement: 'there is no added value gained from involving third sector organisations in producing services'. Finally, almost two thirds agreed that 'the effective delivery of services was dependent on the involvement of third sector organisations'.

## Role of the Third Sector

Third sector organisations were overwhelmingly described as playing a significant role in specialist expertise and service provision to asylum seekers in Scotland, particularly by respondents working in strategic

*Table 8.1* Nature of relationships with third sector organisations

| Type of relationship with third sector organisation | Frequency | Percentage |
|---|---|---|
| Partnership | 26 | 61.9% |
| Contractual | 4 | 9.5% |
| Part of a network | 21 | 50% |

N.B. eight counts (19%) of missing data

*Table 8.2* Types of third sector organisation involvement

| Types of third sector organisation involvement | Frequency | Percentage |
|---|---|---|
| Informal conversations | 32 | 76.2% |
| Formal meetings | 31 | 73.8% |
| Consultation | 22 | 52.4% |
| Community meetings | 25 | 59.5% |

N.B. seven counts (16.7%) of missing data

positions. The case study clearly demonstrated three roles for the third sector during the planning and delivery of social welfare services for asylum seekers in Scotland: mediator, collaborator and advocator. The examples presented in the proceeding analysis emphasise that the role of third sector was not simply to fill gaps in public service provision— although the research identified this as a significant role of the sector— but was also to operate within a wider service system and satisfy the various needs of the asylum seeker community in Glasgow.

The third sector was invariably described as playing a key role in creating dialogue between asylum seekers and both public service organisations and policymakers, through the role of *mediator* (Berger and Neuhaus, 1978). Indeed, third sector organisations were often described as sitting between service providers/policymakers and asylum seekers:

> This would probably come through Citizen's Advice, Refugee Council and those kinds of support forums. I think the advantage of doing it in that . . . it's not just one person asking us.
>
> (Government Agency)

When asked whether they represented asylum seekers to public service providers, over half of respondents responded positively (54.8%). The majority of these respondents agreed to some extent (86.52%) that their knowledge of asylum seekers was 'valued' by service providers. A similar proportion (82.59%) also agreed to some extent that 'Service providers listen to what I have to say because I'm acting on behalf of service users'. Nearly two thirds of respondents (65.52%) disagreed to some extent with the following statement: 'Service providers don't act on the advice I give them'. Finally, 82.6% of respondents in this section agreed to some extent that 'Asylum seeker voices are represented by the organisation I work for'. The case study also showed high regard for third sector organisations among policymakers who generally viewed them as adding value to public services and contributing to their effectiveness. The overwhelming argument was that the third sector played a fundamental role in creating dialogue between asylum seekers and public service providers/ policymakers through a position of trust.

> People who . . . are quite vulnerable and might not necessarily trust the state or indeed the private sector. But the third sector can actually effectively reach out to these people and can transform their lives, and have an effective track record of being able to do that.
>
> (Scottish Government Policymaker)

Through their role as service provider and mediator, third sector organisations were described as occupying a prime position through which they could foster trust and co-operation. In particular, the view of the Charity among other third sector organisations was overwhelmingly positive. Respondents were generally at pains to explain the importance of the Charity's role as mediator (Berger and Neuhaus, 1978) due to their close links and knowledge of asylum seekers in Glasgow. The Charity was viewed as supporting the inclusion of asylum seekers and refugee and community organisations. It was portrayed as a key link in the chain, bonding organisations on the ground with strategic players: '[The Charity] are very involved with the Government . . . we get information back and that information that our group gathers gets fed back through that structure as well' (Young Person's Group). Notwithstanding their fundamental role, the Charity was also noticed to be a powerful organisation with strong links with the Scottish government and the wider third sector. Thus, although this was not directly evidenced in terms of service production, the Charity could also potentially play the role of disabler, by steering the agenda to its own accord rather in reflection of the needs of service users (Brenton, 1985; Pestoff et al., 2006). As a mediating structure, the Charity was able to include asylum seekers as a marginal group in service production who may or may not have the capacity to articulate their own needs (Kearns, 1995; Haugh and Kitson, 2007).

The Charity was also a key player in establishing the Framework for Dialogue structures and also expended time and energy ensuring asylum seekers contributed to its own strategic objectives as an organisation. The role of the Charity, in particular, was described by policy respondents and service managers alike as crucial to participative co-production, offering a platform through which asylum seekers could be consulted and their views fed back to strategic players. The Scottish government, for example, did not tend to engage with asylum seekers directly, instead funding the Charity and other third sector organisations to provide services to asylum seekers and capitalising on their closeness to asylum seekers and the trust they had built up through service relationships which enabled them to gather their views. One policy respondent described her role as one of co-ordination and said that any other departments that were thinking about altering any policies affecting asylum seekers would be advised to contact the Charity before doing so (Scottish Government Policymaker). As such, there was an expectation that the Charity would have the appropriate structures in place to consult asylum seekers. One such important platform funded by the Scottish government was the Framework for Dialogue Groups that were established to consult asylum seekers through third sector organisations. The Framework for Dialogue Groups were described as providing 'a refugee/asylum seeker voice in the assessment of need process and the development of service bids' (Charity Manager). This structure provided a means through which asylum seekers could raise any issues with services to those sitting in more strategic positions.

> So what you've got now on the basic level is people who get together on a neighbourhood level and they can in some cases take issues up to service level locally or at a bigger level. And they can take issues up with government in various ways, both at the Scottish level and the Westminster level.
>
> (Charity Manager)

A Scottish Refugee Policy Forum had also been constituted during the time of the empirical research and its primary role was to lobby MPs, MSPs and the Home Office around issues pertinent to asylum seekers in Scotland. The forum could also be used for policymakers in the Scottish government to consult asylum seekers, although respondents admitted that this had not been done (Scottish Government Policymaker). A fundamental aim of the Scottish Refugee Policy Forum was one of capacity building, to 'provide asylum seekers and refugees with a direct voice' (Scottish Government Policymaker). It was established by the Charity and was composed of various refugee community organisations, which meant the views of asylum seekers could be easily accessed. It also had links into the Framework for Dialogue structures and Integration Networks which existed across the city and were attended by various organisations providing services to asylum seekers to plan services through a collaborative approach.

The case study also emphasised the *collaborative* role of the third sector in Scotland, with third sector organisations typically being described as partners of government. The geographical landscape was repeatedly described as making Scotland conducive to inter-organisational working, as were the structures that had developed since the initial dispersal of asylum seekers, and working together was also thought to prevent duplication and result in service improvements. Asylum seekers and refugee services were well established in Glasgow, within the confines of the regulations and laws coming out from the UK government, which made it easier for organisations to work together. Respondents suggested that there was less need for wrangling over substantive issues because agencies from both the public and third sectors had a history of working together and had laid the foundations of asylum seeker and refugee services down together.

Comparisons to England were made often when the issue of partnership working was discussed; due to the geography of Scotland, being a relatively small area and having asylum seekers housed mainly in the City of Glasgow, rather than spread through the many Boroughs of London, partnership working was considered easier north of the border. Various respondents also mentioned a Scottish mindset towards, and history of, partnership working when asked about their relationships with other organisations (e.g. Scottish government Policymaker, Accommodation Provider Strategic Manager). Collaborative relationships were uncovered both during service delivery where organisations worked together to support the delivery process by sharing resources and information, but also existed at a strategic level where organisations worked together to engage with asylum seekers to feed into service planning. For example, respondents spoke of the network approach that has been established in Glasgow through Community Planning Partnerships, where partners from across sectors worked together to engage service users.

> individual agencies engage with a particular client group and then two months later a different agency will engage with the same client group. . . . And all that does is confuse the client group. So we're a partnership, so we are insisting on collective engagement. . . . And that hopefully will . . . reduce the amount of engagement but will strengthen the quality of engagement.
>
> (Community Planning Partnership)

All Community Planning Partners signed up to partnership working where part of this commitment involved effective community engagement. Thus, there was an expectation on partners that they would engage with the community that they served: 'So partners are increasingly engaging through neighbourhood initiatives, engaging with communities around their priorities and delivering services or shaping the services around those priorities' (Community Planning Partnership). Here, the emphasis was not on engaging asylum seekers specifically, but all disadvantaged groups within the community, as well as the third sector organisations that advocated on their behalf or provided services. Nevertheless, there was some discussion from respondents over whether asylum seekers should be considered a distinct group or mainstreamed under the broader category of race. Some respondents said the categorisation promoted a more integrated approach to service planning and delivery: 'you need to bring together where there are common issues and try and strengthen their voice' (Community Planning Partnership). However, others questioned this approach and cautioned the grouping of asylum seekers with migrants and established ethnic minority groups, arguing that each have distinctive needs which would make it difficult to plan and deliver blanket services (Charity Service Manager).

In documentation from the Young Persons' Group, 'partnership' was used to describe the set-up of the group. However, the analysis also highlighted the broad aims of the Young Persons' Group: to engage with other organisations, influence the policy and practice of partners and create innovative approaches through 'partnership'.

> The Social Inclusion Partnership was not designed to be directly involved with service delivery. It set out to influence the policy and practice of its partners and to link into existing agencies which

provided services to care leavers. By linking into existing partner-ships and joint planning frameworks, there was a greater opportu-nity for the innovative approaches that were developed to become part of the mainstream activities of partners.

Partnership was also referenced on the operational level, during the deliv-ery of services; for example, the Framework for Dialogue Groups dis-cussed the partnership between the Charity and Scottish government to support public service delivery. In the Humanitarian Organisation docu-ments, reference to 'partnership' tends to be associated with joint proj-ects or services and is also related to making improvements to services and the asylum system. Church B referred to 'partnerships' with local organisations. Working 'together' was used as a way of describing the partnership approach in Scotland (e.g. the Humanitarian Organisation). Documentation from the Integration Network confirmed that partner-ship working was also conducted around the planning of services locally.

Policymakers and service managers alike discussed the benefits of part-nership working and two such advantages were avoiding duplication of work or over-engagement. Indeed, there was a feeling among respon-dents that time was limited and the focus should be on delivering high quality services that meet asylum seekers' needs. Respondents also noted that although participative co-production was important, asylum seek-ers could suffer from consultation fatigue should all organisations try to engage them on similar issues and therefore a unified approach should be taken. Respondents also considered the consequences for their business and sustainability of working together, not simply whether there will be positive implications for the service users. Reduced public spending was also identified as a trigger for increased partnership working, which one policy respondent suggested was likely to result in bigger contracts from government bodies which the third sector could only effectively compete for through collaborative working. However, respondents also noted the associated challenges of bringing contracts together, particularly with regards to the implications for service quality:

> often the smaller the contract then the more personalised the level of service. So if you are bringing contracts together, you should be very, very careful of that, treating them in such a way that doesn't have a negative impact on the quality of the service
>
> (Scottish Government Policymaker)

Nevertheless, the same respondent argued that collaborative working between the for-profit sector and third sector could also draw on the benefits that typically characterise each sector 'because you can get some of the economies of scale that the private sector are perhaps able to deliver, but with some of the personalisation of services that you get with the third sector' (Scottish Government Policymaker). Third sector organisations which collaborated with for-profit organisations were described as adopting 'more business-like ways of operating' while maintaining the core social benefit that they wish to deliver at the heart of their business. This suggests the idea of mimetic isomorphism that was forwarded by DiMaggio and Powell (1983), whereby third sector organisations model themselves on their 'more successful' counterparts in order to win contracts. The challenge is, nevertheless, that they may lose their unique characteristics and particularly their 'closeness' to service users which enables them to deliver personalised services (Pifer, 1967; Bode, 2006).

Although respondents suggested they did less work around *advocacy* than when asylum seekers had first come to Glasgow, there was still a place for advocacy and larger third sector organisations generally sat in a good position to raise concerns or lobby. The Charity, Humanitarian Organisation and Woman's Voluntary Organisation, for example, played multiple roles; they delivered services, contributed to service planning and worked on an adversarial basis to represent asylum seekers and campaign on their behalf. Respondents said that they worked to ensure that asylum seekers received appropriate services from public sector organisations and that structures were in place for integration. The Humanitarian Organisation, for example, provided an orientation service which was described as a 'key refugee service, which provides one to one volunteer support to asylum seekers or refugees to help them with the integration process, to help them to access statutory services' (Humanitarian Organisation).

Larger third sector organisations, in particular, were generally described as occupying a good position to raise concerns or lobby against issues despite this strong undercurrent of joint working. Indeed, various third sector organisations played a dual role, managing services and working on an adversarial basis to represent asylum seekers and campaign on their behalf around issues of immigration and for improved services. The perception around this adversarial role differed among respondents. Some public officials described this role as: 'Not helpful, not productive because this is an ideal opportunity for them, literally, to get up on their soapbox'. Others considered it to result in more fruitful discussions which led to awareness and understanding of the landscape and parameters within which different organisations were working, as long as the role was played in a professional way; feet stamping and making demands was not appropriate.

> when you go into a meeting now and somebody gets up and starts to rail against the Borders Agency and the Government and you now kind of look at them and go, really? You're talking nonsense. If you are a refugee in Glasgow and you want support and access in

education, it's there. If you want support and access in employment, it's there. If you want support in improving integration, it's there.

(Humanitarian Organisation)

Gathering evidence and contributing to negotiations was deemed the way forward. There was a strong suggestion in the research that well established third sector organisations were in a position to collate the needs of asylum seekers as a community and discuss these with strategic players and policymakers. However, the dual role of service provision and advocacy was also regarded as challenging in some cases:

> I think sometimes there's been a bit of role confusion, because if somebody acts as a provider of a service and, if you like, takes the Prime Minister's shilling, if you like, then they are part of, like it or not, an operational partnership . . . And then if an organisation stands back and then criticizes that, it can be difficult.
>
> (Accommodation Provider Strategic Manager)

The Charity played a central role, not only sitting on the Integration Networks, but also being funded directly by the Scottish government to provide services to and consult with asylum seekers. It also played a key adversarial role, working directly with asylum seekers (providing services and representing their needs to others) and lobbying the Government Agency around issues of immigration policy that are pertinent to asylum seekers. The Charity had strong links with organisations such as the Accommodation Provider and Humanitarian Organisation. Both of these organisations also sat on the Migration Network and therefore contributed on a strategic level with others like the Charity, Scottish government and Government Agency (co-governance). The Scottish Refugee Policy Forum (SPRF), which represented refugee community organisations, also fed in at the strategic level and benefited from links to the Framework for Dialogue structures.

## Inter-organisational Relationships: Co-management and Co-governance

This research evidenced in line with Osborne (2006) and Klijn (2008) that hierarchies, markets and networks co-exist. In the case of asylum seekers, immigration policies were determined by central government and as such, hierarchy prevailed with strict control placed upon asylum seekers' status and entitlement, which was regulated by the Home Office. Despite this centralised control, services were delivered both by the public sector organisations and third sector organisations who competed for government contracts in the market, but also worked together in partnerships and networks, on various levels, to plan and deliver services. Indeed, the empirical study identified various inter-organisational relationships between public service organisations. Co-management was found where third sector organisations were contributing to public service delivery (Brandsen and Pestoff, 2006; Pestoff et al., 2006) while co-governance referred to instances where third sector organisations contributed to both the planning and delivery of public services (Vidal, 2006; Brandsen and Pestoff, 2006). Given that these organisational modes of co-production are in operation concurrently, one respondent described the challenge of working on these three levels simultaneously:

> It's almost like three-dimensional chess. . . . You know those kiddie books you get about joining up the dots? Sometimes that's what it feels like, you know. You go from one meeting to another meeting and what you try and do is make the link and build onto the next stage.
> (Humanitarian Organisation)

## Co-management

In terms of *co-management*, the Scottish government funded various third sector organisations to *deliver* services for asylum seekers, ranging from support around integration to the provision of drop-in centres or arts and crafts activities. The third sector played a core role in service provision for asylum seekers and the trust built through service relationships—essentially co-construction—was important for the Scottish Government, which consulted asylum seekers through organisations such as the Charity.

One clear example was of a contractual relationship between the Government Agency and the Accommodation Provider to provide housing to asylum seekers. The contract was subject to 'huge financial penalties' for any mistakes on the part of the Accommodation Provider and this formed the basis of a strained relationship between the two parties.

> We think we should work in partnership with them. It's more, you're the contractor; you signed a contract, get on with it . . . and they can make huge mistakes. No wee . . . big, big mistakes. And we can't do anything about it . . . the staff get a bit annoyed.
> (Accommodation Provider Service Manager)

The relationship was made more difficult by the geographical distance between the two parties and the sheer size of the Government Agency, which made effective communication difficult. The contract also had implications for the extent to which the Accommodation Provider could advocate on behalf of asylum seekers. Speaking about detention centres, the service manager said 'we were all moaning. The staff were moaning about it but we can't. . . . We're the contractor'.

However, co-management was not restricted to government contracts. It was also found to exist between organisations delivering services on the ground; partnership working was key. For example, the two
churches studied provided shared crèche services to enable asylum seeker
women to make use of other services. This relationship was described as
unproblematic because both partners had the same aims: 'it does go quite
smoothly because we're both going for the same thing'. However, other
relationships were more strained. The Accommodation Provider and the
Arm's Length Local Authority also worked in partnership to deliver a
service aimed at promoting integration among young asylum seekers and
the indigenous population, but the relationship was described as challenging, lacking both clear lines of communication and trust.

As mentioned earlier, links across organisational boundaries and the
exchange of information were crucial both to the asylum process and to
the delivery of appropriate public services to meet individuals' needs. The
Accommodation Provider and Churches spoke of sharing information
with various statutory agencies and referring asylum seekers onto service
providers in reaction to individual needs. Some relationships were more
formal than others. Church B, for example, had not established any formal partnerships with statutory agencies, but exchanged information and
advice as and when required:

> that lady today, she may have to be taken from the Housing Service
> or the Homelessness Service . . . to the Social Work Department, so
> therefore in that sense we're working with them but not in terms of
> partnership with them. We're really just using them.

### Co-governance

*Co-governance* was demonstrated by the presence of service planning
and delivery networks operating in the city. This organisational mode
of co-production was evidenced on three levels: strategic policymaking,
operational planning and neighbourhood planning.

First, at the strategic level, the National Stakeholders Forum, which
was convened in London by the Home Office, existed to discuss issues
pertinent to asylum seekers. It was attended predominantly by third
sector organisations, although a representative from the Convention of
Scottish Local Authorities (Cosla) also sat on the group. This Forum
was described by respondents working in strategic positions as showing
an adversity to working in silos. Interestingly, this discussion also highlighted that the Charity and Accommodation Provider were sitting on
national groups which the Scottish government was not party to. However, there was criticism over the size of the group and the absence of a
pre-agenda which made it difficult to prepare and contribute effectively:

'so it tends to be, you get the papers, you turn up, there's presentations, there's discussions, agenda item moves onto the next one' (Accommodation Provider Strategic Manager). Organisations such as Accommodation Provider, the Scottish Government, the Government Agency and the Charity also sat together on a Strategic Partnership Group that discussed policy at this level. The Scottish Refugee Policy Forum, which represented various refugee community organisations, also fed into the strategic level.

Despite having access to strategic deliberations, one respondent complained that Scotland tended to be 'tagged on, rather than an integral part to that [policy] cycle' (Accommodation Provider Strategic Manager). In particular, the challenge of engagement around immigration issues existed at various levels, for the Scottish government, the third sector, public sector organisations and asylum seekers living in Scotland. Indeed, not only is immigration reserved to the UK government under Schedule 5 of the Scotland Act 1998, the conception of asylum seekers as non-citizens limits their political agency and, as such, they have no route through which to influence the content or direction of immigration policies. Nevertheless, a respondent from the Government Agency provided a conflicting view, citing examples where external stakeholders have been involved in workshops across the UK, providing them with opportunities to contribute to primary and secondary legislation. The challenge for the Government Agency was an unwillingness of certain parties to talk and listen: 'But it's not helpful, it's not productive when they come to meetings with a pre-set agenda and they're not willing to listen or discuss' (Government Agency).

Second, various third sector organisations and public sector agencies collaborated on Integration Networks to share information and work together to plan services on an operational level (public funds were distributed to these Integration Networks via Community Planning Partnerships). Integration networks were responsible for developing their own Integration Plans: 'it comes from the bottom. . . . These guys know what they're talking about because they do it day in day out. . . . If it was any other way it simply wouldn't function' (Voluntary Community Organisation Accommodation Provider). This again points to the importance of the third sector's mediating role, which positions them as close to asylum seeker service users and in touch with their needs (Berger and Neuhaus, 1978). Interestingly, co-governance at the operational level, supported by effective structures, was described as critical to the success of co-governance at the strategic level: 'people need to form alliances and do preliminary work outside that group to make it work' (Accommodation Provider Strategic Manager).

Integration Networks were established as a means of providing deeper forms of engagement, providing an opportunity for various organisations that represent asylum seekers to sit around the table and contribute to the development of an operational strategy.

> that network then brings together an action plan, a kind of menu of activities for the year. And should ensure that menu is influenced and informed by asylum seeker service users. . . . That you engage them effectively in the design of the services and you're checking those services off with service users. Are these the services that they want? Are they at the right time? Do they make sense to you? Do they work? And in that way, I think, you're going to get a much richer, much more effective grassroots involvement.
>
> (Community Planning Partnership)

The Integration Networks were also described as playing a dual role, being used both as a means of planning services across organisational boundaries—as has been discussed—and also connecting to Framework for Dialogue groups operating at the neighbourhood level. Eight such groups were in operation across Glasgow and acted both as 'information provision networks' and 'consultation mechanisms'. Policymakers and service managers alike discussed the benefits of creating dialogue with asylum seekers and avoiding duplication of work or over-engagement.

> individual agencies engage with a particular client group and then two months later a different agency will engage with the same client group. . . . And all that does is confuse the client group. So we're a partnership, so we are insisting on collective engagement. . . . And that hopefully will . . . reduce the amount of engagement but will strengthen the quality of engagement.
>
> (Community Planning Partnership)

The organisations sitting on the Integration Networks were involved in planning services together during scheduled development days where they drew up the parameters of the Integration Plan. The Integration Networks could be described as cooperative networks (Head, 2008); they were generally task-focused, taking the form of regular meetings within which organisations from across sectors participated while maintaining their identities. The members of the Integration Networks were working on the ground and were therefore thought to benefit from a closeness to service users with whom they had developed relationships and, by consequence, understood their needs. Having relevant organisations and agencies sitting around the table, sharing information and communicating with one another was therefore said to improve service provision. The effectiveness of planning was dependent upon people sitting round the table, raising pertinent issues:

> once the Plan's all done and dusted and it's all been agreed, somebody comes and says, 'Oh by the way, half the asylum seeking population

have real Mental Health problems, so why's that not in the Plan. . . '
Well, why did you not come to the Development Day, and you could
have raised it then?

(Public Service Organisation)

Although the Integration Networks were generally described as effective, relationships were not necessarily continued on a day-to-day basis
due to time pressures and financial constraints. This was particularly the
case for smaller service providers: 'I think the difficulty for most people
is time and resources now . . . you get caught up with your own sort
of thing' (Small Charity). This highlighted the challenge for organisations in balancing priorities. Indeed, working in a silo until the service
was established was sometimes considered to be an appropriate precur-
sor to engaging with other organisations. However, other respondents
described networking as a core element of their job. Networking at the
operational level was important for the adult literacy service manager
from the Development Organisation, for example, who was looking to
build links, exchange information and promote interest in services: 'I go
into all the integration networks as well . . . to let people know who I am,
which services I've got and through that I'm getting referrals'.

At this level, a practitioners' network was also in operation, as was the
Scottish Stakeholders' Forum which was 'led' by Government Agency in
Glasgow and included the Scottish Government, Glasgow City Council,
COSLA, Edinburgh City Council, the Scottish Refugee Council, British
Red Cross, the Victims of Torture, the Legal Practitioners' Forum, the
International Office of Migration and the Strathclyde Police and Health.
Although the Forum was used primarily to discuss national issues at
a local level, it was also used as a means of picking up local issues to
be taken to the national meetings. Indeed, respondents spoke at length
about developing a shared Scottish agenda that could be portrayed at the
UK level.

Third, at the neighbourhood level, eight Framework for Dialogue
groups were in operation across Glasgow. These groups acted both as
'an information provision network and [as a] consultation mechanism or
participation mechanism'. As neighbourhood groups they were described
as important mechanisms through which operational issues could be filtered up to strategic decision-making level, as they had direct links with
the Scottish Refugee Policy Forum and the Charity, which sits on various
strategic groups.

> So what you've got now on the basic level is people who get together
> on a neighbourhood level and they can in some cases take issues up
> to service level locally or at a bigger level. And they can take issues
> up with government in various ways, both at the Scottish level and
> the Westminster level.

(Charity)

Framework for Dialogue Groups and Integration Networks were also described as having 'conterminous boundaries', with each sharing the function of 'building bonds' (Charity). However, time constraints, resourcing issues, language barriers were all recognised as barriers that impede the involvement of Framework for Dialogue groups during Integration Network planning sessions. Thus, there was a reliance on the community development workers to act as a conduit between the two structures. However, one manager recognised that such a role may result in them being viewed 'as gatekeepers or seem to be keeping people out' (Public Service Organisation). Indeed, although third sector organisations play a core role in enabling the inclusion of marginalised groups (e.g. Burt and Taylor, 2004; Elstub, 2006; Haugh and Kitson, 2007), the discussion in Chapter 5 questioned whether the involvement of third sector organisations genuinely enhances co-production, through the strength of collective action, or actually diminishes it by placing the third sector organisation in between the individual service users and service provided (Brenton, 1985; Pestoff et al., 2006).

There were also instances—particularly during the observations—where the mechanisms for co-production appeared to be used more for the benefit of the organisation rather than the asylum seekers using the service. For example, the observation of the Framework for Dialogue Groups was dominated by the service manager although it was supposed to be led by the asylum seeker participants. Although there was some consideration that the responsibility for the Framework for Dialogue Groups may be placed with asylum seekers in the future, this was closely associated with resourcing issues rather than an attempt to bypass any effects mediation has on co-production. In the case of Church B, which described its services as being co-designed by service users during the service encounter, tokenistic forms of participative co-production were noted during the observation.

### Enabling Inter-organisational Relationships

The evidence suggested that four factors enable inter-organisational relationships. First, personal relationships across organisational boundaries were important both on an operational and strategic level. Respondents generally described relationships at the operational level as being fostered and supported by positive relationships existing between strategic managers. This was evidenced strongly in the relationship between the senior members of the Charity and Accommodation Provider. Indeed, respondents noted the Accommodation Provider's early reluctance to inter-organisational working, which had changed both as a result of having established core services and the approach of the senior manager. The positive working relationship between the strategic managers was translated on the operational level, with service managers and front-line staff communicating with each other and sharing information on a day-to-day basis in order to meet the basic needs of asylum seekers coming into Glasgow.

Respondents emphasised that at the organisational level, individual personal relationships were essential to co-management and co-governance, confirming the arguments in the literature that inter-personal relationships and trust are crucial during the exchanges between organisations (Ring and Van de Ven, 1992; Gulati, 1995; Zaheer et al., 1998). Respondents described going to college together or how many people started out in the Charity as colleagues and have since moved to various other organisations operating in the field. As a result, they had established close working relationships as colleagues, which had been transferred into the current roles where they worked for different organisations.: 'I knew X at college in the 1980s. . . . And I guess as a Community Development service, we are such a shrinking band of workers, that we kind of cling to each other' (Public Service Organisation). Trust was, by consequence, described as developing over time through frequent and close interaction (Gulati, 1995; Nooteboom et al., 1997; Tsai and Ghosal, 1998) and between *individuals* rather than organisations (Ring and Van De Ven, 1994; Gulati, 1995; Zaheer et al., 1998; Kale et al., 2000). It was considered to be a central element which can make or break relationships: 'the key to a partnership, if you can get trust. . . . You can have one or two partners that you don't particularly like, but can tolerate. If you all hated one another, it would just fall apart and we've seen it at certain times' (Local Authority Arm's Length Company).

Respondents also spoke of the benefits of face-to-face interactions in developing improved working relationships across organisational boundaries and the dangers of no personal contact and high staff turnover (Nooteboom et al., 1997) for effective collaborative working. Little trust was found to exist between organisations contracted to work for the Home Office, with limited face-to-face contact or indeed clear lines of communication existing at the operational level. In contrast, the relationship between the Accommodation Provider and Charity seemed strong. As two key organisations from the public and third sectors, the relationship was founded upon that of the strategic players at the top of the organisation, which seemed to be forged also at the operational level with front-line staff sharing information and working together to meet the service needs of clients.

Second, the Charity held a strong position within the landscape of social welfare service planning and delivery for asylum seekers. It was respected and valued by the Scottish government, asylum seeker service users and other third sector organisations alike and, as a result, played a significant role in delivering services, advocating on behalf of asylum seekers, mediating between asylum seekers and government and also in a collaborative relationship with other service providers (through Integration

Networks). Its position therefore enabled the Charity as a mediator to consult asylum seekers and reflect their needs to the government in a productive way and also supported inter-organisational relationships to plan services at the operational level. Respondents working on the front line suggested, for instance, that it was the job of their managers to negotiate and raise concerns with the Scottish government, suggesting there were lines of communication from the operational to strategic level.

Third, the geography of Scotland and Glasgow in particular was described as conducive to partnership working: 'it's the biggest village in the planet . . . I mean if you're stuck with something, you'd pick up the phone to who you would see as a colleague, because you used to work with them' (Humanitarian Organisation). Various respondents also mentioned a Scottish mindset towards and a history of inter-organisational working. However, this was particularly challenging during the early days of a service, with the need to establish effective services prioritised over networking and relationship-building:

> It was grim to begin with. We were at each other's throats. . . . And it took a wee while to kind of introduce some sort of agreed mechanism that we could start communicating.
>
> (Local Authority Arm's Length Company)

> I didn't go out proactively to the Scottish Government, to Glasgow City Council. We were very eager, heads down, kind of wanting to develop what we felt were really good resources.
>
> (Humanitarian Organisation)

Fourth, the capacity to develop inter-organisational relationships was generally viewed as having to proceed with the development of established services. Respondents said that working in silos was sometimes necessary to develop the parameters of the service, after which inter-organisational relationships could be successfully developed, suggesting that this was sometimes restricted to service delivery rather than planning.

### Challenges of Inter-organisational Relationships

Four challenges associated with working in collaboration with the third sector in the planning and delivery of social welfare services for asylum seekers were also identified through the empirical research. First, respondents noted the challenge in involving organisations that are sufficiently skilled and funded to ensure the effective delivery of services that match the needs of service users:

> [The] key challenge is for the public sector to recognise the fact that where you've got services which are being delivered to . . . people

who are particularly vulnerable, you do need to ensure that the actual service user itself, and their representative bodies in the third sector, are able to play that role in deciding the services . . . it's being able to ensure that the Third Sector is, or that the budgets are sufficient for those services where the services are being delivered to those vulnerable individuals who need a greater degree of personalisation of care.
(Scottish Government Policymaker)

The second key challenge for inter-organisational working, regardless of which organisations were party to the relationships, was time. The Government Agency in Glasgow was found to act essentially as an operational body that dealt with claims for asylum rather than setting the policy agenda. Although the respondent from the Government Agency spoke of having 'personal working relationships with people', she also pointed out the barrier to working across organisational boundaries: 'the staff are so busy with the asylum cases and working through such a heavy case load that they don't have that time for interaction with stakeholders'. The respondent recognised that although there 'should be' partnership working between operational staff and local agencies, such engagement often takes a back seat due to other work commitments and if there are 'too many people working in too many work streams and in too many different jobs. . . [or in] a silo approach' (Government Agency). However, she further reflected that with a backlog of asylum cases still to be considered, maintaining effective working relationships is crucial to completing the day job: 'it's really important that we maintain the working relationships that we've established over the 5/6 years and we're working hard to do that'.

The third challenge was mistrust for counterparts across organisational boundaries. There was some concern among smaller third sector organisations, in particular, that requests for inter-organisational working arose out of a desire to 'piggy back on your success' (Church B). Another respondent described a situation where organisations working with asylum seekers acted as gatekeepers, until they were sure of the benefit that might result from inter-organisational working.

> You've got to have a good relationship with the organisers before you can actually get to the service users because if they don't like you they're like 'well, what can you do for us?' So we need to be very sensitive and very aware of how . . . establishing our links and then building up trust and then going out to deliver.
> (Women's Voluntary Organisation)

Other respondents suggested a fear of other organisations overstepping the boundaries and taking their responsibilities: 'There's always a fear, particularly when you work with partners, that everybody will start wandering into everybody else's patch' (Local Authority Arm's Length

Company). This was associated with a fear of losing funding as a result of other players taking over core functions and therefore having a negative impact upon the lifespan of the organisation.

Finally, a significant challenge for inter-organisational working was where the organisations had different or competing agendas. For example, respondents generally described the Government Agency as more challenging to work with, given the differences between the UK and Scottish Government's approach to integration. However, larger third sector organisations suggested that the Government Agency was willing to listen to views as long as they were distilled and based on evidence.

## Summary: Inter-organisational Relationships

This chapter confirms the presence of organisational forms of co-production in the case of asylum seeker welfare service provision in Glasgow. The analysis has shown that various welfare services are delivered to asylum seekers in Glasgow from a range of organisations, including small community organisations, larger third sector organisations and public sector organisations. The social welfare services provided to asylum seekers included statutory services such as housing (under a contract with the Home Office) but were dominated by responsive services provided by the third sector that aimed to fill gaps in service provision and meet the needs of asylum seekers (e.g. English classes and drop-in sessions), as well as information provision about the services available. Such services were typically funded by the Scottish government and were closely tied to the aim of integrating asylum seekers.

In confirmation of Wren's (2007) research, the third sector was described as playing a leading role in supporting asylum seekers; this case has shown that their role has been one predominantly of collaborator and mediator during operational planning and service delivery, although some organisations also retained an important advocacy role. The majority of questionnaire respondents said they were working with third sector organisations during service production, particularly during service delivery, but third sector organisations were also described as playing a key mediating role, facilitating dialogue with the asylum seekers they represent and public sector organisations/policymakers.

Organisations from across sectors were described as collaborating together through individual partnerships and broader networks during service delivery and planning, pointing to the presence of both co-management and co-governance. Examples of co-management took the form of government contracts, with third sector organisations being funded to provide various services to asylum seekers that supported the Scottish government's goals around integration. Co-management was also evidenced at the operational level, with organisations working together to deliver shared services. Co-governance, by contrast, took place at various points including the strategic, operational and neighbourhood levels and included examples where organisations worked together to plan services. Both types of relationships were enabled by various factors including the geography of Scotland, which was conducive to partnership working, the strategic direction of leaders within large organisations from the third and public sectors and the existence of established relationships of trust. Inter-organisational working was promoted by the Scottish government but was also deemed by some as a personal choice. However, the analysis also identified barriers to inter-organisational relationship building, including mistrust, lack of time to work together and competing agendas.

The discussion in this chapter points to the importance of the inter-organisational relationships during the planning and delivery of public services. Taken with the analysis presented in Chapter 7, this suggests that the entire landscape of social welfare service production needs to be understood, including the roles of individuals through co-construction, participative co-production and co-design; and, importantly, the different organisations though co-management and co-governance in order to develop a comprehensive understanding of how social welfare services are planned and delivered. However, a number of challenges were also presented that impede co-management and co-governance. These included time constraints, working to different agendas and a lack of trust among prospective partners.

# References

Berger, P. L. and Neuhaus, R. J. (1978). *To empower people: the role of mediating structures in public policy*. Washington, DC: American Enterprise for Public Policy Research.

Bode, I. (2006). Disorganised welfare mixes: voluntary agencies and new governance regimes in Western Europe. *Journal of European Social Policy*. (16,4), 346–359.

Brandsen, T. and Pestoff, V. (2006). Co-production, the third sector and the delivery of public services. *Public Management Review*. (8,4), 493–501.

Brenton, M. (1985). *The voluntary sector in British social services*. London: Longman.

Burt, E. and Taylor, J. (2004). Striking the regulatory balance in the unique case of the voluntary sector. *Public Money and Management*. (October), 297–300.

DiMaggio, P. and Powell, W. W. (1983). The iron cage revisited: collective rationality and institutional isomorphism in organizational fields. *American Sociological Review*. (48,2), 147–160.

Elstub, S. (2006). Towards an inclusive social policy for the UK: the need for democratic deliberation in voluntary and community associations. *Voluntas*. (17,1), 17–39.

Gulati, R. (1995). Does familiarity breed trust? The implications of repeated ties for contractual choice in alliances. *The Academy of Management Journal*. (38,1), 85–112.

Haugh, H. and Kitson, M. (2007). The third way and the third sector: new labour's economic policy and the social economy. *Cambridge Journal of Economics*. (31), 973–994.

Head, B. (2008). Accessing network-based collaborations: effectiveness for whom? *Public Management Review*. (10,6), 733–749.

Kale, P., Singh, H. and Perlmutter, H. (2000). Learning and protection of proprietary assets in strategic alliances. *Strategic Management Journal*. (21,3), 217–237.

Kearns, A. (1995). Active citizenship and local governance: political and geographical dimensions. *Political Geography*. (14,2), 155–175.

Klijn, E. H. (2008). Governance and governance networks in Europe. *Public Management Review*. (10,4), 505–525.

Nooteboom, B., Berger, H. and Noorderhaven, N. G. (1997). Effects of trust and governance on relational risk. *The Academy of Management Journal*. (40,2), 308–338.

Osborne, S. (2006). Editorial: the new public governance? *Public Management Review*. (8,3), 377–387.

Pestoff, V., Osborne, S. P. and Brandsen, T. (2006). Patterns of co-production in public services. *Public Management Review*. (8,4), 591–595.

Pifer, A. (1967). *Quasi non governmental organizations*. New York: Carnegie Corporation.

Ring, P. S. and Van de Ven, A. H. (1992). Structuring cooperative relationships between organization. *Strategic Management Journal*. (13), 483–498.

Ring, P. S. and Van de Ven, A. H. (1994). Developmental processes of cooperative interorganisational relationships. *The Academy of Management Review*. (19,1), 90–118.

Sales, R. (2002). The deserving and undeserving? Refugees, asylum seekers and welfare in Britain. *Critical Social Policy*. (22), 456–478.

Tsai, W. and Ghosal, S. (1998). Social capital and value creation: the role of intrafirm networks. *The Academy of Management Journal*. (41,4), 464–476.

Vidal, I. (2006). Reflections on the market, networking and trust. *Public Management Review*. (8,4), 583–589.

Wren, K. (2007). Supporting asylum seekers and refugees in Glasgow: the role of multi-agency networks. *Journal of Refugee Studies*. (20,3), 391–413.

Zaheer, A., McEvily, B. and Perrone, V. (1998). Does trust matter? Exploring the effects of interorganisational and interpersonal trust on performance. *Organization Science*. (9,2), 141–159.

# Part 3

# Co-production in a Complex Service System

## Social Inclusion and Citizenship

# 9  Co-production in a Complex Public Service System

## The Implications for Social Inclusion and Citizenship

## Abstract

This chapter discusses the implications of asylum seeker co-production for social inclusion and citizenship. It presents the argument that, as *public service users*, asylum seekers will *always* play an active role in the process of public service production through co-construction, but that their role can also be extended through participative co-production and co-design. The discussion examines these modes of co-production alongside co-management and co-governance to suggest that the five modes are operationalised within a complex public service system. The differentiation of co-production in this way and the presentation of the different modes within a complex model has important implications for citizenship and social inclusion. While none of the three modes of individual co-production provide asylum seekers with legal citizenship status, each provides an opportunity for asylum seekers to *act* like citizens. Furthermore, co-production supports social inclusion because of the strong relational dimension that underpins each of the five modes, but it is argued that the distinctive Scottish context was also an important factor supporting the inclusion of asylum seekers.

## Introduction

The case of asylum seekers presented in the previous chapters has served to sharpen the focus on co-production and, in particular, the fact that co-production—through co-construction—is integral to the process nature of services and is critical to the debate. The analysis has indicated that co-production, in the five modes differentiated in Chapter 5, takes place in the context of social welfare services provided to asylum seekers in Scotland and that co-production starts from their role as public service users.

This chapter builds on the previous discussion to present the implications of co-production—in its various dimensions—for the inclusion of asylum seekers and for citizenship. It starts by presenting a multi-dimensional model of co-production that is based on an integration of the theory and empirical analysis presented respectively in Parts 1 and 2 of this book. It then argues that the integral nature of co-production during the service relationship, the support of integration policy and the focus on integration during operational planning and public service delivery have supported the broad agenda of social inclusion and may even lay the foundations towards a partial route of citizenship for asylum seekers.

## Asylum Seekers' Social Welfare Services and Co-production

The analysis and discussion presented earlier confirm the existence of co-production at its most basic level through co-construction, implying that, as public *service users*, asylum seekers will *always* play an active role in service delivery due to the inseparable nature of production and consumption. This implies a service systems approach (Osborne et al., 2015) that starts from the basic premise of treating public services as processes within which the service user plays a key role (Osborne and Strokosch, 2013). Such a formulation advocates for the Public Service Logic through its emphasis of the complex and interconnected processes of co-production, some of which can be enabled (or obstructed) but all of which can be managed by public service organisations to achieve the public sector's primary goal of value creation for individual service users and wider society (Alford, 2016). The discussion has further shown—through the application of the conceptual frameworks—that in the case of asylum seekers, co-production can be extended beyond co-construction, which exists as an integral dimension of public service delivery. It has emphasised that, even as non-citizens, asylum seekers as public service users are never passive and they therefore play a more or less active role under each individual mode of co-production. The evidence pointed to the existence of participative co-production, mainly through consultation used during operational planning, as well as consumer mechanisms such as choice and complaints' procedures. Co-design was also found—albeit to a lesser extent—with public service organisations facilitating service user involvement by encouraging asylum seekers to contribute their expertise to customise and personalise services. It follows then that the organisation delivering the service ultimately controls whether and how co-construction is extended into either participative co-production or co-design. Indeed, there was a widespread view among policy respondents and service managers alike that, as public service users, asylum seekers should be and were engaged in public service production. The difference in opinion came over the issue of when asylum seekers should co-produce; that is whether co-production is restricted to service delivery or whether it is extended into service planning and design. In the case of Church A, for example, co-production was limited to the service encounter through co-construction, while the Humanitarian Organisation, by comparison, promoted 'non-directional advocacy' and encouraged asylum seeker service users to take the lead in the planning and delivery of their own services through co-design.

The analysis and discussion have further suggested that co-production is not limited to the involvement of public service users, but can also take place at the organisational level. The third sector has been described as playing a crucial role in the planning and delivery of public services for asylum seekers and has suggested that social welfare services for asylum seekers are produced through a series of inter-organisational relationships, where organisations work together to deliver (co-management) and/or plan services (co-governance). Through co-management, there was a need to exchange and share information about asylum seekers and also refer them onto other public services to ensure that complex needs were met. On the whole, the relationships uncovered by the research were positive, although there were some instances of mistrust and poor communication that made working together challenging. Personal relationships between service managers across organisational boundaries were of particular importance in facilitating co-management and co-governance. Trust was described as developing over time through frequent and close interaction (Gulati, 1995; Nooteboom et al., 1997; Tsai and Ghosal, 1998), with service managers having been to college together or previously working together.

Three models of co-governance were apparent at the strategic, operational and neighbourhood levels. At the strategic level, good relationships among key players in Scotland such as the Charity and Accommodation Provider facilitated inter-organisational working. Strong personal relationships between individuals across organisational boundaries and particularly between those at the top who were responsible for steering the direction of the organisation were important. By contrast, the relationship with the Government Agency was described as more fraught. The distance and lack of face-to-face contact made relationships difficult and respondents described Scotland as being tagged onto policy rather than integral to it. At the operational level, Integration Networks formed joint planning sessions to draw together expertise, knowledge and resources with the aim of providing needs-led services and promoting integration into Scottish society. However, such inter-organisational relationships were not replicated on a day-to-day basis given time constraints and resource issues. The Framework for Dialogue Groups at the neighbourhood level were essential, supporting asylum seeker integration by providing a structure to facilitate service user participation (Pestoff, 2012). The Framework for Dialogue Groups fed into Integration Networks, offering a means by which to be connected to and informed by service users and also provided public service providers a mechanism through which to directly consult asylum seekers.

Co-management and co-governance were not operating in silos, with complexity and cross over between the two organisational forms of co-production. Relationships were dynamic, with organisations working on Integration Networks to plan services at the operational level (co-governance) and concurrently working together on smaller projects to deliver services together (co-management) or working with other organisations on an informal basis to refer asylum seekers with specific needs. They were also challenging in terms of time and resources and when relationships between service managers across organisational boundaries lacked trust and communication.

## Co-production in a Complex Public Service System

The analysis presented in Chapters 7 and 8 clearly shows that the five modes of co-production do not operate in isolation but within a complex landscape of public service production. Co-productive relationships were operating on three levels and this work sought to explore particularly those at the micro level between public service organisations and service users (or groups of service users) and the meso level between organisations from the public, for-profit and third sectors. At the macro level, government policies particularly from the Scottish government were also significant both in influencing the direction and shape of services (i.e. services funded by the Scottish government were underpinned by a focus on social inclusion and integration) and also encouraging inter-organisational working (e.g. Community Empowerment [Scotland] Act 2015). The five dimensions of co-production are now brought together in a model presented in Figure 9.1, which combines the insights about

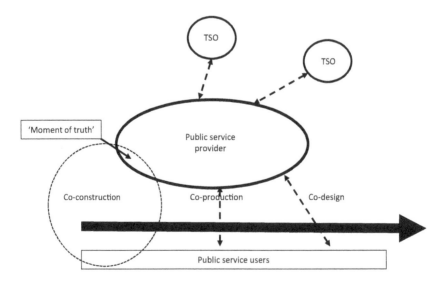

*Figure 9.1* A public service system view of co-production

co-production at the individual and organisational levels within a complex public service system. As such, the model suggests that the interactions of various stakeholders in co-productive relationships operating concurrently are essential to the production of public services.

On the most basic level and fundamental to the debate on co-production, the model depicts a multifaceted picture of public service production that is supported by a series of interconnected and overlapping relationships and emphasises that co-production at the individual level co-exists with functioning inter-organisational relationships between the public service organisations and various other organisations, including (but not exclusively) third sector organisations (TSO). This moves beyond the earlier and more simplistic conceptualisation of co-production which focused on the overlap between two organisations or between a service organisation and service users (Brudney and England, 1983). That overlap remains important as it emphasises the relational and process nature of public services and 'the moment of truth' during service interactions, but it misleads us into thinking that co-production is about only one relationship, when in reality various forms of co-production likely exist, not only between public service staff and service users, but also across organisational boundaries and sectors. This is a concern that is also raised by Trischler and Charles (2019, p. 19) who argue that the sustained focus on 'dyadic exchanges does not consider the dynamism and complexity of public problems' who suggest the application of a service ecosystem lens to examine public policy design. Although it has not been the focus here, Trischler and Charles (2019) and others (see, for example, Skalen et al., 2015) rightly argue that such complexity also extends beyond the micro and meso levels to include the macro, which would include an examination of how public value has been constructed and the various actors and processes that are involved in defining policies and legislation.

All of the organisations delivering services examined in the asylum seeker case study, regardless of sector, spoke of developing some kind of relationship with asylum seekers during service delivery (co-construction), which is why the diagram situates public service users at the bottom, to represent how they—as public service users—feed into the process. The other two extended modes of individual co-production are also positioned here and exist on a continuum, showing that while co-construction is integral to public service production, service users can become more active in public service production when mobilised by public service organisations. This emphasises co-construction as a fundamental component of service delivery, while participative co-production and co-design are 'added on', with their nature and impact therefore being controlled by the organisation delivering the service (Osborne and Strokosch, 2013).

In reality though, public service production is more complicated than the discrete interactions between service organisations and public service users, involving various stakeholders at different points in the service cycle. As discussed previously, public service organisations are not producing manufactured goods in an isolated factory setting that are later consumed by service users at a different location. Rather they produce intangible *services* that are consumed at the same time as they are produced and importantly, their production is facilitated within a complex environment, which can include multiple relationships across organisational boundaries. The organisation producing the service is therefore positioned at the centre of the model, but additional organisations can also contribute to production, perhaps under a government contract (co-management) or by working in partnerships or networks to plan and deliver services (co-governance). The case study analysis highlighted that neither co-management nor co-governance was reliant upon the presence of individual forms of co-production. Rather, inter-organisational working was often described, by service managers, as a requirement of funding (policy around the third sector and community planning places a strong emphasis both on inter-organisational working) and a preferred working style. However, the findings further suggest that service improvement is better rooted in forms of co-management and co-governance that are connected to and informed by services users. The third sector played a crucial role in this sense, as it was typically viewed as a mediator (Berger and Neuhaus, 1978) that was close to service users and knowledgeable about their needs, but also connected to other organisations and therefore had the necessary capacity to signpost service users to other services and also advocate on their behalf to government.

The two-headed arrows displayed in the model reflect the interactive nature of the relationships between organisations, which has significant implications for how co-production is understood and managed. Co-management and co-governance occurred at different levels within the same organisations, with strategic managers working together across organisational and sectoral boundaries to influence national policy or develop a coordinated strategic plan, while operational managers worked together to negotiate shared premises for service delivery or support services to help asylum seekers into critical services.

When applied to the case of asylum seekers and the design and delivery of the social welfare services they receive, this illustration provides a useful visualisation of the reality of co-production at the individual and inter-organisational levels. If, for example, the Accommodation Provider is positioned at the centre of the diagram as a housing provider for asylum seekers in Glasgow, various co-productive relationships are revealed. The depiction would show the organisation, through its front-line staff, co-constructing services with asylum seeker service users. The Accommodation Provider was also party to various networks and had both effective and challenging working relationships with other organisations in the sector. It was, for example, funded by the Home Office to provide housing, and its employees sat on various networks and groups at the neighbourhood, operational planning and strategic planning levels. It also had a particularly close and effective working relationship with other organisations such as the Charity; at this level, the relationship between senior managers was described as one of friendship and trust.

The model presented here is thus an important progression beyond the transactional and linear approach traditionally applied to public service production under the product-dominant reasoning that has been followed in much of the public administration literature (Osborne et al., 2013). From this traditional perspective, public services are understood as being designed and delivered by public service organisations working in isolation and consumed separately by service users. Instead, the model portrays a relational approach between various parties in order to reflect the pluralistic and fragmented nature of public services where interactions take place across organisational boundaries, between sectors and with public service users (Osborne et al., 2015). Instead of working alone to produce services—as they have traditionally been portrayed—public service organisations operate within a complex public service delivery system, including the public sector, third sector, service users (and their families), for-profit sector and local communities through the five modes of co-production. A key issue that has emerged from the discussion is that co-construction, participative co-production, co-design, co-management and co-governance are not mutually exclusive; different combinations of such relationships are likely to take place to plan and deliver any service (Brandsen and Pestoff, 2006; Pestoff, 2012).

Other public sector examples can also be applied to this model to highlight its applicability. In the case of an oncology patient, for example, the complexity of the service system is evident. Co-construction is enacted between the patient and their GP (at a local doctors' surgery), specialist doctors (at hospital) and nurses (at hospital). But the service process involved in such care is more complicated than the relationships of co-construction, despite the value creating potential of service encounters (Vargo and Lusch, 2008). Each of these healthcare professionals most likely work together to deliver a full healthcare service to the individual patient (co-management) and a Health Board oversees the complete care package being offered, taking decisions on how the patient should be treated (e.g. surgery, chemotherapy, radiotherapy). Other organisations are involved too, such as charities that might provide psychological support to the patient referred on from his/her doctor (co-governance), and the NHS buying the necessary drugs for treatment from private pharmaceutical companies (co-management).

In another example, in the case of education, the service relationship exists between front-line staff (teachers) and primary service users (pupils), which is the locus of co-construction, but in reality the service system is again more complicated. Participative co-production takes place in this example when pupils supplement their learning at home through revision and study; this may be supported by their parents, which suggests co-production can also involve indirect service users (Pestoff, 2006; Bovaird, 2007; Alford, 2014). Co-design may also be present in some education systems—such as the one currently operating in Scotland under the Curriculum for Excellence—where primary school pupils are encouraged to take responsibility for the content and nature of their education and therefore supposed to influence and shape operational planning. At another dimension, parents sit on the Parents Association and may, therefore, play a key role in the effective running of the school (co-governance) and the school may also have relationships with other public service organisations that contribute to specific areas of education (e.g. a representative from the Fire Brigade may provide sessions in the school to teach the children about fire safety). The school will also be answerable to the Local Authority (co-governance) and may also have relationships with other schools in the area in order to share resources (co-management).

A third example that again confirms the complexity of co-production in the service system is the case of a family subject to the intervention of social services. A family would most probably have a direct relationship with a social worker (co-construction) but their role is not played out in isolation. To provide the service, the social worker would most likely have various relationships with other service providers, such as schools, doctors' surgeries, dentists or community organisations providing services to the family. An important point here is that these relationships are likely established over time through day-to-day interactions by individual staff members across organisational boundaries (Ring and Van de Ven, 1994). The communication and collaborations between individuals within these organisations are therefore critical to the support that a social worker can provide to individual service users.

## Fostering Social Inclusion and Integration Through Co-production

The literature has discussed participation as a core dimension of public service production that supports asylum seeker inclusion, with particular reference to Ager and Strang's (2008) framework on integration, which has formed the basis of the agenda for social inclusion of asylum seekers in Scotland. It is therefore necessary to discuss the implications of co-production—in its various dimensions—for the integration of asylum seekers. The analysis has shown that asylum seekers occupy a position as *public service users*, and as such their participation in the service relationship through co-construction and during service planning through participative co-production and co-design may have important implications for their integration.

The approach to integration in Scotland differs from the UK government's stance of non-integration until refugee status has been awarded and also sits in general conflict with the exclusionary policies on immigration made at the UK level (Cemlyn and Briskman, 2003; Williams, 2006). Respondents described the Scottish government as occupying a relatively powerless position when it came to immigration policy and legislation, which are reserved to the UK government, and therefore had no say over the outcome of asylum cases. Nevertheless, the challenge for the Scottish government was more complicated because immigration laws and policies of deterrence have persistently sought to limit the rights and entitlements of asylum seekers (Sales, 2002). As discussed in Chapter 6, asylum seekers were typically housed in deprived areas on a no-choice basis, were not permitted to work for remuneration and could not vote. Such positioning is likely to have a negative impact on their social inclusion. Various respondents explained that, from the Scottish perspective, integration should start as soon as asylum seekers arrive in the country due to strong economic drivers and a commitment to maintaining a Scottish population of above five million. This focus was reinforced by policy rhetoric, with the New Scots Strategy defining integration as a long-term process to which early engagement with asylum seekers is crucial. The analysis of the empirical findings suggests that this rhetoric has translated into practice, with third sector organisations delivering services encouraged to think about integration in order to secure government funding. Indeed, the majority of the welfare services examined were geared around integration, with the remit of services including preparing asylum seekers for work, integrating them with British culture and among asylum seekers of different nationalities and the indigenous community (Strokosch and Osborne, 2017).

The Scottish government aimed to start the process of social inclusion as quickly as possible through opportunities for volunteering and education, suggesting that integration was being facilitated (Ager and Strang, 2008). English for Speakers of Other Languages courses were offered, for example, because they were considered to have a beneficial impact upon community integration and also prepared asylum seekers for entering the workforce should their application be successful. Data gathered from Church A, Church B, the Young Person's Group, Development Organisation and Humanitarian Organisation further emphasised that integration was an underpinning goal of the services. Church A, for example, offered drop-in sessions, craft groups and English classes and the service manager described these as offering a 'social and safe environment' where asylum seekers could 'integrate and socially interact'. As a key element of integration, social capital (Ager and Strang, 2008) was also developed and supported particularly by smaller community organisations which aimed to integrate asylum seekers within their own community of other people seeking asylum and the indigenous population.

Importantly the model presented in Figure 9.1 does not only present the complexity of co-production within a public service system, but also suggests that if co-production in its various modes supports social inclusion, then this depends not only on the actions and interactions of service users and public service organisations, but on the complex interactions operating within any given service system, at which the service user through co-construction sits at the heart. Public service organisations were, for example, responsible for providing access to services and enabled integration by facilitating social connections and bonds (Ager and Strang, 2008), but asylum seekers entering the country also had responsibility for integrating themselves through, for example, learning the language to facilitate social interaction and engagement with the local community.

Furthermore, organisations were not providing public services in isolation, but worked across sectors to plan and deliver services, emphasising then the importance of various actors within any given service system and reinforcing the argument made by Ager and Strang (2008) that successful integration depends on the contributions of all sectors of society. In the case of asylum seekers, social networks had been established mainly through the work of small community organisations to lessen the impact of isolation and promote integration through the development of friendships and relationships with both front-line service staff and other service users. These friendships were thought to offer support for social inclusion in line with the arguments presented by Spicer (2008) and Nash et al. (2006), by offering asylum seekers assistance to access core public services, but also providing them with essential emotional support. Service providers from the public and third sectors alike also showed a divergence away from the core service task to focus on more social welfare type services that would help to integrate asylum seekers into Scottish society. For example, those working on the front line for the Accommodation Provider offered support and advice on an individual basis where they could, going beyond the main objective of checking the accommodation to ensure the well-being of asylum seekers.

Various third sector organisations acted as mediating structures, helping asylum seekers access public services, another element of Ager and Strang's framework of integration. Church A, for example, referred asylum seekers on to other public service providers to ensure that their basic needs were met. The third sector was also a vital cog in the chain which created dialogue between asylum seekers and both public service organisations and policymakers. The Charity, for example, played a central role being funded by the Scottish government to consult asylum seekers and also acted as a key link in bonding other third sector organisations to strategic players. Framework for Dialogue Groups operating in the city were also an important mechanism for the inclusion and integration of asylum seekers. Third sector organisations and particularly the Charity were crucial to the development of the Framework for Dialogue structure in Glasgow, suggesting that their role in empowering asylum seekers as a collective group had been important. The Framework for Dialogue Groups were regarded largely as an important mechanism through which asylum seekers' voices could be collated and fed back to public service providers and policymakers.

The analysis has shown that the effective management of co-construction during service interactions can offer a process through which communication with asylum seeker service users is facilitated, which can enable participative co-production and co-design. Consultation was, for example, conducted through participative co-production, typically during the service encounter, where public service organisations could gather the views of asylum seekers while also benefiting from the 'moment of truth' within the encounter which provided access to active and engaged service users.

### Developing and Managing Relationships to Support Social Inclusion

Importantly, the political context in Scotland and specifically the promotion of social inclusion, from both the government at the strategic level and public service organisations working on the ground, elevated co-production as part of the process of social inclusion. Emphasising the integration of asylum seekers as soon as they entered the country impacted service delivery, encouraging public service staff to build relationships with asylum seekers and also involving service users through extended forms of co-production. However, the argument here is not that the differentiated modes of co-production can be relied on to support integration; given the inherently relational nature of each of the types of co-production presented in this book, the success of each is dependent upon the effective management of these relationships. The issue for public service managers then, is not simply managing service production from an individualistic stance, but the governance of a complex service system (Osborne et al., 2015) that can involve co-production on multiple levels. Because co-production is about relationships, the focus within this complex service environment should arguably be how to harness and utilise the skills and knowledge which service users and the various stakeholder organisations bring to the process of service production.

The theory suggests that all three modes of individual co-production are predicated upon buy-in from front-line employees, managers and professionals (Boyle et al., 2006; Crowley et al., 2002) and their capacity to develop and maintain effective, trusting relationships with service users; this was confirmed by the case study analysis. In other words, the service relationship and individual interactions during service encounters which are the basis of co-construction can be managed and are essential to the quality of a service and the satisfaction of service users with their service (Vargo et al., 2008). Nash et al. (2006) also emphasise the importance of front-line staff in enabling and supporting integration. They argue that specialist knowledge among those working in social welfare and community service is critical to integration:

> They can encourage host communities to be well prepared in order that they may accept immigrants, refugees and asylum seekers. They can facilitate community education through publicity campaigns and integration projects to assist the (re)settlement process for immigrants and refugees. They can help host-society children to learn more about the lives and customs of children from different ethnic backgrounds. These are all ways in which civic and social integration can be encouraged to enhance participatory citizenship.
>
> (Nash et al., 2006, p. 359)

At the operational level, there was a strong impetus towards the integration of asylum seekers in Scotland and the service encounter was often used as a means of developing relationships with asylum seekers to promote integration. Indeed, service providers from the public and third sectors alike showed a divergence away from the core service task (e.g. policing) to focus on more social welfare type services that would help to integrate asylum seekers into Scottish society.

Co-construction plays a core element in the effective management of public services on a day-to-day basis but is dependent upon the extent to which public service managers and front-line staff realise and apply this. The service management theory suggested relationship marketing as a potential means of managing service users and, specifically the relationship with the service provider, to promote co-production and achieve greater value from the service (Ramirez, 1999; Gronroos, 2009). This relationship existed primarily between the service and front-line staff within the organisation. Its emphasis was on inter-dependent, collaborative and long-term relationships based on trust, communication and commitment and where the service user is viewed as a partner (Gummesson, 1998; Wright and Taylor, 2007; Kinard and Capella, 2006). Adopting such an approach would, nevertheless, require that public service managers were aware of co-production in its various modes. There was however some variance in whether front-line staff developed a 'friendship' with service users or maintained a professional relationship. The larger organisations tended to establish professional boundaries in order to 'protect' staff, while smaller community organisations were more inclined to develop personal relationships. The development of these types of relationships was not confined to the community sector, however, with one example of a public sector organisation developing friendships in order to build trust in order to deliver a more effective service, the focus of which was integration. For co-construction, trust was crucial to building initial relationships with asylum seekers to ensure they had access to required services and that their needs were satisfied as a result. Indeed, building trust with asylum seekers through the service encounter was considered fundamental not only to the improvement of public services, but to enable asylum seekers to build what Ager and Strang (2008) have termed social connections and bonds in the community with the asylum seeker and indigenous populations. The service encounter (the initial 'moment of truth') was used to build trust with vulnerable asylum seekers who needed dedicated support. The work of the Accommodation Provider is a good example of this: building relationships with newly arrived asylum seekers was a key goal of front-line staff despite the aim of the service being housing provision and the challenges involved in developing relationships, which were significant.

Service encounters and the relationships that developed through co-construction were also key constructs through which participative co-production and co-design could be applied, capitalising on close relationships of trust to offer customised services and make service improvements. For participative co-production, various respondents expressed the need to provide genuine opportunities for asylum seekers to have their voices heard, rather than offering tokenistic forms of involvement. Although, the analysis highlighted that providing a right to participate or voice and choice did not necessarily equate with asylum seeker opportunities to make strategic decisions in practice. Building trust was also fundamental to co-design. A core aim of the Orientation Service offered by the Humanitarian Organisation, for instance, was to foster a one-to-one relationship based on trust in order to 'help them with the integration process'. However, building trust was also perceived as a significant challenge for organisations delivering services particularly given the marginalised nature of asylum seekers. Although service encounters are critical sites for integration, for certain groups, such points of access do not exist. For example, the service manager from Church A recognised a challenge in accessing male asylum seekers who did not utilise the drop-in services provided; there was as a result no point of access to assist this group with their claims for asylum or their broader public service needs.

The network approach in this case was functioning effectively through established relationships of partnership, collaboration and friendship, which highlighted the importance of operationalising co-management and co-governance to support social inclusion. The literature suggested that effective support systems may operate at the local level, particularly with regards to inter-organisational networks. Because dispersal was involuntary and asylum seekers faced a complex array of negative factors such as poor housing, language difficulties, discrimination, isolation and access problems to social welfare, social exclusion was a key factor. Networks were promoted as ways of offering practical support, including assistance in accessing other services, interpreters and emotional support (Bloch, 2000; Spicer, 2008). In Glasgow the establishment of networks was initially challenging because asylum seekers were relatively new to the city but evidence suggests that local third sector organisations have been effective in developing support mechanisms for asylum seekers. Research conducted by Wren (2007) confirmed this, finding that, between 2000 and 2003, a total of ten networks were established in Glasgow, which had led to the development of community-based activities such as church drop-ins and language support. In her exploration of these networks, Wren found that some had been more successful at engaging statutory agencies and likewise some were better at actively involving asylum seekers. This was also demonstrated through this case study; although there was strong agreement among respondents who were planning and delivering services in Glasgow that asylum seekers should be involved in networks, their involvement was often concentrated during the service relationship or appended through participative co-production (mainly through consultation) due to various factors, including a professional ambivalence to deeper forms of engagement and logistical issues such as language barriers.

More broadly, building and sustaining inter-organisational relation-ships was deemed necessary for effective partnership working and, linked to this, the successful delivery of services to meet both the individual needs of services users and those of the wider community, one of which was social inclusion. This has important implications for public service management and how inter-organisational relationships are managed to improve service production. Individual personal relationships and trust were essential to co-management and co-governance (Ring and Van de Ven, 1992, Gulati, 1995, Zaheer et al., 1998). Respondents generally spoke positively of partnership and networking, as these relationships allowed them easy access to advice and help. They said that established structures and organisational remits created a viable environment for inter-organisational relationships. Inter-organisational working was linked to strong personal relationships between individuals in organisa-tions, particularly between those at the top who were responsible for steering the direction of the organisation but were also notable on the operational level. Furthermore, the Charity was placed in a central posi-tion both as a key service provider for asylum seekers but also as a link between organisations.

## Are Asylum Seekers 'Acting Like Citizens'?

Participation has been framed in the literature as a core human and citi-zenship right (Powell, 2002; Brannan et al., 2006; Lister, 2007) and co-production offers a key facet of the debate on the participation of asylum seekers. Significantly, asylum seekers do not have citizenship status or the associated rights, with the concept of citizenship being constructed tradi-tionally as a means of excluding outsiders while protecting the rights of the indigenous population (Cemlyn and Briskman, 2003; Choules, 2006; Tyler, 2010). As discussed earlier, the lack of citizenship rights afforded to asylum seekers has had substantial implications for their inclusion in society, not least the negative implications for their potential to engage with democratic structures, obtain paid employment and access social welfare services.

The type of participation that is constructed through the dimensions of co-production differentiated in this work extend beyond traditional conceptualisation of participation that focuses on the role of citizens or customers (Strokosch and Osborne, 2016). In line with the classical view of co-production found in the public administration literature, this work has argued that the delivery of quality public services is dependent on participation (Ostrom, 1989). The difference here has been the focus on the service relationship and the 'moment of truth' as a core and integral dimension of co-production.

In Chapter 6, Choules' (2006) conceptualisation of citizenship was defined as having three core dimensions: membership of a political community, membership of a community of shared character and membership of a welfare state. In the Scottish context, the inequality embedded in the stratified system of social rights, which limits asylum seekers' access to public services and singles them out as a visibly in-need group distinct from mainstream society (Sales, 2002), is deepened both through notions of citizenship that have been constructed as a means of excluding outsiders and through the 'demonisation' of asylum seekers by politicians and the media (Cemlyn and Briskman, 2003; Choules, 2006). Their lives are regulated and constrained by immigration laws, and they are forbidden to work for remuneration, which potentially impedes their capacity to integrate into society. Taken together, these factors effectively preclude them from membership of Choules' first category of citizenship—though not necessarily from the subsequent two. Although they are clearly not part of a political community, as a distinct group of asylum seekers, they arguably have membership of a smaller community of shared character— Choules' second category of membership required for citizenship. Furthermore, asylum seekers *are* positioned as public service users, which suggests that they also fulfil the third category of Choules' elements of citizenship: membership of a welfare state.

Although none of the three modes of individual co-production discussed here provide asylum seekers with what Lister (2003) would describe as citizenship status, interestingly, the analysis suggested that co-production is not dependent on citizenship. Rather, each provides an opportunity for asylum seekers to play a more or less active role in the service production process. This arguably offers asylum seekers a way of *acting* like citizens (Lister, 2003), albeit in a partial and significantly restricted capacity. Asylum seekers cannot vote, participate in paid employment or move freely, but they can and do play an active role in public service production through co-production as *public service users*. Importantly, through co-construction, asylum seeker service users are always active in public service delivery as a result of the inseparability of production and consumption (Nankervis, 2005; Gronroos, 2007). The level of service user activeness can be extended through participative co-production or co-design, but this depends ultimately upon the policy direction towards social inclusion and the extended forms of co-production, public service managers' disposition towards co-production and perhaps, most importantly, the willingness and ability of front-line staff to build and sustain relationships with service users.

Furthermore, Niiranen (1999) focused on the collective dimension of citizenship. Although asylum seekers cannot participate in democratic structures open to the indigenous population, there are examples of them—as a collective—being involved and working in partnership with public service organisations to achieve service improvements but also broader public policy goals such as integration. Indeed, the empirical research uncovered different instances where asylum seekers were consulted as a distinctive group of service users. Given the central role of the third sector in the production of public services for asylum seekers in Scotland, there may be another route for asylum seeker participation. There was also a strong suggestion in the research that well-established third sector organisations were in a position to collate the needs of asylum seekers as a community and discuss these with strategic players and policymakers. Framework for Dialogue Groups that were managed by the Charity, for example, were key constructs through which the views of asylum seekers could be gathered and disseminated to those planning and delivering services. This could be viewed as providing asylum seekers with a collective voice, another element that may also contribute to their capacity to *act* like citizens (Alford, 2002).

## Summary: Co-production, Social Inclusion and Citizenship

This chapter has argued that as *public service users*, asylum seekers will *always* play an active role in the process of public service production through co-construction, but that their role can be extended and appended by public service organisations through participative co-production and co-design. The discussion has also suggested that co-production on the organisational level takes place through co-management and co-governance, respectively, where organisations work in collaborative relationships to deliver and plan services. No one mode of co-production was found to be reliant on another form of co-production, although co-construction was evidenced in each of the public services studied. Thus, individual forms of co-production do not preclude the organisational forms and because an organisation has, for example, facilitated participative co-production, this does not mean that the co-construction no longer took place, or that co-design could not also be endorsed. Significantly, the analysis here has shown that the various modes of co-production are operationalised within a complex public service system where the actors work together to differing extents and in several types of relationship to plan and deliver services.

None of the three modes of individual co-production presented here provides asylum seekers with legal citizenship status, but it has been argued that each provides an opportunity for asylum seekers to *act* like citizens, albeit in a partial and significantly restricted capacity. Co-production, and specifically co-construction that exists through the service relationship, has been suggested as the starting point for the process of integration, offering a core participatory role for asylum seekers accessing social welfare services through their interactions with front-line service staff. Co-production, in its various forms, has also been argued to support social inclusion because of its strong relational dimension, but the strong impetus to integration is also clearly supported in Scotland at the policymaking and operational levels despite the conflict with immigration policies that apply to the whole of the UK and which prescribe an approach of marginalisation.

This chapter has also discussed the organisational forms of co-production and the implications of co-management and co-governance for social inclusion. It has suggested that the integration of asylum seekers depends on the complex interactions of the public sector, third sector, communities and service users. Such interactions were described as friendships that had established over time at the strategic and operational levels through trust building. The discussion has further confirmed the key role played by the third sector in mediating between asylum seekers and other organisations, opening up an important avenue for participative co-production.

# References

Ager, A. and Strang, A. (2008). Understanding integration: a conceptual framework. *Journal of Refugee Studies*. (21,2), 166–191.

Alford, J. (2002). Why do public-sector clients coproduce? *Administration and Society*. (34,1), 32–56.

Alford, J. (2014). The multiple facets of co-production: building on the work of Elinor Ostrom. *Public Management Review*. (16,3), 299–316.

Alford, J. (2016). Co-production, interdependence and publicness: extending public service-dominant logic. *Public Management Review*. (18,5), 673–691.

Berger, P. L. and Neuhaus, R. J. (1978). *To empower people: the role of mediating structures in public policy*. Washington, DC: American Enterprise for Public Policy Research.

Bloch, A. (2000). Refugee settlement in Britain: the impact of policy on participation. *Journal of Ethnic and Migration Studies*. (26,1), 75–88.

Bovaird, T. (2007). Beyond engagement and participation: user and community co-production of public services. *Public Administration Review*. (67), 846–860.

Boyle, D., Clark, S. and Burns, S. (2006). *Hidden work: co-production by people outside paid employment*. York: Joseph Rowntree Foundation.

Brandsen, T. and Pestoff, V. (2006). Co-production, the third sector and the delivery of public services. *Public Management Review*. (8,4), 493–501.

Brannan, T., John, P. and Stoker, G. (2006). Active citizenship and effective public services and programmes: how can we know what really works? *Urban Studies*. (43,5–6), 993–1008.

Brudney, J. L. and England, R. E. (1983). Toward a definition of the co-production concept. *Public Administration Review*. (January–February), 59–65.

Cemlyn, S. and Briskman, L. (2003). Asylum, children's rights and social work. *Child and Family Social Work*. (8), 163–178.

Choules, K. (2006). Globally privileged citizenship. *Race, Ethnicity and Education*. (9,3), 275–293.

Crowley, P., Green, J., Freake, D. and Drinkwater, C. (2002). Primary care trusts involving the community: is community development the way forward. *Journal of Management and Medicine*. (16,4), 311–322.

Gronroos, C. (2007). *Service management and marketing: customer management in service competition* (3rd ed.). Chichester: John Wiley & Sons.

Gronroos, C. (2009). Marketing as promise management: regaining customer management for marketing. *Journal of Business and Industrial Marketing*. (24,5), 351–359.

Gulati, R. (1995). Does familiarity breed trust? The implications of repeated ties for contractual choice in alliances. *The Academy of Management Journal*. (38,1), 85–112.

Gummesson, E. (1998). Implementation requires a relationship marketing paradigm. *Journal of the Academy of Marketing Science*. (26,2), 242–249.

Kinard, B. R. and Capella, M. L. (2006). Relationship marketing: the influence of consumer involvement on perceived service benefits. *Journal of Services Marketing*. (20,6), 359–368.

Lister, R. (2003). *Citizenship: feminist perspectives* (2nd ed.). Basingstoke: Palgrave Macmillan.

Lister, R. (2007). From object to subject: including marginalised citizens in policy making. *Policy and Politics*. (35,3), 437–455.

Nankervis, A. (2005). *Managing services*. Cambridge: Cambridge University Press.

Nash, M., Wong, J. and Trlin, A. (2006). Civic and social integration: a new field of social work practice with immigrants, refugees and asylum seekers. *International Social Work*. (49,3), 345–363.

Niiranen, V. (1999). Municipal democracy and citizens' participation. In Rouban, L. (ed.), *Citizens and the new governance*. Amsterdam: IOS Press.

Nooteboom, B., Berger, H. and Noorderhaven, N. G. (1997). Effects of trust and governance on relational risk. *The Academy of Management Journal*. (40,2), 308–338.

Osborne, S. P., Radnor, Z., Kinder, T. and Vidal, I. (2015). The SERVICE framework: a public-service-dominant approach to sustainable public services. *British Journal of Management*. (26,3), 424–438.

Osborne, S. P., Radnor, Z. and Nasi, G. (2013). A new theory for public service management? Toward a (Public) service dominant approach. *American Review of Public Administration*. (43,2), 135–158.

Osborne, S. P. and Strokosch, K. (2013). It takes two to tango? Understanding the co-production of public services by integrating the service management and public administration perspectives. *British Journal of Management*. (24), S31–S47.

Ostrom, E. (1989). Microconstitutional change in multiconstitutional political systems. *Rationality and Society*. (1,1), 11–50.

Pestoff, V. (2006). Citizens and co-production of welfare services. *Public Management Review*. (8,4), 503–519.

Pestoff, V. (2012). Co-production and third sector services in Europe: some critical conceptual issues. In Pestoff, V., Brandsen, T. and Verschuere, B. (eds.), *New public governance, the third sector and co-production*. New York: Routledge.

Powell, M. (2002). The hidden history and social citizenship. *Citizenship Studies*. (6,3), 229–244.

Ramirez, R. (1999). Value co-production: intellectual origins and implications for practice and research. *Strategic Management Journal*. (20), 49–65.

Ring, P. S. and Van de Ven, A. H. (1992). Structuring cooperative relationships between organization. *Strategic Management Journal*. (13), 483–498.

Ring, P. S. and Van de Ven, A. H. (1994). Developmental processes of cooperative interorganisational relationships. *The Academy of Management Review*. (19,1), 90–118.

Sales, R. (2002). The deserving and undeserving? Refugees, asylum seekers and welfare in Britain. *Critical Social Policy*. (22), 456–478.

Skalen, P., Kotaiba, A. A. and Edvardsson, B. (2015). Cocreating the Arab spring: understanding transformation of service systems in contention. *Journal of Service Research*. (18,3), 250–264.

Spicer, N. (2008). Places of exclusion and inclusion: asylum-seeker and refugee experiences of neighbourhoods in the UK. *Journal of Ethnic and Migration Studies*. (34,3), 491–510.

Strokosch, K. and Osborne, S. P. (2016). Asylum seekers and the co-production of public services: understanding the implications for social inclusion and citizenship. *Journal of Social Policy*. (45,4), 673–690.

Strokosch, K. and Osborne, S. P. (2017). Co-producing across organisational boundaries: promoting asylum seeker integration in Scotland. *Voluntas*. (28,5), 1881–1899.

Trischler, J. and Charles, M. (2019). The application of service ecosystems lens to public policy analysis and design: exploring the frontiers. *Journal of Public Policy and Marketing*. (38,1), 19–35.

Tsai, W. and Ghosal, S. (1998). Social capital and value creation: the role of intrafirm networks. *The Academy of Management Journal*. (41,4), 464–476.

Tyler, I. (2010). Designed to fail: a biopolitics of British citizenship. *Citizenship Studies*. (14,1), 61–74.

Vargo, S. L. and Lusch, R. F. (2008). Service-dominant logic: continuing the evolution. *Journey of the Academy of Marketing Science*. (36), 1–10.

Vargo, S. L., Maglio, P. P. and Archpru Akaka, M. (2008). On value and value co-creation: a service systems and service logic perspective. *European Journal of Management*. (26), 145–152.

Williams, L. (2006). Social networks of refuges in the United Kingdom: tradition, tactics and new community spaces. *Journal of Ethnic and Migration Studies*. (32,5), 865–879.

Wright, G. H. and Taylor, A. (2007). Strategic partnerships and relationship marketing in healthcare. *Public Management Review.* (7,2), 203–224.

Wren, K. (2007). Supporting asylum seekers and refugees in Glasgow: the role of multi-agency networks. *Journal of Refugee Studies.* (20,3), 391–413.

Zaheer, A., McEvily, B. and Perrone, V. (1998). Does trust matter? Exploring the effects of interorganisational and interpersonal trust on performance. *Organization Science.* (9,2), 141–159.

# 10 Conclusions

## Abstract

This chapter discusses the conclusions and starts with a presentation of the integrated account of co-production which draws together the public administration and service management perspectives. It discusses the importance of both streams of literature in framing and understanding co-production and, importantly, argues that their integration supports greater analytical clarity of the concept through its dis-aggregation into five distinct modes. The chapter then discusses the empirical case of asylum seekers in receipt of social welfare services in Glasgow and argues that, through the conceptualisation of co-production presented here, there are potential implications for citizenship and social inclusion, but that these are influenced also by various factors within the external environment. The final section in this chapter suggests the implications of the broader discussion for policymakers and public service managers, who through the application of the model presented here will be better equipped to understand the various modes of co-production and how they might be more effectively supported and managed.

## Introduction

Co-production is an ambiguous concept, being used to describe different types of service user involvement in both policy design and service planning and delivery (Voorberg et al., 2015). There has been a call for further work around the conceptualisation of co-production and, for the purposes of this analysis, the focus has been on the operational level of public service planning and delivery.

The examination of the literature highlighted the conceptual difference that exists between the literature on co-production from the public administration and service management perspectives. The classic public administration narrative on co-production has much to offer the debate and, particularly, its analysis of the appended and participative modes of co-production including the following: the motivations to co-produce

(Alford, 2009), the enablers and obstacles to the operationalisation of co-production (Alford, 2014) and the various roles and experiences service users might play in co-productive relationships (Bovaird, 2007). Co-production from this perspective has clear transformative potential as it suggests more than giving service users a say in their services through evaluation, but rather a deeper influence and ownership over the services they receive. However, the public administration view of co-production also incorporates certain challenges that are typical to that of traditional forms of participation by presenting co-production as an appended dimension of the service production process. Insights from the service management literature, by contrast, shift the focus to the integral role of the service user in the production of public services and have been argued to offer a better starting point for conceptualising about co-production. This literature defines co-production as a central construct, existing as an integral dimension of the service production process (Gronroos, 2007). Co-production from this perspective emphasises not only the relational interaction between service provider and service user but the interdependency between the two during service delivery, as a result of the inseparability of production and consumption.

Building on these two streams of literature, the model presented in Chapter 4 suggests that co-production at the level of individual service users can be operationalised in three ways through co-construction, participative co-production and co-design. This model was then extended in Chapter 5, again through an integration of the theories on inter-organisational relationships from the public administration and service management literature, but with a focus on inter-organisational relationships to enable the exploration of the role of third sector organisations during the operational level of service planning and delivery.

## An Integrated Perspective on Co-production

By integrating insights from two distinct perspectives (public administration and service management) the discussion has sought to enhance the understanding of co-production in a public service setting by differentiating three distinct modes of co-production at the level of individual service users and two further modes at the organisational level. This framework provides greater clarity in discussing the co-production of public services and has enabled its dis-aggregation from one larger, somewhat vague concept, into separate conceptually rigorous elements. This permits for greater analytical rigour, which has been a criticism of the conceptualisation of co-production in both literatures (Gronroos and Voima, 2013; Voorberg et al., 2015).

The essential argument presented in the public administration literature is that co-production offers an alternative approach to service production where public service staff have been positioned as designing and delivering services alone. Co-production, from this perspective, has forwarded a relational approach where two parties jointly contribute inputs in the creation of output (Parks et al., 1981; Bovaird, 2007, 2009; Alford, 2014; Pestoff, 2006, 2012). This literature has been significant in understanding how co-production can be linked to individual and community participation in the planning of public services and also its limitations in practice. Although Ostrom's early work pointed to a dependency on service users who jointly create service quality through co-production with organisations delivering services (Ostrom, 1989), the public administration literature has evolved with a strong normative dimension that suggests that the participation offered by co-production is affixed to the service production process during either service delivery or planning as a way of improving democracy by increasing participation (Denhardt and Denhardt, 2015) or to improve services (Pestoff, 2014). It has been argued that in its traditional formulation co-production offers a potentially tokenistic approach to the involvement of service users, and it has also been criticised by some for offering an unequal opportunity to participate, being prejudiced towards certain sections of society that are more inclined to participate (Bovaird, 2007; Crompton, 2018). Furthermore, the application and operationalisation of co-production has also been formulated within a product-dominant logic under the New Public Management, which has had a hegemonic influence on public service reform across many countries since the 1980s. The discipline of public management has traditionally drawn on management theory derived primarily from the manufacturing sector and therefore likens public services to manufactured goods where production and consumption are distinct processes (Osborne and Strokosch, 2013). This has emphasised a linear approach to service production as the standard arrangement; in theory and practice, public services are understood as being designed and delivered by public service organisations working in isolation and are consumed separately by public service users. Co-production has, by consequence, largely been conceptualised, in a way, to traditional forms of participation, as an appended mechanism of empowerment that is controlled by those in power; staff exercise control over the application, nature, extent and impact of co-production. Co-production is then a voluntary and conscious act on the part of both the public service organisation and the service user, but its application, scope and impact are controlled ultimately by the public service organisation. From the classical perspective then, co-production is seen as a normative, voluntary, good that should create value to the public service production process, but is not intrinsic to it.

Recent academic work has suggested that such comparisons are problematic and do not accurately describe or understand the process of public service production (Osborne and Strokosch, 2013; Osborne et al., 2013, 2016). The work presented here has contributed to that debate.

Drawing on the service management literature, the argument presented here has added another analytical layer to co-production, positing that the service user *always* plays an active and integral role in public service production through co-construction because of the process nature of services and the inseparable nature of production and consumption (Vargo and Lusch, 2008). The service management perspective arguably therefore improves our understanding of the nature of the co-production of public services by individual service users, by providing a more accurate description of the service production process at an operational level. It helps us to understand the inherent role of co-production in the delivery of any service through co-construction.

Locating the various types of co-production was achieved through an examination of the defining characteristics of each mode within the case study sub-units. The three modes of individual co-production were distinguished by the following characteristics. *Co-construction* was defined as an inherent component of service production due to the nature of services, which are characterised by the inseparability of production and consumption (Normann, 1991; Nankervis, 2005; Gronroos, 2007). As such, co-construction is *involuntary and unavoidable* on the part of both the service user and public service organisation and its relational dimension forms the basis of the daily operations of any service. While the goal of this mode is service quality through a positive service user experience at the point of service delivery, *participative co-production* is concerned with achieving added value through service improvement or a broader social goal. The mechanisms supporting participative co-production have been divided into two categories. They have on one hand been associated with the New Public Management agenda and the marketisation of public services, empowering service users as consumers who can exercise choice, complaints and evaluation during service delivery (e.g. Greener, 2007) and, on the other, with mechanisms typically associated with citizen participation such as consultation, where the locus of service user involvement is during service delivery and planning (see, for example, Pestoff, 2006; Bovaird, 2009). Service users can thus take on a more active role in service production than co-producing solely through consumption. However, the type and extent of the role they play in co-production is determined by the public service organisation, depending on what goal is aspired to. Finally, *co-design* is based upon an integrated view of the public administration and service management theories, with the goal of service reform and innovation. Co-design is characterised by the embedded involvement of service users throughout the service production process (rather than simply during service delivery as is the case in co-construction), where their experience or 'sticky' knowledge is valued by public service staff designing or re-designing services as being important for the innovation and personalisation of the service, but which is difficult for service providers to acquire and transfer (von Hippel, 1998). This suggests that service users' contributions during service design serve to build their needs and experiences into the design process which supports the development of a needs-led service (Steen et al., 2011). Co-design, therefore, starts from the premise that service users play an integral role in service production (through co-construction) but seeks to build on and benefit from the service users' knowledge of their own experiences to innovate the service during service planning. The potential for value creation therefore extends beyond the 'moment of truth' to all points of interaction with the service user during the production process.

Co-production has been further differentiated at the organisational level according to the locus of involvement by third sector organisations during service production. Co-management describes instances where organisations contribute to service *delivery* and co-governance refers to the role of organisations in the planning *and* delivery of services (Brandsen and Pestoff, 2006; Pestoff et al., 2006). Although the focus here has been the role played by third sector organisations during co-production, it has been noted that the organisational modes of co-production could be applied to organisations from across the public and for-profit sectors too. The arguments presented here have suggested that these organisational forms of co-production exist in their own right and are not reliant on the presence of individual forms of co-production. In the case study, co-management was evidenced through both government contracts with third sector organisations to deliver services and also through relationships between public service organisations delivering services. Co-governance was demonstrated through three layers of public service planning and delivery networks that were operating in the city on the strategic, operational and neighbourhood levels. Furthermore, both inter-organisational modes operated concurrently with each other and the three individual modes of co-production.

The differentiation of co-production at an organisational level is a point of particular importance in our understanding of how public services are planned and delivered. The analysis and discussion have presented a multifaceted depiction of service production, within which the various individual and organisational dimensions of co-production inter-connect and overlap. This highlights that public services are not delivered in a linear fashion—as they have been conceptualised traditionally—but in a complex system that involves various organisations from across the public, for-profit and non-profit sectors and also includes a fundamental role for public service users and those front-line staff interacting with them (Osborne et al., 2015; Skalen et al., 2015; Trischler and Charles, 2019).

## Co-production, Citizenship and Social Inclusion

The empirical case has emphasised that co-production—through its integral categorisation and its appended forms—has the potential to have political implications around citizenship and social inclusion, but its practice and impact are shaped very much by the external environment; in the case of asylum seekers in Scotland, the nature of co-production has been influenced by the Scottish government's largely positive reaction to asylum seekers.

The fact that co-production is integral to the process nature of services has implications for asylum seekers and their potential for inclusion within society. The analysis and discussion confirm the existence of co-production in its different dimensions and importantly, suggests that, as public service users, asylum seekers will always play an active role in the process of public service production through co-construction. Chapter 6 described asylum seekers as a marginal and disenfranchised group who do not possess the political agency necessary for citizenship (Haikio, 2010). Indeed, asylum seekers were generally described as 'powerless', with immigration legislation and policies restricting their capacity to contribute to civic life. However, significantly for this debate, they were described as *public service users* and as such their involvement in the co-production of services was generally regarded as integral to service production. Public service providers spoke of the importance of asylum seeker co-production to ensure buy-in and use of the services. This leads to a juxtaposition of their status and the role they can play through the co-production of services. Asylum seekers' role as public service users highlights the contradiction, of their lack of citizenship status, because they are not members of the polity with their potential for citizenship through their shared community and the role they can play in the welfare state through the co-production of services. Although asylum seekers are not privy to the economic and political participation afforded to legal citizens, they played an integral role in the co-construction of the public services they used and had further opportunities to co-produce through participative co-production and co-design, which were employed at the discretion of service providers who subscribed strongly to the agenda of social inclusion, of which participation through co-production was key.

The discussion has emphasised that none of the modes of individual co-production discussed here provide asylum seekers with legal citizenship status—or are intended to. What they offer is a route towards a partial and restricted form of 'citizenship in practice' where they can *act* as citizens (Lister, 2003)—albeit in a reduced capacity—through their position in the welfare state as public service users. Co-production does not have a positive impact upon their case for asylum, nor does it permit those seeking asylum to contribute on a political or economic level. However, in its various forms, co-production promotes and facilitates their social inclusion through the involvement of asylum seekers at the operational level of public service production. It is their role as co-producer that offers a community typically identified by its marginalised and powerless attributes a participatory role that promotes their inclusion in society. Co-production has, for instance, allowed asylum seekers to establish trusting relationships with service providers and supports their inclusion into Scottish society. The approach in Scotland aligns strongly to the perspective forwarded by Ager and Strang (2008), although it was limited in the sense that the asylum process and access to a constrained system of welfare benefits were administered by the UK government. Indeed, the social, political and legal backdrop facing asylum seekers made integration particularly challenging; asylum seekers are situated in a socially disadvantaged position and cannot participate in paid employment, but are provided with accommodation, education and health, all of which fall under Ager and Strang's (2008) framework of integration. Despite their limited rights and entitlements, this study demonstrated a strong impetus to integrate asylum seekers through the co-construction during the day-to-day management of service encounters. Various service providers examined also chose to implement and manage participative co-production (and to a lesser extent co-design) to effect change and service improvement.

This research has also shown how asylum seeker integration has been promoted in Scotland, highlighting certain important factors which were not included in Ager and Strang's framework, such as policy direction and the disposition of organisations providing public services towards co-production, integration and inter-organisational working. The political context in Scotland and specifically the promotion of integration by the Scottish government filtered down to the operational level. The goal of integration also underpinned many of the services provided by third sector organisations, such as English language provision and building relationships among asylum seekers and with the indigenous population (Ager and Strang, 2008). Some organisations, such as the Accommodation Provider and Church A, also diverged from core tasks to promote integration and facilitate social inclusion.

The analysis has further evidenced that asylum seeker integration can be promoted through co-management and co-governance, but that other factors such as government policy, geography, established services, personal relationships and structures of participation are key to both integration and inter-organisational relationships. The propensity for inter-organisational working through co-management and co-governance was supported by Scottish government policy and legislation such as the Community Planning Act. The third sector was invariably described by the case study research as playing a key role in planning and delivering public services to asylum seekers. This was evidenced by the survey findings and past literature which showed a high regard for third sector organisations, which were generally viewed as adding value to public services and contributing to their effectiveness, confirming the arguments made in the literature (Wren, 2007). The geography, along with established structures, clear organisational remits and personal relationships created a viable environment for inter-organisational relationships.

Indeed, asylum seeker services were well established in Glasgow, making it easier for organisations to work together. Respondents suggested that there was less need for wrangling over substantive issues because agencies across sectors had a history of working together and have laid down the foundations of asylum seeker services together. There was less of a role for advocacy, but larger third sector organisations generally sat in a good position to raise concerns or lobby against issues despite this strong undercurrent of inter-organisational working.

## Implications for Public Service Management

The analysis presented here may be used to aid policymakers and public service managers to clarify and better understand the roles played by various parties in planning and delivering public services and how these relationships of co-production might be more effectively utilised and managed to create public service improvement and transformation.

There has been a dearth of research on asylum seekers and their role in the production of public services and it has been argued that this study group has sharpened the focus on co-production. Although asylum seekers are a very particular case, insight from this study will be applicable in other areas of practice. There are continuing concerns about disengagement with the political process (Lister, 2003) and co-production may offer an alternative way through which to involve people as public service users, but, importantly, it also provides a unique opportunity for public services to be shaped and informed by service user knowledge and expertise (von Hippel, 1994). This suggests that not only does co-production offer the normative dimension that has been widely discussed in the public management literature around its capacity to reform democracy (Pestoff, 2006; Denhardt and Denhardt, 2015) but also, predominantly through the reconceptualisation of public services as relational processes that are dependent upon the contributions of service users, co-construction can be managed on a day-to-day basis for the purpose of service improvement.

By exploring the nature and processes of co-production on both the organisational and individual levels, this work has suggested that, by recognising and differentiating co-production through its various modes, service production may be more effectively managed. As discussed in earlier chapters, public service delivery has traditionally been conceptualised as something to be authorised by public service professionals, with the service user taking a largely passive role in the process. In reality though, it is impossible to deliver any services without co-construction and it is through this understanding of the service production process that relationships and how they are managed become of crucial importance.

The fact that co-construction is a fundamental dimension of the service relationship has significant implications for the application and management of co-production; as an integral dimension of the service relationship co-construction should be managed effectively to create a positive service experience. In this sense, the capacity and willingness of front-line service staff to build and sustain relationships with service users is of significant import. The importance of the service interaction suggests two key issues for public service management. The first is that public service users play an active role during the service delivery process (Nankervis, 2005; Gronroos, 2007; Normann, 1991) through co-construction. The second is the emphasis on service interactions as processes, which suggests that quality and satisfaction rely on the interaction that exists during 'the moment of truth' (Gronroos, 2007), and as such the role of front-line staff is critical. Their role is to manage the service interaction and develop an effective relationship with service users to create service user satisfaction (Lovelock and Young, 1979; Gummesson, 1998; Gronroos, 2009); conversely, if the relationship breaks down it is likely to destroy such satisfaction. Indeed, building trust with asylum seekers was fundamental to the improvement of public services for a vulnerable group, pointing to a potential role for relationship marketing in public service management. Public service managers therefore need to recognise the process and relational dimensions of public services and the importance of managing service interactions to support the co-construction of a positive service experience (Gronroos, 2000).

Public service managers' disposition towards co-production is also important, particularly in relation to the appended modes of co-production— participative co-production and co-design—which are applied at the behest of public service organisations. The differentiation of the three modes of individual co-production suggests that while there may be times where participative co-production or co-design are appropriate and necessary (e.g. to foster innovation), if the aim is service improvement it may be more effective and efficient to invest in service interactions ('the moment of truth') rather than redirecting resources to, for example, consult service users to participate in a distinct element of the service. This may involve, for example, staff training to support them in developing relationships with vulnerable service users. By implication then, this suggests a more pragmatic approach to co-production, where the adoption of the appended modes are selected only when they are necessary to improve service quality or support innovation and not conducted simply as evidence of consultation (which may in fact not be genuine) (Osborne et al., 2013). An important question for public managers is, therefore, whether to invoke expensive forms of co-production, such as consultation, or instead focus of the interface between public service users and front-line staff during service encounters and the effective management of that relationship.

The analysis has further suggested that public service organisations do not produce services in isolation, nor is the relationship between the service user and public service staff the only important interaction within public service production. Rather public services are designed and delivered within a complex service system that involves various actors within organisations and across sectors who interact through co-management and co-governance to plan and deliver services to meet service users' and the wider community's needs. The complexity of the service system and the operation of the various dimensions of co-production suggest that it is not only the individual modes of co-production that require effective management. Building and sustaining relationships across organisational boundaries is necessary for successful partnership working and, linked to this, the successful delivery of services to meet needs. Relationship marketing may also therefore have an important role to play in co-management and co-governance. In Glasgow, the third sector played a central role in planning and delivering services and contributing to strategic decision-making (particularly in Scotland). Its involvement facilitated the meeting of complex asylum seekers' needs, one of which was integration and there was clear evidence of third sector organisations working across organisational boundaries in the pursuit of each of these roles. Ultimately, this had implications for practice and specifically how inter-organisational relationships might be best managed to promote the necessary levels of communication and trust to facilitate effective co-management and co-governance. Managing relationships across the public service delivery system, with not only public service users but other stakeholders and organisations from various sectors, opens up the potential for public service organisations to tap into both user knowledge and professional expertise to the benefit of the service and everyone involved. Furthermore, the complexity of the service system also suggests that the inter-connections between the individual and organisational modes of co-production need to be managed to facilitate the alignment of relationships between the individual service users, operational service providers and strategic decision-makers to ensure each is aspiring to the same goals.

Overall, the depiction of a complex public service system where services are designed and delivered through various relationships at the individual and organisational levels is significant. It moves beyond a simple linear conception of public service production, which has been traditionally used within the field of public administration, within which the roles of producers and service users have been demarcated into specific spheres of planning/design, delivery and consumption. Instead, it depicts a complex process that involves various interactions between multiple organisations from across sectors and with public service users. Understanding service production in this way arguably facilitates the improved management of public services through a clearer and more accurate articulation of the roles played by public service staff, stakeholders and, perhaps most importantly, public service users.

# References

Ager, A. and Strang, A. (2008). Understanding integration: a conceptual framework. *Journal of Refugee Studies*. (21,2), 166–191.

Alford, J. (2009). *Engaging public sector clients: from service-delivery to co-production*. Basingstoke: Palgrave Macmillan.

Alford, J. (2014). The multiple facets of co-production: building on the work of Elinor Ostrom. *Public Management Review*. (16,3), 299–316.

Bovaird, T. (2007). Beyond engagement and participation: user and community co-production of public services. *Public Administration Review*. (67), 846–860.

Bovaird, T. (2009). Strategic management in public sector organisations. In Bovaird, T. and Loeffler, E. (eds.), *Public management and governance* (2nd ed.). London: Routledge.

Brandsen, T. and Pestoff, V. (2006). Co-production, the third sector and the delivery of public services. *Public Management Review*. (8,4), 493–501.

Crompton, A. (2018). Inside co-production: stakeholder meaning and situated practice. *Social Policy Administration*, 1–14.

Denhardt, J. V. and Denhardt, R. B. (2015). *New public service: serving, not steering* (4th ed.). New York: Routledge.

Greener, I. (2007). Choice or voice? Introduction to the themed section. *Social Policy and Society*. (7,2), 197–200.

Gronroos, C. (2000). Creating a relationship dialogue: communication, interaction and value. *The Marketing Review*. (1,1), 5–14.

Gronroos, C. (2007). *Service management and marketing: customer management in service competition* (3rd ed.). Chichester: John Wiley & Sons.

Gronroos, C. (2009). Marketing as promise management: regaining customer management for marketing. *Journal of Business and Industrial Marketing*. (24,5), 351–359.

Gronroos, C. and Voima, P. (2013). Critical service logic: making sense of value creation and co-creation. *Journal of the Academy of Marketing Science*. (41,2), 133–150.

Gummesson, E. (1998). Implementation requires a relationship marketing paradigm. *Journal of the Academy of Marketing Science*. (26, 2), 242–249.

Haikio, L. (2010). The diversity of citizenship and democracy in local management reform. *Public Management Review*. (12,3), 363–384.

Lister, R. (2003). *Citizenship: feminist perspectives* (2nd ed.). Basingstoke: Palgrave Macmillan.

Lovelock, C. H. and Young, R. F. (1979). Look to consumers to increase productivity. *Harvard Business Review*. (57, May–June), 168–178.

Nankervis, A. (2005). *Managing services*. Cambridge: Cambridge University Press.

Normann, R. (1991). *Service management: strategy and leadership in service business* (2nd ed.). West Sussex: John Wiley & Sons.

Osborne, S. P., Radnor, Z., Kinder, T. and Vidal, I. (2015). The SERVICE framework: a public-service-dominant approach to sustainable public services. *British Journal of Management*. (26,3), 424–438.

Osborne, S. P., Radnor, Z. and Nasi, G. (2013). A new theory for public service management? Toward a (Public) service dominant approach. *American Review of Public Administration*. (43,2), 135–158.

Osborne, S. P., Radnor, Z. and Strokosch, K. (2016). Co-production and the co-creation of value in public service: a suitable case for treatment? *Public Management Review*. (18,5), 639–653.

Osborne, S. P. and Strokosch, K. (2013). It takes two to tango? Understanding the co-production of public services by integrating the service management and public administration perspectives. *British Journal of Management*. (24), S31–S47.

Ostrom, E. (1989). Microconstitutional change in multiconstitutional political systems. *Rationality and Society*. (1,1), 11–50.

Parks, R. B., Baker, P. C., Kiser, L., Oakerson, R., Ostrom, E., Ostrom, V., Percy, S. L., Vandivort, M. B., Whitaker, G. P. and Wilson, R. (1981). Consumers as co-producers of public services: some economic and institutional considerations. *Policy Studies Journal*. (9,7), 1001–1011.

Pestoff, V. (2006). Citizens and co-production of welfare services. *Public Management Review*. (8,4), 503–519.

Pestoff, V. (2012). Co-production and third sector services in Europe: some critical conceptual issues. In Pestoff, V., Brandsen, T. and Verschuere, B. (eds.), *New public governance, the third sector and co-production*. New York: Routledge.

Pestoff, V. (2014). Collective action and the sustainability of co-production. *Public Management Review*. (16,3), 383–401.

Pestoff, V., Osborne, S. P. and Brandsen, T. (2006). Patterns of co-production in public services. *Public Management Review*. (8,4), 591–595.

Skalen, P., Kotaiba, A. A. and Edvardsson, B. (2015). Cocreating the Arab spring: understanding transformation of service systems in contention. *Journal of Service Research*. (18,3), 250–264.

Steen, M., Manschot, M. and De Koning, N. (2011). Benefits of co-design in service design projects. *International Journal of Design*. (5,2), 53–60.

Trischler, J. and Charles, M. (2019). The application of service ecosystems lens to public policy analysis and design: exploring the frontiers. *Journal of Public Policy and Marketing*. (38,1), 19–35.

Vargo, S. L. and Lusch, R. F. (2008). Service-dominant logic: continuing the evolution. *Journey of the Academy of Marketing Science*. (36), 1–10.

von Hippel, E. (1994). Sticky information and the locus of problem solving: implications for innovation. *Management Science*. (40,4), 429–439.

von Hippel, E. (1998). Economics of product development by users: the impact of 'sticky' local information. *Management Science*. (44,5), 629–644.

Voorberg, W. H., Bekkers, V. J. J. M. and Tummers, L. G. (2015). A systematic review of co-creation and co-production: embarking on the social innovation journey. *Public Management Review*. (17,9), 1333–1357.

Wren, K. (2007). Supporting asylum seekers and refugees in Glasgow: the role of multi-agency networks. *Journal of Refugee Studies*. (20,3), 391–413.

# Index

Note: Page numbers in *italics* indicate figures and page numbers in **bold** indicate tables.

intangibility of 48; integrated
approach to co-production and
68–69, 77; inter-organisational
relationships and 81, 85–86;
limitations of 62–63; participation
and 51; productivity/quality in 136;
public choice theory and 46; Public
Service Logic and 4; relationship
marketing and 59–61, 63, 190;
relationships in 68; value creation
in 47, 52–55, 57–58
services *see* public services
service users *see* public service users
Sharif, G. 113
Sicilia, M. 2, 19, 26, 28, 30, 37,
72, 85
Sigona, N. 115
Sim, D. 109
social capital 110
social citizenship 112–113
social inclusion: asylum seekers and
117, 128, 150, 161–162, 187,
189–191; citizenship and 192–193;
co-production and 16, 188–189;
education and 162; English policies
for 109, 128, 150; networks
and 191–192; relationships
and 190–191; Scottish policies
for 109, 128, 150, 161–162;
service encounters and 190–191;
volunteering and 162
social networks 110–111
social rights 104–107, 111–112,
122
social welfare services: asylum seekers
and 105–107, 151; co-production
and 2; inter-organisational
relationships and 82; New Public
Management and 140; third sector
organisations and 5, 117; *see also*
public services
Somerville, P. 91
Spicer, N. 110, 188
state actors 19
Steen, T. 26
Steen, T. P. S. 17
sticky knowledge 56, 62, 74–75, 77,
145–146, 202
Stoker, G. 21, 114
Strang, A. 110–114, 122, 129, 144,
185, 188, 191, 205
Strokosch, K. 6, 69
Sundeen, R. A. 29

Taylor, A. 59
Taylor, M. 91
third sector organisations:
accountability and 90, 92;
adversarial role of 90, 163–164;
advocacy and 163–164; asylum
seekers and 115–118, 139, 141,
144, 156–164, 174, 205–206;
bureaucracy in 90; co-governance
and 81, 90–94, 165–170;
collaborative role of 160–163;
co-management and 81, 89–90,
93–94, 165–166; co-production
and 82, 88, *88*, 93, *93*, 94;
criticism of 91–92; diversity of 87;
government contracts and 89–90;
integration strategies and 205;
marginalised groups and 88–89; as
mediating structures 5, 81, 86–89,
93, 158–159, 188; modernised
87; non-institutionalised 87;
partnership approach and 160–163;
public services delivery and 87, 89,
91, 93; relationships with **157**; role
of 157–164; social welfare services
and 5, 117; types of involvement
**157**; volunteering and 144
Tocqueville, A. de 112
transactional marketing 58–59
Trischler, J. 183
Trlin, A. 189
trust 76, 85–86, 181, 191, 205
Tummers, L. G. 55
Tyler, I. 113

United Kingdom: asylum seeker
integration in 186; asylum seekers
in 103–106; deterrence policies
104–105, 107, 111; immigration
policies 104–112, 122, 128,
131, 167, 186–187; immigration
statistics in 106; media discourse
on asylum seekers in 107–108;
participation rhetoric in 29; social
rights in 104–105; *see also* Scotland
user participation 72–73

value co-contamination 26
value creation: actors and 53,
57; co-creation and 53–58;
co-production processes for 82;
product-dominant logic and 52, **52**;
service-dominant logic and 52, **52**,